Lecture Notes
in Business Information Processing   238

More information about this series at http://www.springer.com/series/7911

Dietmar Winkler · Stefan Biffl
Johannes Bergsmann (Eds.)

Software Quality

The Future of Systems- and Software Development

8th International Conference, SWQD 2016
Vienna, Austria, January 18–21, 2016
Proceedings

 Springer

Editors
Dietmar Winkler
Institute of Software Technology
    and Interactive Systems
Vienna University of Technology
Vienna
Austria

Stefan Biffl
Institute of Software Technology
    and Interactive Systems
Vienna University of Technology
Vienna
Austria

Johannes Bergsmann
Software Quality Lab GmbH
Linz
Austria

ISSN 1865-1348   ISSN 1865-1356 (electronic)
Lecture Notes in Business Information Processing
ISBN 978-3-319-27032-6   ISBN 978-3-319-27033-3 (eBook)
DOI 10.1007/978-3-319-27033-3

Library of Congress Control Number: 2015955358

Springer Cham Heidelberg New York Dordrecht London

Printed on acid-free paper

Springer International Publishing AG Switzerland is part of Springer Science+Business Media
(www.springer.com)

Message from the General Chair

The Software Quality Days (SWQD) conference and tools fair started in 2009 and have grown to be the biggest conferences on software quality in Europe with a strong community. The program of the SWQD conference is designed to encompass a stimulating mixture of practical presentations and new research topics in scientific presentations as well as tutorials and an exhibition area for tool vendors and other organizations in the area of software quality.

This professional symposium and conference offer a range of comprehensive and valuable opportunities for advanced professional training, new ideas, and networking with a series of keynote speeches, professional lectures, exhibits, and tutorials.

The SWQD conference is suitable for anyone with an interest in software quality, such as software process and quality managers, test managers, software testers, product managers, agile masters, project managers, software architects, software designers, requirements engineers, user interface designers, software developers, IT managers, release managers, development managers, application managers, and those in similar roles.

January 2016   Johannes Bergsmann

Message from the Scientific Program Chair

The 8th Software Quality Days (SWQD) conference and tools fair brought together researchers and practitioners from business, industry, and academia working on quality assurance and quality management for software engineering and information technology. The SWQD conference is one of the largest software quality conferences in Europe.

Over the past years a growing number of scientific contributions were submitted to the SWQD symposium. Starting in 2012 the SWQD symposium included a dedicated scientific program published in scientific proceedings. For the fifth year we received an overall number of 25 high-quality submissions from researchers across Europe, which were each peer-reviewed by three or more reviewers. Out of these submissions, the editors selected five contributions as full papers, for an acceptance rate of 20 %. Further, nine short papers, which represent promising research directions, were accepted to spark discussions between researchers and practitioners at the conference.

The main topics from academia and industry focused on systems and software quality management methods, improvements of software development methods and processes, latest trends in software quality, and testing and software quality assurance.

This book is structured according to the sessions of the scientific program following the guiding conference topic "The Future of Systems and Software Development":

- Software Engineering Processes and Process Modelling
- Requirements Engineering
- Software Architecture
- Software Estimation and Development
- Software Testing
- E-Government Applications

January 2016   Stefan Biffl

Organization

SWQD 2016 was organized by the Software Quality Lab GmbH, the Vienna University of Technology, Institute of Software Technology and Interactive Systems, and the Christian Doppler Laboratory "Software Engineering Integration for Flexible Automation Systems."

Organizing Committee

General Chair

Johannes Bergsmann   Software Quality Lab GmbH

Scientific Program Chair

Stefan Biffl   Vienna University of Technology

Proceedings Chair

Dietmar Winkler   Vienna University of Technology

Organizing and Publicity Chair

Petra Bergsmann   Software Quality Lab GmbH

Program Committee

SWQD 2016 established an international committee of well-known experts in software quality and process improvement to peer-review the scientific submissions.

Maria Teresa Baldassarre	University of Bari, Italy
Mokhtar Beldjehem	University of Ottawa, Canada
Miklos Biro	Software Competence Center Hagenberg, Austria
Matthias Book	University of Iceland, Iceland
Ruth Breu	University of Innsbruck, Austria
Fabio Calefato	University of Bari, Italy
Maya Daneva	University of Twente, The Netherlands
Oscar Dieste	Universidad Politécnica de Madrid, Spain
Frank Elberzhager	Fraunhofer IESE, Germany
Michael Felderer	University of Innsbruck, Austria
Gordon Fraser	University of Sheffield, UK
Nauman Ghazi	Blekinge Institute of Technology, Sweden
Volker Gruhn	University of Duisburg-Essen, Germany
Jens Heidrich	Fraunhofer IESE, Germany
Frank Houdek	Daimler AG, Germany
Slinger Jansen	Utrecht University, The Netherlands
Marcos Kalinowski	Fluminense Federal University, Brazil

Petri Kettunen	Helsinki University, Finland
Ricardo Machado	CCG-Centro de Computação Gráfica, Portugal
Eda Marchetti	ISTI-CNR, Italy
Paula Monteiro	CCG-Centro de Computação Gráfica, Portugal
Juergen Muench	University of Helsinki, Finland
Oscar Pastor Lopez	Universitat Politècnica de València, Valencia, Spain
Mauro Pezzè	University of Lugano, Switzerland
Dietmar Pfahl	University of Tartu, Estonia
Rick Rabiser	Johannes Kepler University Linz, Austria
Rudolf Ramler	Software Competence Center Hagenberg, Austria
Andreas Rausch	Technical University Clausthal, Germany
Barbara Russo	Free University of Bozen-Bolzano, Italy
Ina Schieferdecker	Fraunhofer Institute for Open Communication Systems, FOKUS, Germany
Klaus Schmid	University of Hildesheim, Germany
Rini Van Solingen	Delft University of Technology, The Netherlands
Stefan Wagner	University of Stuttgart, Germany
Dietmar Winkler	Vienna University of Technology, Austria

Sub-reviewers

| Johannes Gmeiner | Marco Körner | Martin Vogel |
| Ravi Khadka | Amir Saeidi | Phillip Wolter |

Contents

Software Estimation and Development

Software Testing

E-Government Applications

Keynote

The Disciplined Agile Process Decision Framework

Scott W. Ambler[1(✉)] and Mark Lines[2]

[1] Toronto, Canada
scott@scottambler.com
[2] Calgary, Canada
mark@scottambler.com

Abstract. The Disciplined Agile 2.0 process decision framework [1] provides light-weight guidance to help organizations streamline their information technology (IT) processes in a context-sensitive manner. It does this by showing how various activities such as solution delivery, operations, enterprise architecture, portfolio management, and many others work together in a cohesive whole. The framework also describes what these activities should address, provides a range of options for doing so, and describes the tradeoffs associated with each option. Every person, every team, and every organization is unique, therefore process frameworks must provide choices, not prescribe answers.

Keywords: Agile · Disciplined · Kanban · Scrum · Agility at scale · DevOps · Information technology department

1 History

To date there have been three major release tiers of this framework:

1. **Disciplined Agile Delivery 0.x.** The framework was originally developed at IBM Rational from early 2009 to June 2012. The IBM team worked closely with business partners, including Mark Lines, and was led by Scott Ambler. IBM Rational Method Composer (RMC) currently supports an early, 0.5 version of the DA framework.
2. **Disciplined Agile Delivery 1.x.** The DA 1.0 release occurred in June 2012 with publication of the first DA book, Disciplined Agile Delivery [2]. Evolution and publication of the DA framework continued at the Disciplined Agile site starting in August 2012. Ownership of the DA framework intellectual property effectively passed over to the Disciplined Agile Consortium [3] in October 2012, a fact that was legally recognized by IBM in June 2014. The focus was on the software delivery process.
3. **Disciplined Agile 2.x.** This is the current version of the framework, initially released in August 2015. The focus is on describing a flexible, context-sensitive approach to the entire IT process.

D. Winkler et al. (Eds.): SWQD 2016, LNBIP 238, pp. 3–14, 2016.
DOI: 10.1007/978-3-319-27033-3_1

2   Why Disciplined Agile?

There are several reasons why an organization should consider adopting the Disciplined Agile framework:

4. **Enable Agile Delivery Teams to Succeed.** The focus of Disciplined Agile Delivery (DA) 1.x [4] was tactical scaling of agile software development strategies across the delivery lifecycle in the range of situations that delivery teams find themselves in. The DA 1.x framework described how agile/lean teams work from beginning to end, showing how all the activities of solution delivery (analysis, design, testing, architecture, management, programming, and so on) fit together in a cohesive, streamlined whole. However, to succeed delivery teams must often work with people outside of the team, such as enterprise architects, operations engineers, governance people, data management people, and many others. For agile/lean delivery teams to be effective these people must also work in an agile/lean manner.

5. **Provide a Coherent Strategy for Agile IT.** The focus of Disciplined Agile 2.x is on strategic scaling of agile and lean strategies across the IT department. IT departments are complex adaptive organizations. What we mean by that is that the actions of one team will affect the actions of another team, and so on and so on. For example, the way that your agile delivery team works will have an effect on, and be affected by, any other team that you interact with. If you're working with your operations teams, perhaps as part of your overall Disciplined DevOps [5] strategy, then each of those teams will need to adapt the way they work to collaborate effectively with one another. Each team will hopefully learn from the other and improve the way that they work. These improvements with ripple out to other teams. The challenge is that every area within IT has one or more bodies of knowledge, and in some cases published "books of knowledge", that provide guidance for people working in those areas. These industry groups and their corresponding bodies of knowledge contradict one another, they are at different points on the agile/lean learning curve, and sometimes they promote very non-agile/lean strategies. At the IT level this can be very confusing, resulting in dysfunction. As you can see in Fig. 1, the DA framework shows how this all fits together in a flexible manner that supports the realities faced in complex adaptive systems.

6. **Support the Lean Enterprise.** A lean enterprise [6] is able to anticipate and respond swiftly to changes in the marketplace. It does this through an organizational culture and structure that facilitates change within the context of the situation that it faces. Lean enterprises require a learning mindset in the mainstream business and underlying lean and agile processes to drive innovation. This includes an IT department that is able to work in an agile/lean manner.

7. **Context Counts.** Every person, every team, and every organization is unique. The implication is that you need a framework that provides you with choices so that you can tailor, and later evolve, an approach to address the situation that you face in practice. Although prescriptive, one-size-fits-all frameworks such as SAFe [7] or Nexus [8] may seem like an attractive solution to your process-related needs at first, the reality is that they often do more harm than good within the organizations that adopt them.

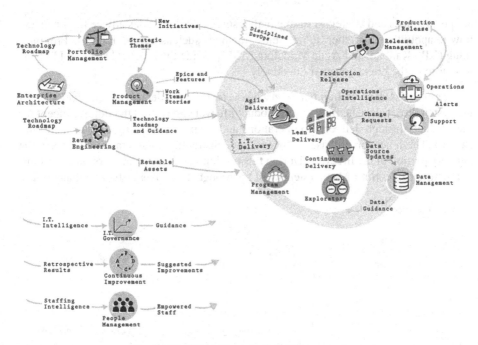

Fig. 1. The Disciplined Agile 2.0 Framework.

3   Tactical Agility at Scale

Many organizations start their agile journey by adopting Scrum because it describes a good strategy for leading agile software teams. However, Scrum is only a small part of what is required to deliver sophisticated solutions to your stakeholders. Invariably, teams need to look to other methods to fill in the process gaps that Scrum purposely ignores. When looking at other methods, there is considerable overlap and conflicting terminology that can be confusing to practitioners as well as outside stakeholders. Worse yet, people don't always know where to look for advice or even know what issues they need to consider. Then to compound the issue many teams find themselves in situations, such as geographically distributed teams or regulatory compliance, which "pure agilists" prefer to ignore.

To address these challenges, the Disciplined Agile (DA) process decision framework provides a more cohesive approach to agile solution delivery. It does this via several strategies.

Strategy #1: DA is a hybrid framework that builds upon the solid foundation of other methods and software process frameworks. One of the great advantages of agile and lean software development is the wealth of practices, techniques and strategies available to you. This is also one of its greatest challenges because without something like the DA framework, it's difficult to know what to choose and how to fit them together. Worse yet, many teams new to agile will adopt a method like Scrum or SAFe as if it's a recipe, ignoring advice from other sources and thereby getting into trouble. The DA framework adopts practices and strategies from existing sources and provides advice for when and how to apply them together. In one sense, methods such as Scrum, Extreme Programming (XP), Kanban, and Agile Modeling (AM) provide the process bricks and DA the mortar to fit the bricks together effectively.

Strategy #2: DA supports a full delivery lifecycle. Figure 2 depicts a high-level view of the system lifecycle. The full system/product lifecycle goes from the initial concept for the product, through delivery, to operations and support and finally to retirement (not shown). The inner three phases – Inception, Construction, and Transition – form the delivery portion of the lifecycle. During this portion you incrementally build a consumable solution over time. Most systems will go through the delivery lifecycle many times.

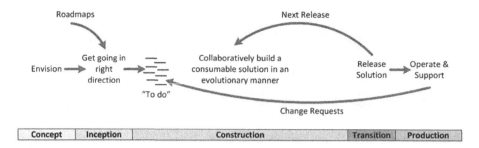

Fig. 2. A high-level view of the system lifecycle.

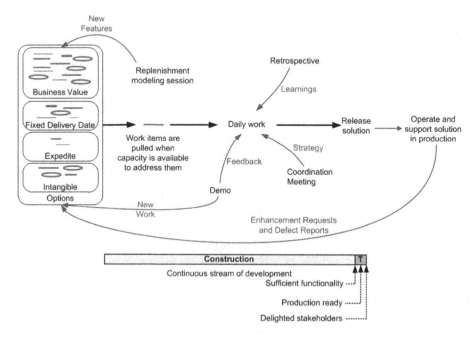

Fig. 3. Disciplined Agile's Continuous Delivery lifecycle.

Strategy #3: DA supports four delivery lifecycles. Because DA is not prescriptive and strives to reflect reality as best it can, it supports four versions of a delivery lifecycle [9]. These lifecycles are: an agile/basic version that extends the Scrum Construction life-cycle; an advanced/lean lifecycle based on Kanban; a continuous delivery lifecycle (shown in Fig. 3); and an exploratory lifecycle based upon a Lean Start-up approach [10]. DA teams will adopt a lifecycle that is most appropriate for their situation and then tailor it appropriately.

Strategy #4: DA is goal-driven, not prescriptive. The DA framework came about from empirical observations of dozens of teams apply agile and lean strategies in dozens of organizations working in different domains around the world. Although there were similarities between how these teams worked every team worked in a unique manner, and every team had spent considerable time and effort determining how to do so. And every team still had improvements to make, and many were struggling with doing so because they didn't have the process background to identify candidate options. It was clear to us that agile/lean teams could benefit from light-weight process guidance that described the range of options available to them.

To do this DA adopted a goal-driven, or capability-based, approach. The delivery goals are summarized in the mind map of Fig. 4. For example, the diagram indicates that when a team is in Inception that they must address goals such as forming the initial team, aligning with the enterprise direction (e.g. follow your corporate roadmaps and guidelines), develop an initial release plan, and explore the initial scope amongst other things. Although every team addresses these goals in some way, every team does so in a different manner and are likely to evolve their approach over time as they learn from experience.

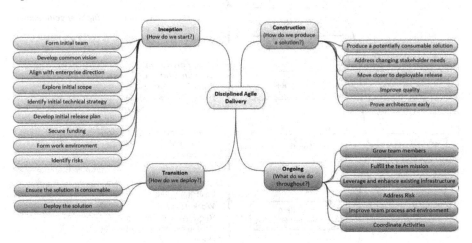

Fig. 4. Delivery goals (capabilities).

To provide teams more detailed guidance as to the process choices they have to address each goal the DA framework introduced the concept of process goal diagrams [11]. A process goal diagram depicts the process factors that should be considered when addressing the goal and then a representative list of options for those goals. Because people around the world are constantly improving upon and identify new practices and strategies the list of options presented in the goal diagrams cannot possibly be definitive. Instead they represent the range of options available, letting people know that choices do exist (regardless of what prescriptive methodologies imply) and that sometimes some choices are distinctly better than others (again, regardless of what prescriptive method-ologies imply).

Let's work through an example. Figure 5 depicts the goal diagram for Explore Initial Scope, a goal that you should address at the beginning of a project during the Inception phase. Where some agile methods will simply advise you to populate your product backlog with some initial user stories, the goal diagram makes it clear that you might want to be a bit more sophisticated in your approach. What level of detail should you capture, if any (a light specification approach of writing up some index cards and a few whiteboard sketches is just one option you should consider)? What view types should you consider (user stories are one approach to usage modeling, but shouldn't you consider other views to explore the data or the UI)? Default techniques, or perhaps more accurately suggested starting points, are shown in bold italics. Notice how we suggest that you likely want to default to capturing usage in some way, basic domain concepts (for example, via a high-level conceptual diagram) in some way, and non-functional requirements in some way. There are different strategies you may want to consider for modeling. You should also start thinking about your approach to managing your work. In DA, we make it clear that agile teams do more than just implement new requirements, hence our recommendation to default to a work item list over Scrum's simplistic

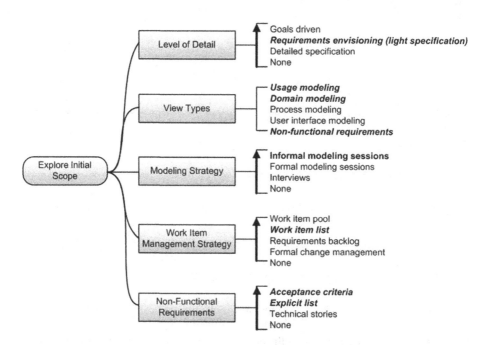

Fig. 5. The process goal diagram for Explore Initial Scope.

Requirements Backlog strategy. Work items may include new requirements to be implemented, defects to be fixed, training workshops, reviews of other teams' work, and so on. These are all things that need to be sized, prioritized, and planned for. Finally, the goal diagram makes it clear that when you're exploring the initial scope of your effort that you should capture non-functional requirements – such as reliability, availability, and security requirements (among many) – in some manner.

There are several fundamental advantages to taking a goal-driven approach to agile solution delivery. First, a goal-driven approach supports process tailoring by making process decisions explicit. Second, it enables effective scaling by guiding you through tailoring your strategy to reflect the realities of the scaling factors that you face. Third, it makes your process options very clear and thereby makes it easier to identify the appropriate strategy for the situation you find yourself in. Fourth, it takes the guesswork out of extending agile methods and thereby enables you to focus on your actual job, which is to provide value to your stakeholders. Fifth, it makes it clear what risks you're taking on and thus enables you to increase the likelihood of project success. Sixth, and this may not be a benefit, it hints at an agile maturity model.

Strategy #5: DA enables tactical scaling. When many people hear "scaling" they often think about large teams that may be geographically distributed in some way. This clearly happens, and people are clearly succeeding at applying agile in these sorts of situations, but there's often more to scaling than this. Organizations are also applying agile in compliance situations, either regulatory compliance that is imposed upon them or self-selected compliance (such as CMMI and ISO). They are also applying agile to a range

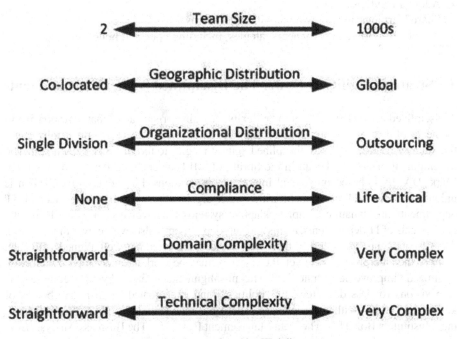

Fig. 6. Scaling factors faced by IT delivery teams.

of problem and solution complexities, and even when multiple organizations are involved (as in outsourcing). Figure 6 summarizes the potential scaling factors that you need to consider when tailoring your agile strategy [12].

Strategy #6: DA teams are enterprise aware. The observation is that DA teams work within your organization's enterprise ecosystem, as do all other teams. Often there are existing systems currently in production, and minimally your solution shouldn't impact them. Better yet, your solution will hopefully leverage existing functionality and data available in production. You will often have other teams working in parallel with your team and you may wish to take advantage of a portion of what they're doing and vice versa. Your organization may be working towards business or technical visions to which your team should contribute. A governance strategy exists which hopefully enhances what your team is doing.

Enterprise awareness is an important aspect of self-discipline because as a professional you should strive to do what's right for your organization and not just what's interesting to you. Delivery teams developing in isolation may choose to build something from scratch, or use different development tools, or create different data sources, when perfectly good ones that have been successfully installed, tested, configured, and fine-tuned already exist within the organization. Disciplined agile professionals will:

- Work closely with enterprise professionals, such as enterprise architects and portfolio managers
- Adopt and follow enterprise guidance
- Leverage enterprise assets, including existing systems and data sources
- Enhance your organizational ecosystem via refactoring enterprise assets
- Adopt a DevOps culture
- Share learnings and knowledge with other teams
- Adopt appropriate governance strategies, including open and honest monitoring.

4   Strategic Agility at Scale: The Disciplined Agile IT Department

A disciplined agile IT department is a flexible learning organization that is responsive to the needs of the organization(s) that it supports and is able to do so in a financially effective manner. DA 2.x extends disciplined agile strategies to the entire IT department. The development of DA 2.x began in the Spring of 2014 under the leadership of Scott and Mark. DA 2.x is based on several important observations. First, every organization is unique, and every IT department within each organization is also unique. Second, IT departments are dynamic complex adaptive systems that evolve over time. Third, the components of IT departments, teams and sub-departments, also evolve over time. Fourth, these components, when left to their own devices, are often not well aligned with each other or the enterprise. Worse yet, these groups may be working under their own locally optimized "improvement strategies." This misalignment is caused by competing leadership visions (or less delicately, by "politics") and exacerbated by disparate bodies of knowledge (BoKs) within our industry: The Agile Manifesto [13]; The Project Management Institute's BoK [14]; The Data Management BoK [15]; The Business Analysis BoK

[16]; The Open Group Architecture Framework (TOGAF) [17]; The Information Technology Infrastructure Library (ITIL) [18]; The Control Objectives for Information and Related Technology (COBIT) framework [19]; and many more.

Although all of these bodies of work provide valuable insight, they each provide their own locally optimized view of how things should work. These views overlap, they provide inconsistent advice, and they are often focused on a single specialty. For example, the BABoK provides a business analyst-centric view, TOGAF provides an architecture centric view, the DMBoK provides a data management centric view, and so on. All great views, but when combined with one another, which is a common approach in most organizations today looking for "best practices", they prove to be an ineffective mishmash. DA 2.x provides a coherent, integrated, high-level view of how an IT department may address all of these key areas in a consistent, flexible, and evolutionary manner. Wherever possible DA 2.x references the effective ideas in these BoKs and supplements them with strategies that are more consistent with modern agile approaches. Figure 1 overviewed the DA 2.x framework.

DA 2.x has been arranged into components called "process blades." Each process blade focuses on a major IT activity, as you can see in the previous diagram. No blade is an island unto itself – each one is involved in workflows with several other blades. The implication is that a change in one area, such as a process improvement or a change in the organizational structure of the people involved, will potentially affect the instantiation of the other blades. This interconnection of processes and organization strategies is a reflection of the fact that IT departments are complex adaptive systems. The process blades are:

- *Agile/Basic*. Describes the end-to-end solution delivery lifecycle for teams working in an agile, or Scrum-based, manner. Project teams who are new to agile, or who find themselves in situations where a regular work cadence is effective for them, will often choose to adopt this lifecycle.
- *Continuous Delivery*. Describes the end-to-end solution delivery lifecycle for teams working in a continuous delivery manner. Product teams who are working in a DevOps environment often adopt this strategy.
- *Continuous Improvement*. Addresses how to support process and organizational structure improvement across teams in a lightweight, collaborative manner; how to support improvement experiments within teams; and how to govern process improvement with the IT department.
- *Data Management*. Addresses how to improve data quality, evolve data assets such as master data and test data, and govern data activities within the organization.
- *Enterprise Architecture*. Addresses strategies for supporting stakeholders; supporting delivery teams; resolving technical dependencies between solutions; evolving the enterprise architecture; capturing the enterprise architecture; and governing the enterprise architecture efforts.
- *Exploratory/Lean Startup*. Describes the end-to-end solution delivery lifecycle for teams working in an exploratory, or "lean start up", manner. Teams who find themselves in situations where rapid innovation is called for often follow this lifecycle.
- *IT Governance*. Addresses strategies for consolidating various governance views, defining metrics, taking measurements, monitoring and reporting on measurements, developing and capturing guidance, defining roles and responsibilities, sharing

knowledge within the organization, managing IT risk, and coordinating the various governance efforts (including EA governance).

- *Lean/Advanced.* Describes the end-to-end solution delivery lifecycle for teams working in a lean, or Kanban-based, manner. Teams who have many small, relatively independent requirements (be they change requests or potential defects) and who are working on an existing solution will often adopt this lifecycle.
- *Operations.* Addresses how to run systems, evolve the IT infrastructure, manage change within the operational ecosystem, mitigate disasters, and govern IT operations.
- *Portfolio Management.* Addresses how to identify potential business value that could be supported by IT endeavors, explore those potential endeavors to understand them in greater detail, prioritize those potential endeavors, initiate the endeavors, manage vendors, and govern the IT portfolio.
- *Product Management.* Addresses strategies for managing a product, including allocating features to a product, evolving the business vision for a product, managing functional dependencies, and marketing the product line.
- *Program Management.* Addresses strategies for managing large product/project teams, allocating requirements between sub teams, managing dependencies between sub teams, coordinating the sub teams (via common or disparate cadences), and governing a program.
- *Release Management.* Addresses strategies for planning the IT release schedule, coordinating releases of solutions (such as release trains or release windows), managing the release infrastructure, supporting delivery teams, and governing the release management efforts.
- *Reuse Management.* Addresses how to identify and obtain reusable assets, publish the assets so that they are available to be reused, support delivery teams in reusing the assets, evolving those assets over time, and governing the reuse efforts.
- *Support.* Addresses how to adopt an IT support strategy, to escalate incidents, to effectively address the incidents, and govern the IT support effort.

The business environment is only becoming more competitive over time, with small nimble organizations competing in international marketplaces with large established competitors. This puts increasing pressure on existing enterprises to respond swiftly and effectively. They only way they can do this is if they have nimble IT departments that are sufficiently responsive. To increase the challenge, IT departments must be able to react to the changing needs of their organization while at the same time keep the existing IT infrastructure running smoothly. The only way that they can do this is by taking a flexible, holistic approach to the business of IT – This is exactly what Disciplined Agile 2.x is all about.

5   Principles for Effective Process Frameworks

The Disciplined Agile process decision framework is guided by the following principles:

- *Choice is good, and making informed choices is better.* Every team is a collection of unique individuals that face a unique situation within the context of a unique organization. One process size does not fit all. To provide choice the DA framework supports four delivery lifecycles and is process goal driven. Most importantly the DA framework describes the tradeoffs involved with a myriad of agile and non-agile practices enabling people to make intelligent decisions regarding which practices to adopt given the current situation that they face.

- *Optimize the whole.* The DA framework addresses the full IT lifecycle, showing how it all fits together. Without an understanding of the larger process environment teams run the risk of locally optimizing their own processes to the detriment of the whole. For example, your data management team may have their own streamlined process based on traditional DAMA strategies, your delivery team may have their streamlined process based on the principles of the Agile Manifesto, and your operations team may have their streamlined process based on ITIL. Yet your overall process is ineffective because these three locally optimized strategies contradict and degrade one another when combined.
- *Every team owns its process.* Teams, and the individuals on them, must be free to improve the way that they work based on their learnings over time. In agile parlance we say that these teams "own their process".
- *Improve continuously.* Individuals, teams, and organizations must strive to continuously learn and improve the way that they work. The DA framework includes the process goal Improve Team Process and Environment which describes options for doing exactly what its name implies. It also has an explicit process blade Continuous Improvement that describes strategies for sharing improvements across teams, thereby speeding up your organization's process improvement efforts.
- *Embrace process change.* IT departments are complex adaptive systems. One implication of this is that any improvements that a team makes is that they change that the team works with other teams, motivating process improvements within those teams. Those changes will motivate improvements on other teams and so on. Disciplined agile teams are enterprise aware and understand that they will need to work with other teams to help them to understand and adopt new innovations, and be prepared to be helped by others to do the same.
- *Repeatable results are far more important than repeatable processes.* Effective teams focus on producing repeatable results, such as delivering high-quality software that meets stakeholder needs in a timely and cost effective manner. Because each team finds themselves in a unique situation, to be most efficient they need to follow a unique process tailored to reflect that situation. That "unique process" may be comprised of a relatively standard lifecycle and common practices such as architecture envisioning, database regression testing, non-solo development, and many others (granted, those practices may be tailored to reflect the situation too). Each team in your organization must be allowed to follow their version of the process, ideally sharing similar process components defined by a common process framework, to achieve the results required of them.
- *Empiricism is far more important than theory.* Observing how well a technique works in practice, and more importantly the context of the situations in which it (doesn't) work is far more valuable to practitioners than theories or prognostications about what should work. Theory has its place, but it is a poor cousin to empiricism.

The DA framework was originally developed based on observations of dozens of organizations worldwide, and has evolved since then based on learnings from many more. Furthermore it is backed up by our ongoing industry research [20].

IT departments are unique, complex adaptive systems. Anyone working in such environments needs a process framework that is sufficiently flexible to address the range of situations faced by your teams. The Disciplined Agile process decision framework is light-weight yet sufficiently flexible to support scaling at both the tactical and strategic levels.

References

1. The Disciplined Agile site. http://DisciplinedAgileDelivery.com
2. Ambler, S.W., Lines, M.: Disciplined Agile Delivery: A Practitioner's Guide to Agile Software Delivery in the Enterprise. IBM Press, New York (2012)
3. Disciplined Agile Consortium. http://DisciplinedAgileConsortium.org
4. Introduction to Disciplined Agile Delivery (DAD) 1.x. http://DisciplinedAgileDelivery.com/introduction-to-disciplined-agile-delivery/
5. Disciplined DevOps. http://DisciplinedAgileDelivery.com/disciplineddevops/
6. Jumbler, J., Molesky, J., O'Reilly, B.: Lean Enterprise: How High-Performance Organizations Innovate at ScaleO'Reilly Media, Sebastopol (2015)
7. Scaled Agile Framework (SAFe). http://ScaledAgileFramework.com
8. The Scaled Scrum Framework. http://Scrum.org/Resources/What-is-Scaled-Scrum
9. Full Agile Delivery Lifecycles. http://DisciplinedAgileDelivery.com/lifecycle/
10. Ries, E.: The Lean Startup. How Today's Entrepenuers Use Innovation To Create Radically Successful Businesses. Crown Business, New York (2011)
11. Process Goals. http://DisciplinedAgileDelivery.com/process-goals/
12. Scaling Factors. http://DisciplinedAgileDelivery.com/agility-at-scale/scaling-factors/
13. The Agile Manifesto. http://AgileManifesto.org
14. PMBoK Guide and Standards. http://pmi.org/PMBOK-Guide-and-Standards.aspx
15. The Data Body of Knowledge. http://dama.org/content/body-knowledge
16. A Guide to the Business Body of Knowledge (BABoK). http://iiba.org/babok-guide.aspx
17. The Open Group Architecture Framework (TOGAF) v9.1. http://opengroup.org/togaf/
18. The Information Technology Infrastructure Library (ITIL). http://axelos.com/best-practice-solutions/itil
19. The Control Objectives for Information and Related Technology (COBIT) framework. http://isaca.org/COBIT/Pages/default.aspx
20. Surveys Exploring the Current State of Information Technology Practices. http://ambysoft.com/surveys/

Software Engineering Processes and Process Modelling

How Scrum Tools May Change Your Agile Software Development Approach

Matthias Eckhart[(✉)] and Johannes Feiner

Internet Technologies and Applications, FH Joanneum, Werk-VI-Strasse 46,
8605 Kapfenberg, Austria
{matthias.eckhart,johannes.feiner}@fh-joanneum.at
http://www.fh-joanneum.at/itm

Abstract. A major problem for distributed Scrum teams is proper communication between the involved parties to ensure the quality of the final product. This is especially true for coordination issues such as sharing requirements, time schedules, to-dos and code artefacts. Hence, Scrum-Masters complain frequently about software tools not suiting their daily needs when supporting agile teamwork, finally leading to the fact of not using a Scrum tool at all. In this paper we describe the extensive interviews held with selected ScrumMasters in which they explained their current tools and the existing gap to their real needs. Within this context, they were able to define the features and aspects they really need. After collecting those requirements for their daily work, we extracted the most wanted ingredients, prioritised them and finally forged them into an Open Source tool called Scrumpy, helping us to present a first solution, which focuses on the agile philosophy of Scrum and the elements needed most by ScrumMasters. Features of Scrumpy include, for example, web-based access to the task board with real-time updates, advanced dashboard visualisation techniques and a sophisticated chat system, which enables effortless communication for distributed teams. Although we already have first anecdotal feedback from users, we plan to improve the tool in a next step by adding more commodity features, perform additional mobile usability tests and systematically evaluate Scrumpy with a large number of end users.

Keywords: Scrum tools · Scrum · Agile software development · Distributed Scrum · Scrum task board

1 Introduction

Understanding potential benefits and risks of Scrum tools is crucial to the success of Scrum in agile organisations, which prefer the use of a software-based tool to assist participants of the Scrum process in handling their daily tasks. Since more and more organisations decide to switch to the agile way of software development [1], the need for a suitable Scrum tool grows substantially [2]. As a result, a vast amount of new products enter the global market, leading to the fact that

© Springer International Publishing Switzerland 2016
D. Winkler et al. (Eds.): SWQD 2016, LNBIP 238, pp. 17–36, 2016.
DOI: 10.1007/978-3-319-27033-3_2

Scrum tool producers try to outsell each other. Although the product may fulfil its brand-promise, there is no guarantee that participants involved in Scrum, benefit from features offered by the Scrum tool in the end.

In the last few years there has been a growing interest in reorganising the organisational structure by establishing remote teams at low-cost locations, in order to reduce personnel expenses [3]. As a consequence, further issues in geographically distributed teams may emerge, such as time differences, technical challenges and cross-cultural communication problems [4]. To overcome collaboration barriers across remote teams, the proper use of Scrum tools may be vital to the success of the company in the long run. This actually raises the question what the essence of a valuable tool for supporting efficient agile development is. The study at hand, therefore, aims at investigating flaws regarding the use and development of Scrum tools that needed to be discussed, addressing the correlation between software-based tools and Scrum.

This paper is structured as follows. The next section, Sect. 2, reviews related work in the field. Section 3 describes the applied research methodology. In Sect. 4 we put forward several determined issues concerning the use of Scrum tools and involved risks that might have a negative impact on the Scrum team's productivity. Section 5 proposes concepts for using Scrum tools more effectively. Furthermore, we present new useful features and potential enhancements that can be implemented in existing Scrum tools. In addition, we provide in Sect. 6 a list of minimum requirements that should be implemented to avoid dissatisfaction among users — suggestions put forward by the interviewed ScrumMasters. In Sect. 7, we introduce our developed Scrum tool based on the listed minimum requirements. Finally, in Sect. 8, we draw some concluding remarks and discuss future work concerning this study and the developed Scrum tool.

2   Related Work

Moe et al. [5] indicate that conflicts between team members may emerge when making the switch to agile software development, since additional work can be incurred, in order to foster self-managing teams. Compared to traditionally managed teams, the characteristics of shared leadership embraces a joint decision-making process which requires a strong team commitment. As a result the individuals' ability to work collaboratively with other team members is fundamental to a self-organising team. In addition, Moe et al. reinforce their doubts regarding a team of specialists, because this culture may encourage an individual autonomy which can result in a lack of focus for the team's goal. Furthermore, they describe that this jeopardy may evolve if each software developer is responsible for a separate module, as they may rarely be involved in other components of the system and consequently tend to get side-tracked. According to their study, developing software with Scrum in a remote setup is likely to exacerbate the issues of an individual leadership. Moe et al. also describe that collocation facilitates communication within the team and fosters the ability to achieve a high level of collaboration, which encourages a break of the hierarchical relationship and as a consequence initiates to build trust and commitment. As stated by Scissors et al. [6], distributed teams may face severe challenges when creating a team culture among individuals from different nationalities. Furthermore, they describe that distributed team members, who rely heavily on nonverbal communication, are particularly prone to conflicts, which may endanger social harmony. In addition, previous research indicates that there is a strong coherence between the communication efficiency and the used communication method. Rayhan and Haque from *Code 71, Inc.* [7] state in their paper that the use of e-mail and Microsoft Excel to manage their remote Scrum team has been proven to be impractical, especially as the team size grew. They also reported that the communication of the daily project status via e-mail posed a distraction for the Scrum team. As a result, they decided to introduce the agile project management software *VersionOne*. However, due to a lack of intuitive user experience design and insufficient support for collaboration, they used *VersionOne* only for time tracking purposes and introduced *Basecamp*, a tool which seemed to fit their needs for managing backlogs. However, transferring artefacts from one tool to another resulted in productivity decrease and consequently engendered the desire to create a seamless process.

A different approach in implementing agile development has been reported by Sarkan et al. [8] who used Scrum tools to support the agile requirements development for software projects at the research and development centre *MIMOS Berhad* in Malaysia. In the initial phase of introducing Scrum, they decided to use *Redmine* for gathering user stories. Although the tool provided an extensive issue tracking system, they recorded bugs in separate tools such as *Rational ClearQuest*. Given that *Redmine* takes full effect of traditional project management, rather than agile methodologies, they decided to substitute the tool with *JIRA*. As a result they could benefit not only from its product backlog features, but also from the task board to monitor the team's progress. In addition, they decided to track issues with *JIRA* which enabled them to link the reported problems to user stories. Furthermore, Sarkan et al. stated in their study that the requirements management effort has been reduced to a minimum degree, owing to the introduction of a Scrum tool. Yet, these findings point towards a tool supported Scrum process, little is known about how ScrumMasters assess the impact of Scrum tools on core Scrum values and principles.

Since there was a shortage in quantitative information related to the needs of a company with regard to Scrum tools, Azizyan et al. [2] conducted a survey to identify the most important aspects of the tools used. They analysed the responses to questions of 120 companies, including collocated as well as distributed team structures. According to their survey results, 65 % of collocated teams and more than 80 % of distributed teams used agile project management tools to support their processes. As a result, we imply that Scrum tools take on an important role in agile software development. Although the study from Azizyan et al. provides comprehensive results about the needs of agile software development companies, further research to determine insights from the ScrumMaster's perspective is still required.

Previous research has indicated that the use of a physical task board in collocated teams is strongly recommended, while the use of its digital equivalent can be regarded as negligible, unless there are substantial reasons which justify its implementation [9]. In contrast, the use of a tool, to support distributed Scrum teams in managing the product backlog, is considered as essential for coordinating the teams at remote locations [10]. Furthermore, the results obtained in [11,12] suggest that particular attention needs to be paid to the characteristics of the Scrum tool's digital task board, as well as to the implementation process when migrating from other platforms such as *SharePoint*.

3   Methodology - A Case Study with Interviews

Since extensive research, for example, by Azizyan et al. [2] has addressed various tools used in 120 different companies, we chose a rather qualitative than quantitative approach in which we identified the role of Scrum tools in agile software development, by taking viewpoints of ScrumMasters into consideration. Therefore, we conducted a case study, interviewing five selected Scrum experts for an in-depth analysis of their experiences in (remote) Scrum teams and their work with current Scrum tools. The male interviewees were acquired via the Scrum User Group Graz (XING) and by directly contacting medium-sized enterprises in Austria. At the time of the study, their average expertise with Scrum was 6.2 years, as ScrumMasters 3.4 years and all of the participants were Scrum Alliance® certified. The average development team size was 8.2, whereas two ScrumMasters out of five had to handle two teams at a time.

The scientific method of our empirical observation did not focus on quantitative (online questionnaires, statistical results), but high qualitative data which we received by means of detailed and thorough semi-structured interviews with Scrum practitioners in winter 2014. We used a holistic approach to examine the real-life context, by asking this small group to report about their positive and negative experiences as well as their suggestions for future improvements. Prior to the case study, we prepared a guideline for the interviews which was split into three parts. The first part covered background information about the participants and the company they are working for, such as experience with Scrum, size of enterprise or the office cubicle (workspace) design. The second part focused on a variety of aspects related to the implemented Scrum processes. For instance, we wanted to examine their Scrum team structure, as well as the Scrum activities carried out. To name a few examples, we asked them about the applied effort estimation technique, the development team size or the iteration planning, in order to achieve a broad range of questions. The last component of our three-part interview primarily dealt with the introduced Scrum tool. To encourage the interviewees to talk about the issues faced owing to the used Scrum tool, we asked questions like *"What are the key problems with digital task board usage?"*, *"Did you configure different access permissions for artefacts in the Scrum tool?"* or *"Which reports are generated for the management?"*. As suggested by Seaman [13], we avoided polar questions for collecting qualitative data, in order to make it easier for participants to expound about the discussed topics. Based on this, we asked 37 open-ended questions in total, within a time frame of 20–60 min. To ensure qualitative research results, we collected data by recording the semi-structured interviews. After the interview sessions were held, we transcribed the recorded audio and subsequently coded our transcript by labelling relevant sections. After we formed a set of codes, we examined the assigned passages in our transcript with respect to repetitions and similarities among the interviewees opinions. Finally, we grouped selected codes which we thought were most important and created themed categories. To gain profound insights into Scrum tools from the perspective of the interviewed ScrumMasters, we interpreted the data.

The limitation of this case study is the small number of participants, which does not really allow to extract statistically relevant data. Nevertheless, based on these findings, we developed a real-time[1] web-based Scrum tool named Scrumpy (see Sect. 7) to examine the link between Scrum and Scrumpy further.

4 Identification of Critical Problem Areas

The following section is devoted to potential deficiencies with regard to Scrum tools and its involved parties. Our aim in this chapter is to raise awareness of several issues concerning the use of Scrum tools, as well as the introduction of the tool in real projects.

4.1 The ScrumMaster's Role as a Critical Success Factor

According to the interviewed experts, it is still prevalent that IT managers do not acknowledge the ScrumMasters' work, since they do not produce any code by themselves. As a result, they often do not hire ScrumMasters, but rather retrain existing project managers or developers. Unfortunately, this leads to wrong organisational change, in which an individual occupies two roles simultaneously, e.g. ScrumMaster and software developer or ScrumMaster and Product Owner. Although personnel cost may be saved, Scrum cannot be used to its full extent and continual improvement may not be achieved in the long run, due to the negligence of the ScrumMaster's duties.

As stated in the agile manifesto, direct communication is the most efficient and effective method of transferring information [14]. One issue that may emerge in this context is the misuse of the Scrum tool as the main way of communicating within a collocated team. Despite the fact that Scrum tools may simplify the act of communicating, especially with distributed teams, they obviously cannot substitute face-to-face communication. This issue is not limited to the live chat features of a Scrum tool, because even the update of a task on the virtual task board will result in a loss of nonverbal communication details such as body

---

[1] Our application is capable of handling live updates, i.e. data changes will be pushed to clients instantly, without the necessity to refresh the page manually.

language or gestures. Findings of the research conducted by Segers [11] confirm our study results that declare physical task boards as a gathering place for the Scrum team which establishes open communication and subsequently improves collaboration since individuals are able to perceive every single movement or unconscious body signal. As a result, meeting participants should be encouraged to start a discussion if discrepancies among the Scrum team members exist. Therefore the ScrumMaster's task and obligation is to raise awareness regarding the importance of communication. The interviewees past experience suggests that this task requires a lot of effort. For that reason, they prefer a strict observance of the roles, allowing the ScrumMaster to focus only on the tasks defined in the Scrum framework, having no other burden with obligations outside his or her remit.

Furthermore, the data obtained from the interviews indicate that ScrumMasters need to take special care of conflicts caused by obsessive micromanagers. The evaluation of the interviews shows that managers tend to check the progress of the Scrum team based on the burn down chart on a daily basis, even though this tool should be designed by and for the development team only. However, managers should definitely have full access to the Scrum tool including the burn down chart provided by the tool, otherwise the process will become non-transparent and eventually will have a strong negative impact on the collaboration between the Scrum team and other parties, due to feelings of anxiety as managers may feel out of control.

4.2   Inflexible Scrum Tools Limit the Agility of Scrum

One of the major advantages of Scrum in comparison to traditional project management is that the stated agile method offers a certain degree of flexibility with regard to the defined processes. Because of this, the Scrum team is able to maintain continuous improvement and consequently may increase efficiency over time. Therefore, it is even worse if the introduced Scrum tool implicitly requires certain parts of the Scrum process, which cannot be bypassed when using the software.

One interviewed expert exemplified this issue by outlining a workaround which allowed the Scrum team to keep up with the sprint rhythm of the Scrum tool if the development team needed an extra sprint for fixing bugs, especially shortly before a major release. Although all increments were finished according to the Definition of Done (DoD), some builds failed after the integration of critical components. As a result, the Scrum team split the sprint of two weeks in half and used one week for integration tests and one week for fixing bugs. Carrying out integrations multiple times during the sprint is certainly the best-case scenario, but unfortunately this is often not attainable in real-world systems.

Another significant point about the inflexibility of Scrum tools concerns the type of effort estimation, specified by the Scrum tool. Since the preferred effort estimation method may vary from development team to development team, a Scrum tool should not predefine the technique to estimate effort. According to our interview results, a Scrum tool should provide a feature to record the estimated effort, but any inputs related to the effort estimation should definitely not be designed as mandatory. This request applies to the effort estimation of user stories as well as tasks, because some development teams may skip the estimation of tasks, due to the fact that this may be too time-consuming. Moreover, the selected effort estimation technique affects also the visualisation method, for the simple reason that the measurement of work progress is often deduced from the estimated effort. For instance, the data unit to visualise the work progress can be hours, story points, user stories or tasks completed. Furthermore, even an overlay of multiple data units may be desired. As a result, the development team should have the opportunity to choose the data unit for visualisation methods, provided by the Scrum tool.

Further concerns stem from the fact that Scrum tools are considered to be hard to adapt with regard to process changes. For instance, if the Scrum team decides to record a new attribute for user stories on the digital task board, extensive configurations may apply which could require reading the documentation. In contrast, the physical task board can easily be changed and is not limited to any settings.

Table 1. A comparison of supported characteristics by the physical task board and its digital equivalent.

Criteria	Physical task board	Digital task board
Ease of change	✓	Problematic
Remote capabilities	✗	✓
Social aspects	✓	Problematic
Versioning	Problematic	✓
Haptic	✓	✗

Find in Table 1 a comparison of several physical and digital task board characteristics.

4.3 Agile Organisational Structures Apart from the Traditional Scrum Framework

The expert interviews revealed that there are tremendous discrepancies between the roles which are specified by the Scrum tool and the roles defined in large-scale organisations. One real-world example of a large-scale organisation is presented in Fig. 1. This organisation type extends the typical Scrum roles by a project manager, a Chief Product Owner (CPO), a Product Manager (PM) and the three cross-divisional roles: Chief Software Architect (CSA), one person in charge of writing the documentation (DOC) and the Quality Assurance Manager (QA).

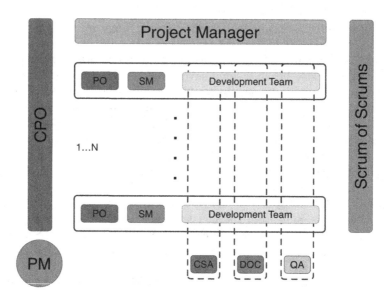

Fig. 1. Organigram of an extended agile organisational structure.

Especially when scaling Scrum in a large enterprise, while remaining agile is desirable, a complete mapping of all the roles in a Scrum tool is often unachievable. After all, the organisation should not be forced to adapt the roles, specified by the Scrum tool but rather the tool should provide a sophisticated role management feature, so that a straightforward mapping of the organisation is attainable or further role separation for the use of the Scrum tool is not needed at all.

4.4 Insufficient Overview of the Digital Task Board Due to a Mass Amount of Information to Display

All interviewed experts complained about an insufficient overview of the digital task board. The main reason for their complaint was that meeting participants may lose the overall context of the discussed tasks when scrolling to the next user story, due to fact that not all of the tasks could be displayed at once, making reading difficult. One interviewee took advantage of this *issue* by forcing the development team to focus only on three user stories at a time. This way, all of the user stories and corresponding tasks in process could be displayed at once and as a consequence, scrolling was unnecessary. However, there is still a demand for an improved design of the task board to display the entire content at once, without compromising readability.

4.5 Scrum Tools Hosted in the Cloud

Numerous producers of web-based Scrum tools, such as *Atlassian*, sell cloud hosting services in addition to the developed product to enable customers a fast and easy launch of the Scrum tool in their organisation. Although cloud hosting may be a more convenient way than deploying the Scrum tool on a self-hosted server, there are a few things worth taking into consideration when using third-party cloud services for hosting a Scrum tool.

First of all, Scrum tools are used to support the agile software development process and therefore need to handle data which may betray customers' privacy to a certain degree. Unfortunately, it cannot be guaranteed that the service provider will not face any data privacy issues. In addition, they often have their own privacy policies, which may exclude coverage for privacy and security liabilities. Nevertheless, the cloud hosting provider should hold a valid industry-standard security certification which verifies a safe hosting environment at a high level.

Secondly, relying on a Scrum tool which is hosted by a cloud service provider could have a huge negative impact on the productivity of the Scrum team, if the tool is not available when needed. Even more attention should be paid to this potential risk, if the Scrum tool is used as a central information system and business relevant data must be accessible all time. Since hosting issues may not be resolved immediately after occurrence, the web-based Scrum tool can be offline for a longer period of time. However, the existence of this problem could not be verified, since all interviewed experts host the Scrum tool in their internal IT infrastructure, due to the previously stated potential risks.

Owing to both of the mentioned reasons, all of the interviewed ScrumMasters recommend the self-hosted solution, because the use of a cloud hosted Scrum tool will result in an undesirable dependency to the service provider. However, Scrum teams in small companies may benefit more from cloud hosted Scrum tools, since they do not have to care about the deployment of the server and the ongoing periodic maintenance tasks.

4.6   Challenges in Introducing Scrum Tools in an Organisation

According to our study, organisations may face problems related to practicing Scrum if the Scrum tool has been introduced at the same time as the agile methodology itself. One of the main risks related to this approach is that the Scrum team may deduce the Scrum process from the features of the Scrum tool. In this way, they will lose all possibilities for continuously improving the Scrum process from the very beginning. As the Scrum tool may provide ready-made processes, the Scrum team often tends to carry out mindlessly instructions the Scrum tool gives. Two interviewed ScrumMasters compared this pitfall to *SAP* implementation failures due to massive internal organisational changes across a variety of business segments in the company. As a result, it is highly recommended to start introducing a Scrum tool after Scrum has been successfully established in the organisation. Especially at an early stage, the use of a physical task board, to visualise the sprint backlog with sticky notes, may be more effective when practicing Scrum. Only after the Scrum team has understood the importance of face-to-face communication, they can try to make the switch to a digital task board, provided by the Scrum tool. Nevertheless, the physical task board should be available at any time during the first sprint conducted with the Scrum tool, allowing the team members to switch back to the old method easily. Ideally, a part of the sprint retrospective meeting should be used to reflect on how the Scrum tool was used during the sprint and if it should be used in future sprints. As a consequence, the Scrum tool should provide features to perform a fast migration, so that an implementation later on in the Scrum process is still attainable.

5   Concepts for Success Regarding the use of Scrum Tools

In this section, we present examples for a better understanding of how to use Scrum tools effectively and make suggestions how they could be improved.

5.1   Agile Software Development with Distributed Teams

The coordination of distributed teams requires a lot of effort to keep the collaboration among distributed team members vibrant, ensuring an ongoing productivity on a high level. Considering the economic aspects of distributing teams globally, it may be worth the management effort. However, beside differences in culture and language problems, also technical issues may emerge. One interviewed ScrumMaster reported that they started to use Skype as a video conferencing tool for their daily Scrum meetings on both of the two locations. The interviewee also pointed out that the use of a HD camcorder instead of an off-the-shelf webcam for live streaming is beneficial in terms of video quality and mobility. Furthermore, the ScrumMaster mentioned that the use of a professional studio microphone is more qualified for the stand-up meeting than a built-in microphone, because it can be passed along from person to person. Although the quality of the video calls was acceptable for streaming the daily Scrum meetings, a professional video conferencing system may be superior if more than two distributed Scrum teams participate.

However, according to the interviewees, recording the physical task board is useless, since meeting participants on other locations cannot read the streamed content of the user stories and the corresponding tasks. Even transmitting high-resolution photos of the physical task board has been proven as inefficient. This issue has been resolved by using a Scrum tool and installing an additional monitor on each location in order to view the digital task board and the video conference simultaneously. In addition, meeting participants may benefit from the use of a screen sharing software for mirroring the Scrum tool, because this way they are able to keep track of the discussed topics. Despite that the proposed solution may work to some extent, the ScrumMaster suggested that the Scrum teams should meet at each others location on a rotating basis at the end, as well as at the beginning of the consecutive sprint, if the project enters a critical stage and the travel expenses are affordable.

5.2 Optimising the Digital Tool Landscape

Scattering documents across multiple tools is a known problem for IT companies in general. Especially in companies which specialise in the development of software, this issue may be even more important since they may need a tool to track down bugs. In addition, specifications for the implementation of the developed product may also be managed on data storage systems or with web content management systems such as *MediaWiki* or *TWiki*. In general, there is a need for a revision control system specifically for documents, on the one hand to prevent data inconsistencies, due to concurrent processing of the same file by multiple users, and on the other hand to keep track of the changes made. According to Møller et al. [15], there is also a requirement for an internal logging feature, which tracks the project's progress and in further consequence provides historical data of everything that has happened during the sprint. Their findings suggest that owing to a Scrum tool's project history feature it would be no longer necessary to review extensively the progress of tasks and ipso facto time can be saved in discussions.

As the software maintenance effort increases by every new tool that will be integrated in the existing IT infrastructure, a Scrum tool which could eliminate other tools currently being used in the organisation would be ideal. For instance, a real-time collaborative editor feature like *Etherpad* could replace document processing tools. Moreover, the interviewed experts confirmed the findings of Sarkan et al. [8] that the integration of a bug tracker in the Scrum tool may simplify the bug fixing process, owing to referenced bugs on the digital task board. As a result, the establishment of the Scrum tool as a single environment like a *one-stop-shop* would not only be cost and time efficient, but also may increase the productivity of the Scrum team. Nevertheless, a Scrum tool capable of being used for many purposes in the context of software development may exhibit an undesirable strong dependence and consequently can become a potential single point of failure.

5.3 Integrated Reporting Solution

If the Scrum team works with the Scrum tool on a regular basis, the tool has great potential to increase efficiency by automating complex analysing and reporting tasks. In particular, measured agile metrics are relevant to managers, so that they can address problems and resolve incidents early enough. Typically, measuring and tracking the velocity is significant to estimate the rate of progress of the development team. In this way, managers can determine the project status to make sure that the arranged delivery date can be met. Furthermore, an evaluation of past impediments may increase the team's productivity if recurring issues can be fixed permanently. As Scrum tools may offer features that are able to extract data for reporting purposes or able to integrate a reporting system seamlessly, they could provide support for analysing and evaluating the team's performance. However, as previously stated, the ScrumMaster should give particular attention to prevent the emergence of a command-and-control leadership style by managers that may cause interferences in the development team's work.

5.4   Simulating the Look and Feel of a Physical Task Board

The design of the digital task board can have a huge impact on the usability of the Scrum tool. According to our results of the expert interviews, the layout of the digital task board should be based on an ordinary physical task board, because the Scrum team members may recognise it as a familiar object to work with. Typically, user stories and the corresponding tasks are displayed as virtual sticky notes in a matrix view. Although the overall design of the digital task board is important, the main focus should be put on the interaction with tasks. The interviewed ScrumMasters emphasised that they prefer drag-and-drop functionality for moving the virtual sticky notes to other task status columns, because this way of interacting is more intuitive than updating the task's status by setting a specific value in a drop-down list, to mention one prominent example. Consequently, users may get more engaged with using the Scrum tool.

In contrast to the capabilities of a physical task board, the digital task board provided by the Scrum tool may also be able to display the user's avatar on the virtual sticky note, showing the responsible team member's particular tasks. In this way, social aspects of an online community can be integrated, increasing the interpersonal trust in distributed teams [16]. In addition, the highlighting of tasks, which remain more than one day in progress, is beneficial for identifying problems or indicating that complex tasks should be broken down into sub-tasks.

5.5   Printable User Stories and Tasks

Scrum teams that want to take advantage of the physical, as well as the digital task board should certainly choose a Scrum tool which provides an export feature for user stories and tasks. In this way, the content of the digital task board can be printed and subsequently attached to a whiteboard or wall. The status of the tasks can then be synchronised manually with the digital task board periodically or at the end of each sprint. One interviewed expert recommended the *JIRA* plugin *Agile Cards* which enables an automated synchronisation by importing a photograph of the physical task board to *JIRA*.

6   Minimum Requirements for Scrum Tools

In the following section, we present minimum requirements that a Scrum tool must meet, as reported by the interviewed ScrumMasters. Not meeting these requirements may cause dissatisfaction among Scrum team members. Since the Scrum team's needs may vary, our aim is to provide a brief overview of fundamental characteristics which a Scrum tool should have implemented to its full extent.

As listed in Table 2, the suggested minimum requirements are deduced from remarks of prior sections, but are not ordered by importance or any other criteria.

Table 2. Determined minimum requirements for Scrum tools, based on our study results, including specific quotations made by the interviewed ScrumMasters.

Minimum requirement	Description	Extracts from the interviews
Information hub	The Scrum tool must be established as the primary source for information regarding the agile development process, in order to eliminate multiple subject-specific tools like Wikis and document management systems	"Developers should use the Scrum tool as a daily companion, assisting users in doing their work by providing relevant information concerning the project."
Usability	According to the ScrumMasters' opinions, the management may agree on a training for eight hours at the maximum, therefore the Scrum tool must be easy to use and consequently require little or no need for training	"As Scrum is easy to understand, the initial training phase for users of a newly introduced Scrum tool should have a similar learning curve. In this particular context, usability is definitely a factor to consider."
Availability	The tool must be available during working hours at the minimum. In case multiple teams are employed globally at different locations, the availability of the Scrum tool must be adapted according to potential time differences	"I have been informed that *iceScrum's* datacenter faced network issues several times which caused a downtime of the Scrum tool and affected customers of their cloud service."
Flexibility	The Scrum tool must preset roles which can be mapped with enterprise organisational structures. Furthermore, the Scrum tool must offer a variety of effort estimation methods and the specified sprint duration must be modifiable	"Whether a Scrum process or any other activity in an organisation is supported by a tool, it should be able to adapt to the given conditions at all times and not vice versa, in the manner of some failed *SAP* implementations."

(Continued)

Table 2. *(Continued.)*

Minimum requirement	Description	Extracts from the interviews
Design of the digital task board	The look and feel of a typical physical task board must be simulated by designing the structure of the digital task board in a similar way and by implementing intuitive interactions for handling virtual sticky notes	"The implemented interaction technique of a Scrum tool which we used prior to *iceScrum* provided a rather inconvenient way of changing the task's status, because the interaction with tasks was based on basic GUI elements like a drop-down menu. As opposed to this way of interacting with tasks, dragging a virtual sticky note from one column to another seems more appealing to me."
Traceability	Changes made to artefacts with the Scrum tool must be traceable via a version control functionality, so that modifications are understandable at any time	"A Scrum tool must provide traceability features, otherwise users are not able to understand the changes made to artefacts. Thus, the artefact's history is fundamental to the comprehension of information involved in Scrum processes."
Customisability	The Scrum tool must provide an interface to enable adaptations, either by customising the existing code of the Scrum tool or by being capable of integrating third-party plugins	"Since the implemented Scrum processes often vary from organisation to organisation, it should be possible to adjust the Scrum tool to specific needs and different environments."
Transparency	Artefacts, managed with the Scrum tool, must be visible for anyone involved in the Scrum process	"The Scrum tool must not limit the access to artefacts, otherwise the implementation of Scrum may be classified as a sinking ship and will result in a failed project or cost overrun."

(Continued)

Table 2. *(Continued.)*

Minimum requirement	Description	Extracts from the interviews
Reporting	Managers must be able to extract useful data concerning the performance of the Scrum team, in order to get a solid source of information regarding the project status	"For now we use an internal website which provides a status report based on various sources of information. Periodically, I export this website as a PDF file and send the document to the management. Since this manual processing is time-consuming, a Scrum tool, which is able to automatically generate detailed reports at regular intervals would be extremely helpful. Furthermore, in my opinion, the Scrum tool's reporting feature should put emphasis on simplicity, so that the project's status is easy to grasp. This could be implemented via a coloured illustration of a traffic light which indicates the current status."
Integrated communication solution	The Scrum tool must provide an integrated real-time one-to-one as well as a group messaging system to simplify communication with distributed teams	"Managing distributed Scrum teams is challenging. However, a Scrum tool can make a significant positive contribution to the collaboration among distributed team members."

7 Scrumpy – An Agile Project Management Tool Designed to Skyrocket Your Team's Productivity

The idea to develop a custom-built, Open Source Scrum tool [17] originated from the need of a lightweight solution which is extensible and allows adjustments which are specific to the environment at hand. Initially, the Institute of Internet Technologies and Applications, a department of the University of Applied Sciences JOANNEUM, used *Scrumy* for managing tasks, but the lack of extensibility in terms of LDAP authentication led to the decision to develop a new Scrum tool in-house. As a consequence, we created a web-based Scrum tool named Scrumpy [18,19] based on the results obtained from the expert interviews. Scrumpy runs on Meteor, a JavaScript framework for building modern real-time web applications. Owing to the integrated real-time web functionality, using the Scrum tool leads to a more vibrant experience, since data changes become immediately visible without refreshing the page.

Our main goal was to build a Scrum tool which can serve as an all-in-one solution, as well as an auxiliary tool which is limited to the digital task board

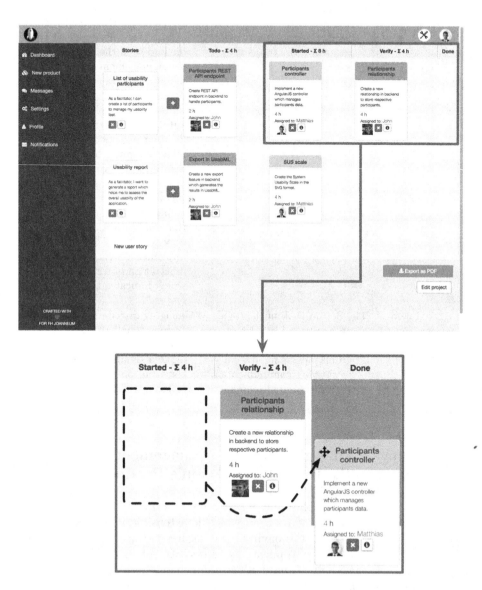

Fig. 2. Users can drag and drop virtual notes in order to update the task's status.

feature. Therefore we created an advanced and a basic mode[2] to meet the user's needs. In contrast to the basic mode, the advanced mode also includes a product management feature with detailed statistics on the progress of the product development, an activity stream which enables Scrum team members to easily track changes and a component for managing backlog items. Furthermore, we integrated the library *ShareJS* into the advanced mode, in order to enable users concurrent editing of documents in real-time. Regardless of the selected mode, user stories and the corresponding tasks can be exported as a PDF document, similar to the *JIRA* plugin *Agile Cards*.

According to the assessed needs concerning the usability of Scrum tools in Sect. 4.4, we used a responsive web design approach to take advantage of high-resolution monitors for displaying as much content as possible and not wasting any empty space. Thus, the appearance of the web application is especially beneficial for viewing the digital task board on a modern big-screen as many user stories and tasks can be displayed at once without the need for zooming. Particular attention has also been paid to the design of interactions with tasks and product backlog items. Since the interviewed experts prefer a natural, intuitive way of handling the tasks, we decided to implement a drag-and-drop function-

Table 3. List of minimum requirements and the stage of development, indicating whether the feature is implemented in Scrumpy.

Minimum requirement	Supported by Scrumpy
Information hub	Scrumpy provides a real-time editor which enables multiple users to work simultaneously on the same document. The integration of a file management system in Scrumpy is planned for future releases
Usability	✓
Availability	Depends on the infrastructure of servers and networks
Flexibility	Scrumpy maps the traditional Scrum roles in the advanced mode and provides two different user levels (administrator and team member) in the basic mode
Design of the digital task board	✓
Traceability	✗
Customisability	✓
Transparency	✓
Reporting	✓
Integrated communication solution	✓

---

[2] The basic mode is not necessarily intended for Scrum teams, but rather for any team, who wants to manage work visually via a task board.

ality. As a result, users are able to prioritise the product backlog or update the task's status by dragging the backlog item or the virtual sticky note to specific drop zones. Figure 2 shows the digital task board of Scrumpy's basic mode and the way how users interact with tasks.

Although Scrumpy is intended for professional use, we implemented features which should integrate social aspects of a typical online community. For instance, users are able to setup profile pages, upload avatars and chat with other registered members. In this way, the collaboration across globally distributed Scrum teams may be strengthened.

In spite of Scrumpy's huge feature set, we are planning to improve the existing components and continually implementing more functionality. For instance, Scrumpy does not provide a feature to define acceptance criteria for user stories. Furthermore, we plan to implement an internal calendar to schedule appointments and sync it with cloud services like *iCloud*. Last but not least, the integration of *ownCloud* would be desirable.

Find in Table 3 the implemented features according to the identified minimum requirements from Sect. 6.

8   Conclusion and Future Work

The expert interviews revealed problem areas regarding Scrum tools that tend to be crucial to the success of any agile Scrum project. Those issues are not only related specifically to the improper use, but also to the implementation of a Scrum tool in an organisation. For instance, we discovered that the ScrumMaster may face challenging tasks in maintaining effective conversations among team members, since chatting on a Scrum tool is a poor substitute for face-to-face communication. Furthermore, Scrum tools may not be able to map various types of enterprise agile organisational structures completely, which can cause a lack of transparency. This study also investigated problems concerning the introduction of Scrum tools and the hosting of the tool in the cloud, which should be used in caution, since privacy and availability issues may be faced. In contrast, we also analysed how Scrum tools can be used effectively and presented possible feature concepts to improve them.

The practical implications of our study can be summed up as follows. Scrum-Masters are sceptical towards the use of Scrum tools in collocated teams, because they appreciate the benefits of face-to-face communication which may be harmed due to the improper use of the tool. Although they think that Scrum tools can be very helpful if they have been introduced in an organisation properly, they certainly prefer a tool-free start of the first agile project, especially if Scrum team members are not familiar with agile-oriented processes. After the first couple of sprints have been successfully completed and the participants respect the agile principles as well as values, they can try to make the shift to a tool-supported Scrum workflow. However, according to the interviewed ScrumMasters, the use of a Scrum tool in a remote setup is almost essential. In this context, we noticed that ScrumMasters who work with distributed teams reconsider their toolset with an emphasis on collaboration features.

Since Scrumpy has not been assessed in real-world contexts, the prototype will be extensively evaluated in the next phase of the development process. This procedure will be done in two steps. First, we want to introduce Scrumpy in a Scrum-based software development course at our university and in further consequence establish the tool as an information hub for students to manage their project work. After that, we want to introduce Scrumpy in local agile software development companies to examine the Scrum tool in a real-world example. Based on this evaluation, we also intend to extend the functionality of Scrumpy in our future research. In addition, future work will also involve usability tests in a desktop and mobile setup, to improve the overall usability of the application and determine if the application can be used on mobile devices.

References

1. The Standish Group International. CHAOS MANIFESTO 2013 - Think Big, Act Small (2013). http://www.versionone.com/assets/img/files/CHAOSManifesto 2013.pdf
2. Azizyan, G., Magarian, M.K., Kajko-Mattson, M.: Survey of agile tool usage and needs. In: Agile Conference 2011, AGILE 2011, pp. 29–38. IEEE Computer Society, August 2011. doi:10.1109/AGILE.2011.30. ISBN: 978-0-7695-4370-3
3. Heller, R., Laurito, A., Johnson, K., Martin, M., Fitzpatrick, R., Sundin, K.: Global teams: trends, challenges and solutions. In: Cornell Center for Advanced Human Resource Studies. Partner Meeting, CAHRS 2010, May 2010. https://est05.esalestrack.com/eSalesTrack/Content/Content.ashx?file=4578f59e-21b3-4a2c-bbfe-63e53af3f5dc.pdf
4. Damian, D., Lassenius, C., Paasivaara, M., Borici, A., Schroter, A.: Teaching a globally distributed project course using scrum practices. In: Proceedings of 2nd Workshop on Collaborative Teaching of Globally Distributed Software Development, CTGDSD 2012, pp. 30–34. IEEE Computer Society (2012). doi:10.1109/CTGDSD.2012.6226947. ISBN: 978-1-4673-1818-1
5. Moe, N.B., Dingsoyr, T., Dybå, T.: Overcoming barriers to self-management in software teams. IEEE Softw. **26**(6), 20–26 (2009). doi:10.1109/MS.2009.182
6. Scissors, L., Shami, N.S., Ishihara, T., Rohall, S., Saito, S.: Realtime collaborative editing behavior in USA and Japanese distributed teams. In: Proceedings of the SIGCHI Conference on Human Factors in Computing Systems, CHI 2011, Vancouver, BC, Canada, pp. 1119–1128. ACM (2011). doi:10.1145/1978942.1979109. ISBN: 978-1-4503-0228-9
7. Rayhan, S.H., Haque, N.: Incremental adoption of scrum for successful delivery of an IT project in a remote setup. In: Melnik, G., Kruchten, P., Poppendieck, M. (eds.) Agile 2008 Conference, AGILE 2008, pp. 351–355. IEEE Computer Society, August 2008. doi:10.1109/Agile.2008.98
8. Sarkan, H., Ahmad, T., Bakar, A.: Using JIRA and redmine in requirement development for agile methodology. In: 2011 5th Malaysian Conference Software Engineering (MySEC), pp. 408–413, December 2011. doi:10.1109/MySEC.2011.6140707
9. Perry, T.: Drifting toward invisibility: the transition to the electronic task board. In: Agile, AGILE 2008, Conference, pp. 496–500, August 2008. doi:10.1109/Agile.2008.62

10. Berczuk, S.: Back to basics: the role of agile principles in success with an distributed scrum team. In: Agile Conference (AGILE), pp. 382–388, August 2007. doi:10.1109/AGILE.2007.17
11. Segers, J.: Analysis of a paper-and software-based scrum task board. M.A. thesis. Universiteit Twente, September 2012. http://essay.utwente.nl/62136/
12. Uy, E., Rosendahl, R.: Migrating from SharePoint to a better scrum tool. In: Melnik, G., Kruchten, P., Poppendieck, M. (eds.) Agile 2008 Conference, AGILE 2008, pp. 506–512. IEEE Computer Society, August 2008. doi:10.1109/Agile.2008.69. ISBN: 978-0-7695-3321-6
13. Seaman, C.: Qualitative methods in empirical studies of software engineering. IEEE Trans. Softw. Eng. **25**(4), 557–572 (1999). doi:10.1109/32.799955. ISSN: 0098-5589
14. Beck, K., Martin, R.C., Schwaber, K., Sutherland, J., Fowler, M.: Principles behind the agile manifesto (2001). http://agilemanifesto.org. Accessed 12 January 2001
15. Møller, L.S., Nyboe, F.B., Jørgensen, T.B., Broe, J.J.: A scrum tool for improving project management. In: Flirting with the Future, Prototyped Visions by the Next Generation, Proceedings of the 5th Student Interaction Design Research Conference (SIDeR 2009), pp. 30–32 (2009)
16. Bente, G., Ruggenberg, S., Kramer, N.C., Eschenburg, F.: Avatar-mediated networking: increasing social presence and interpersonal trust in net-based collaborations. Hum. Commun. Res. **34**(2), 287–318 (2008). doi:10.1111/j.1468-2958.2008.00322.x
17. Eckhart, M.: Scrumpy on GitHub, May 2015. https://github.com/Matthias Eckhart/Scrumpy
18. Eckhart, M., da Silva, E.V.: Scrumpy – An Agile Project Management Tool Designed to Skyrocket Your Team's Productivity, May 2015. http://scrumpy.meteor.com
19. Eckhart, M.: Product description of Scrumpy on KMU-goes-mobile, May 2015. https://kmu.fh-joanneum.at/scrumpy

Towards Business Process Execution Adequacy Criteria

Antonia Bertolino, Antonello Calabró[✉], Francesca Lonetti,
and Eda Marchetti

Istituto di Scienza e Tecnologie dell'Informazione "A. Faedo",
Consiglio Nazionale delle Ricerche (CNR), via G. Moruzzi 1, 56124 Pisa, Italy
{antonia.bertolino,antonello.calabro,
francesca.lonetti,eda.marchetti}@isti.cnr.it

Abstract. Monitoring of business process execution has been proposed
for the evaluation of business process performance. An important aspect
to assess the thoroughness of the business process execution is to monitor
if some entities have not been observed for some time and timely check
if something is going wrong. We propose in this paper business process
execution adequacy criteria and provide a proof-of-concept monitoring
framework for their assessment. Similar to testing adequacy, the purpose
of our approach is to identify the main entities of the business process
that are covered during its execution and raise a warning if some entities
are not covered. We provide a first assessment of the proposed approach
on a case study in the learning context.

Keywords: Business process · Monitoring · Adequacy criteria ·
Learning assessment

1 Introduction

Nowadays, more and more industrial organizations are using Business Process
Model and Notation (BPMN) for process modeling. The main benefits of BPMN
commonly rely on the possibility of having a simple and standard notation for
creating a description of processes (in terms of participants and activities) and
develop executable frameworks for the overall management of the process itself.
Monitoring the business process execution represents a key aspect both for business process management and business process validation. Existing works [1–3]
focus on monitoring and analysis of the factors that influence the performance of
business processes. Specific key performance indicators (KPIs), including time
based and cost based parameters, are defined together with their target values
based on business goals. In this paper, we focus on monitoring the adequacy
of the business process execution by defining coverage based adequacy criteria
and a proof-of concept framework able to assess the BPMN execution adequacy.
The main idea is to assess if a business process execution is *adequate*, i.e., if all
the main entities (activities, connection objects, swimlanes, etc.) of interest of

© Springer International Publishing Switzerland 2016
D. Winkler et al. (Eds.): SWQD 2016, LNBIP 238, pp. 37–48, 2016.
DOI: 10.1007/978-3-319-27033-3_3

the business process are covered during its execution or if the business process execution misses some of them with consequent unexpected behaviour or security flaw. Our proposal extends a more generic notion of adequacy criterion, presented in our previous work [4], by defining and implementing an instantiation of this adequacy criterion for the business process execution. However, the goal of this paper is not to assess the monitor adequacy as in [4], but the adequacy of the business process execution using monitoring facilities for measuring the proposed adequacy criteria. The main idea is to define what are the relevant entities that we would expect to observe during BPMN execution and hence to set adequacy criteria on such entities, using monitoring facilities for observing and reporting about the percentage of entities that have been covered during business process execution. In such way we can become aware that some expected entities (for instance activities or swimlanes) have not been covered for some time, and then timely check whether this happens because something is going wrong during business process execution or this is simply due to a temporary decrease of users interest for those entities. This idea takes inspiration from coverage-based test adequacy that have been extensively studied in software testing, e.g. referring to coverage of entities in the program control-flow or data-flow [5], and nowadays constitutes a fundamental instrument for test suites evaluation. Similarly to testing adequacy, we introduce here the notion of business process execution adequacy. A difference with the traditional notion of testing adequacy is the concept of observation window, namely the period along which the business process execution is assessed. It is out of scope in this paper to address the problem of how to set the length of the observation window. We refer to [4] for an overview of existing methodologies for properly setting the length of such observation window.

The contribution of this paper can be summarized into: (i) the definition of business process execution adequacy criteria; (ii) a proof-of-concept framework able to measure the BPMN execution adequacy; (iii) a preliminary assessment of the proposed proof-of-concept framework on a case study developed in the learning context.

The remainder of this paper is structured as follows: Sect. 2 introduces business process modeling notation and the notion of testing adequacy; Sect. 3 illustrates the business process execution adequacy criteria whereas Sect. 4 describes the architecture of a proof-of-concept framework able to measure the BPMN execution adequacy. Section 5 provides a preliminary assessment of the proposed approach. Finally, Sect. 6 puts our work in context of related work whereas Sect. 7 concludes the paper also hinting at future work.

2   Background

This section introduces the background behind the proposed approach. Specifically, we first present some key concepts of the Business Process Modeling Notation and then we focus on test coverage as adequacy criterion in software testing.

Business Process Modeling Notation. Business Process Model and Notation (BPMN) is a standard notation by the Object Management Group (OMG) [6] for specifying business process. BPMN provides a graphical notation for supporting business process management that allows to fill the gap between technical users and business users by providing a notation that is intuitive to business users and able to represent complex process semantics. There are three basic types of sub-models within an end-to-end BPMN model: Processes (Orchestration), Choreographies, and Collaborations. The five core notation elements of BPMN are: (i) flow objects that allow to model event, activity, and gateway; (ii) data items that model data within the process flow and are represented by four elements: data objects, data inputs, data outputs, and data stores; (iii) connection objects that connect the flow objects to each other and are: sequence flow, message flow, and association; (iv) swimlanes to model process participants; (v) artifacts (group and text annotation) are used to provide additional information about the process.

Testing Adequacy. In software testing, coverage of entities of program control-flow or data-flow is a test adequacy criterion that has been proposed as an indicator of testing effectiveness for selection and evaluation of different test cases. Code coverage e.g. is measured as the fraction of program code that is executed at least once during the test execution. Various code coverage criteria have been suggested [7], including statement coverage, decision coverage, path coverage, C-use coverage, P-use coverage, etc. whereas different coverage metrics have been proposed for different languages and application domains. The correlation between code coverage and fault detection capability has been extensively studied but it remains nowadays a controversial issue. Some previous studies [7,8] show that high code coverage implies high software reliability and low fault rate. Experimental studies [9] focus on coverage testing and mutation testing in order to investigate the relationship between code coverage and fault detection capability of a test suite. Others studies [10] show that the relationship between code coverage and fault detection varies under different testing profiles and it is affected by the different code coverage metrics. In this paper we propose to measure the adequacy of the business process execution by identifying what are the relevant entities to be covered and by assessing if all of them, or otherwise what percentage, have been covered. It is out of scope of this paper to investigate the relationship between business process coverage and fault detection.

3   Defining Business Process Execution Adequacy

In this section we introduce the generic concept of business process execution adequacy, without considering a specific coverage measure or application domain.

In test coverage criteria, a set of requirements that a test suite must fulfill is established and it is mapped onto a set of entities that must be covered when the test cases are executed, as for instance all statements or all branches of a program control-flow. The coverage criterion is satisfied if all the entities are covered; otherwise, the percentage of covered entities represents a quality measure of the test suite.

The intuitive motivation behind measuring test coverage is that if some entity has never been tested, it might contain undetected faults. Obviously, the converse reasoning does not apply: if we had covered all entities and detected no failure, this does not necessarily imply that the program is correct. In a similar way, we propose here to assess the adequacy of the business process execution by identifying what are the relevant entities to be covered and by assessing if all of them, or otherwise what percentage, have been executed. To do this, we propose a proof-of-concept monitoring framework to observe and collect business process execution traces and measure the coverage of the entities belonging to these traces. As for test adequacy, the motivation behind assessing business process execution adequacy is that if some entities are not covered, we cannot exclude that these might hide some problem or security flaw. Similarly to the notion of testing session, namely the period along which the test adequacy is measured, we define the observation window as the length of a considered observation period associated to the business process execution coverage measure. Intuitively, a sliding observation window over a time measurement unit can be established, which could be either continuous (e.g. the execution traces collected in the last 120 s) or discrete (e.g., the most recent 15 traces). The proposed business process execution adequacy criteria extend a general monitoring adequacy criterion presented in [4], by defining and implementing an instantiation of this adequacy criterion for the business process execution.

In the rest of this section the generic concept of business process (BP) execution adequacy criterion, without binding its definition to a specific coverage measure, is introduced. In fact, the notion of business process execution adequacy is neutral with respect to both the entities to be covered (i.e. activity, tasks, paths and so on) and the application domain. In the next section the generic concept of business process execution adequacy criterion is instantiated considering three different entities of the business process (Activity Entity, Sequence Flow Entity, Path Entity) and a set of coverage adequacy criteria is presented.

Definition 1. *Denote $r_i \in R$ the i-th entity to be covered, and by $\delta_i \in \Delta$ the length of its associated observation window. The business process execution adequacy criterion C dynamically measures the coverage on R for a given entity i at each time unit t as follows:*

$$C[R, \Delta](t) = \frac{\sum_{i=1}^{|R|} \lambda_i(t)}{|R|}$$

where for $r_i \in R$ and $\delta_i \in \Delta$

$$\lambda_i(t) = \begin{cases} 1 & \text{if } r_i \text{ is covered at least once in } [t - \delta_i, t] \\ 0 & \text{otherwise.} \end{cases}$$

According to this definition the length of δ_i could be different for each r_i, or could be the same for all entities. In summary the definition of business process execution adequacy introduces the following concepts:

- an "adequate business process execution" is a business process execution on which a set of entities r_i to be covered in a window δ_i is defined (this is similar to the instrumentation phase of coverage testing);
- a monitoring tool that, at every instant t, can provide a coverage measure as in Definition 1 and, if this is less than 1, can provide a list of those entities that have not been covered;
- an entity that is not covered is an entity of the business process that has not been executed for some time. In such a case a warning message could be raised by the monitoring tool.

3.1 Entity Definition

Inside a business process execution the definition of what is an entity to be covered can be provided at different levels and with different targets. We consider the following definitions:

Definition 2 (Activity Entity). *Given a BP, an activity entity is one of the activities specified in the BP that can be executed at least once.*

Definition 3 (Activity Coverage Domain). *Considering a BP, the activity coverage domain is the set of all the activity entities of the BP.*

Definition 4 (Percentage of Activity Coverage). *With reference to Definition 1, the percentage of activity coverage at time t is given by $100*C$, where R is the activity coverage domain.*

Consequently, at a given instant a business process execution is adequate with respect to the activity coverage criterion if the percentage of activity covered is 100 % (or greater than an established threshold level).

Definition 5 (Sequence Flow Entity). *Given a BP, a sequence flow entity is one of the sequence flow[1] specified in the BP that can be executed at least once.*

Definition 6 (Sequence Flow Domain). *Considering a BP, the sequence flow coverage domain is the set of all the sequence flows entities of the BP.*

Definition 7 (Sequence Flow Coverage). *With reference to Definition 1, the percentage of sequence flow coverage at time t is given by $100*C$, where R is the sequence flow coverage domain.*

Consequently, at a given instant a business process execution is adequate with respect to the sequence flow coverage criterion if the percentage of sequence flow entities covered is 100 % (or greater than an established threshold level).

Definition 8 (Path Entity). *Given a BP, a path entity is one of the paths specified in the BP that can be executed at least once.*

---

[1] Sequence Flow is used to show the order in which activities of a process will be performed. A Sequence Flow connection is represented with a solid line and a solid arrowhead in a Business Process Model.

Definition 9 (Path Domain). *Considering a BP, the path coverage domain is the set of all the path entities of the BP.*

Definition 10 (Path Coverage). *With reference to Definition 1, the percentage of path coverage at time t is given by 100*C, where R is the path coverage domain*

Consequently, at a given instant a simulation is adequate with respect to the path coverage criterion if the percentage of path entities covered is 100 % (or greater than an established threshold level).

4 Framework

With reference to Fig. 1, we present in this section the components of a proof-of-concept framework able to measure the business process execution adequacy, we have implemented:

- BPMN Path Explorer. This component is in charge to explore and save all the possible entities (Activity Entity, Sequence Flow Entity, Path Entity) reachable on a BPMN. The paths extraction is realized by an optimized unfolding algorithm that exploits advantages provided by the use of BPMN 2.0. The goal is to derive an acyclic graph, defining a partial order on its nodes. In particular, the exploration reduces the required space and time thanks to a more efficient management of the interleaving among different activities, taking into account the characteristics of a BPMN 2.0 model and of pools, parallel and exclusive gateways, and tasks sending and receiving messages within the model. More details about the BPMN exploration approach are in [11]. Once

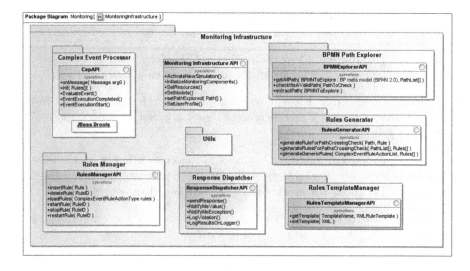

Fig. 1. Framework components diagram.

extracted, the paths will be provided to the Rules Manager that through the Rules Generator will create, using the templates of rules stored into the Template Manager, a set of rules that aims to check the coverage of all the feasible paths of the business process.

- Complex Event Processor (CEP). It is the rule engine which analyzes the events, generated by the business process execution. Several rule engines can be used for this task like Drools Fusion, VisiRule, RuleML. Our instance is realized using Drools Fusion [12], that is able to detect patterns and monitor the business process execution adequacy.

- Rules Generator. The Rules Generator is the component in charge to generate the rules needed for the monitoring of the business process execution. It uses the templates stored into the Rules Template Manager. These rules are generated according to the specific adequacy criterion to be assessed and the entities to be covered. For each entity, the rule generator generates one corresponding rule for the CEP. A generic rule consists of two main parts: in the first part the events to be matched (the entities to be covered) are specified; the second part includes the events/actions to be notified after the rules evaluation (the *covered* attribute is set to true if the entity is covered).

- Rules Template Manager. This component is an archive of predetermined rules templates that will be instantiated by the Rules Generator. A rule template is a rule skeleton, the specification of which has to be completed by instantiating a set of template-dependent placeholders. The instantiation will refer to appropriate values inferred from the specific adequacy criterion to be assessed. Once the synthesis of the new set of rules is completed, the new rules are loaded by the Rule Generator into the Rules Template Manager.

- Rules Manager. The complex event detection process depends directly from the operation done by the Rules Manager component which is in charge to load and unload set of rules into the complex event processor and fire it when needed.

- Response Dispatcher. The Response Dispatcher is a registry that records the business process execution adequacy monitoring requests. Once it receives the advice of a rule firing or pattern completion from the CEP, it stores coverage information. It elaborates statistics about the overall percentage of the covered entities and raises warning messages for the entities that are not covered to the consumer/requester of the business process adequacy evaluation.

5 Preliminary Assessment

In this session we present a preliminary assessment of the proof-of-concept framework presented in Sect. 4 on a case study in the learning context, developed inside the Learn PAd European project [13]. The main goal of the Learn PAd project is to foster an innovative learning platform for Public Administrations, based on enriched business process models, where the steps performed by the learner during a learning session are associated to the execution of the entities of a business process.

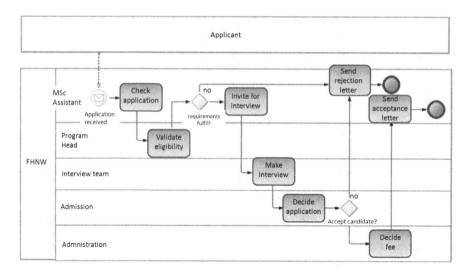

Fig. 2. Overview of the student admission process (from [14]).

The proposed business process execution adequacy criterion can be applied for providing some business process coverage measurements useful for assessing the adequacy of a business process based learning session. The intuitive motivation of using the proposed business process execution adequacy criterion for evaluating a learning session is that if some part of the business process has never been executed, the learner might have not exercised important steps of the business process and therefore his/her acquired knowledge could not be completed. To assess the adequacy of a learning session it is important to identifying what are the relevant entities to be covered and monitoring if all of them, or otherwise what percentage, have been observed. Through the analysis of data monitored over the learning session, the learner from one side can become conscious of the level of knowledge he/she acquired and can receive an evaluation/score of the progress done. Form the other side he/she can have a clearer picture of his/her exploration over a learning session, i.e. to know exactly the entities (either the events, or message interactions, or business patterns) so far not executed, so either to timely decide how to continue the learning activity or get his/her evaluation score.

The business process considered in this preliminary assessment, presented in Fig. 2, is the mock-up of the real process "Student Admission" described in [14], that refers to the process for regulating the admission of applicants to the study program MSc in Business Information Systems (BIS) within the school of business at FHNW.

In this section we applied the proposed business process execution adequacy criteria and the implemented proof-of-concept framework described in Sect. 4, to the business process presented in Fig. 2. The observation window for the assessment of the business process execution adequacy criteria has been fixed to the

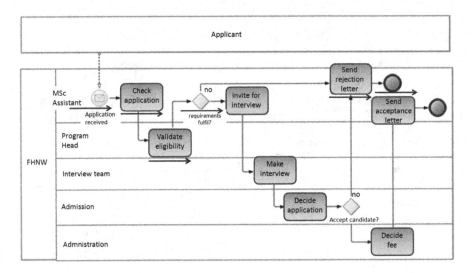

Fig. 3. Activity entities monitored over a learning session (Color figure online).

duration of a learning session because it coincides with a complete examination process of a student.

In the performed learning session we varied the following independent variables:

- Coverage Criterion (CC): this parameter indicates the entities to be covered, i.e., CC ∈ activity, path[2]. The activities for the BP of Fig. 2 are for instance: *Invite for interview, Make Interview, Send acceptance letter* and so on. The cardinality of activity coverage domain for the BP of Fig. 2 is 13, whereas that of path coverage domain is 3;
- Coverage Threshold (CT): this parameter indicates the coverage threshold according to which the business process execution is considered adequate.

In the fist step of our experiment the entity has been defined at the granularity of activity. The percentage of activity coverage within the established observation window was 6/13 *100 = 46,15 where: 6 was the number of activity entities monitored in the observation window (the activity entities marked with a (blue) arrow in Fig. 3); 13 is the cardinality of the activity coverage domain. Since the learning adequacy level established were 100 % of the activity entities, the performed learning session were not adequate with respect to the activity coverage criterion.

In a second step of the experiment, the entity has been defined at the granularity of path and the set of monitored (executed) path entities that have been observed in the observation window was represented just by the one marked with blue arrows in Fig. 4. In this case the percentage of path coverage within

---

[2] Note that for this specific business process path entity coincides with sequence flow entity.

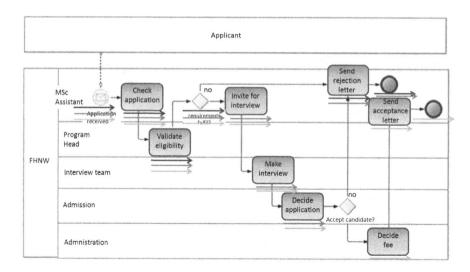

Fig. 4. Path entities monitored over a learning session (Color figure online).

the established observation windows is $1/3*100 = 33$ where: 1 is the number of path entities monitored in the observation window, 3 is the cardinality of path coverage domain. Since the learning adequacy level established in the observation window were 33 % of the path entities, the considered learning session is adequate with respect to the path coverage criterion.

6   Related Work

The adoption of business process modeling promotes and makes easier the use of model-based approaches for verifying the dynamic distributed systems. Monitoring is assuming a key role for tracking the states of a business process and for evaluating its execution performance [1,15]. Particular interest has been dedicated to "smart" monitoring approaches, i.e., monitors enhanced beyond the passive observation of system executions, with the aim of preventing or anticipating potential risks. As a trend, several researchers start to consider monitoring a useful instrument to observe the behavior of business processes not only to report about problems that have already occurred but also to predict likely problems in the near future.

However, most of the predictive approaches remain limited to the elaboration of the passively captured executions. A first attempt to provide a monitoring approach also able to raise a warning of not having observed for some time interesting behaviours or situations is presented in [4] where the general concept of monitor adequacy and two adequacy criteria for service compositions are provided. This approach takes inspiration from the passive testing approaches, which refer to the observation of the input/output behavior of a system during normal operation for the purpose of detecting faults [16]. Our proposal extends the general adequacy criterion presented in [4] by providing the definition of a business process execution adequacy criterion and a proof-of-concept monitoring framework able to assess the business process execution adequacy. Differently from existing approaches on monitoring of business process that focus on QoS metrics and continuous evaluation of key performance indicators (KPI), our goal is to measure the adequacy of business process execution by identifying what are the relevant entities to be covered and by assessing if all of them, or otherwise what percentage, have been covered. This idea is similar to testing adequacy where coverage of entities of program control-flow or data-flow is a test adequacy criterion for assessing the test effectiveness. We refer to [17] for an overview on coverage measurements and coverage-based testing tools.

In the context of learning, that is the application domain of the proposed case study, contemporary Learning Content Management Systems (LCMSs) provide rather basic feedbacks about the learning process, such as simple statistics on technology usage or low-level data on students activities (e.g., page view). Some tools [18] have been developed for providing feedbacks on the learning activities by the analysis of the user tracking data in order to propose customized learning paths that learners can follow according to their knowledge and learning requirements. Our proposal applied to the model based learning allows to assess the adequacy of a learning session by providing feedback on the executed learning activities and identifying the learning paths that are not covered.

7   Conclusion and Future Work

In this paper we introduced the notion of business process execution adequacy and provided a proof-of-concept monitoring framework able to measure the proposed adequacy criteria. We presented a first assessment of the proposed approach on a case study developed inside the Learn PAd European project [13]. Even if preliminary, the experimentation evidenced the effectiveness of the proposed approach in providing some measures about the coverage of a business process, useful for evaluating the adequacy of the associated learning session.

In future work we intend to perform a more extensive assessment of the approach to evaluate its costs and benefits. We plan to refine and enhance the proposed business process execution adequacy notion in order to consider the adequacy relative to a specific role and/or level of the business process and provide the associated relative coverage measures. A further research direction deals with investigating on the length of the observation window, namely the period along which the business process execution is assessed.

Acknowledgements. This work has been partially funded by the Model-Based Social Learning for Public Administrations project (EU FP7-ICT-2013-11/619583).

References

1. Wetzstein, B., Leitner, P., Rosenberg, F., Brandic, I., Dustdar, S., Leymann, F.: Monitoring and analyzing influential factors of business process performance. In: Enterprise Distributed Object Computing Conference, pp. 141–150 (2009)
2. Bertoli, P., Dragoni, M., Ghidini, C., Martufi, E., Nori, M., Pistore, M., Di Francescomarino, C.: Modeling and monitoring business process execution. In: Basu, S., Pautasso, C., Zhang, L., Fu, X. (eds.) ICSOC 2013. LNCS, vol. 8274, pp. 683–687. Springer, Heidelberg (2013)
3. Calabró, A., Lonetti, F., Marchetti, E.: Monitoring of business process execution based on performance indicators. In: The Euromicro Conference Series on Software Engineering and Advanced Applications (SEAA) (2015)
4. Bertolino, A., Marchetti, E., Morichetta, A.: Adequate monitoring of service compositions. In: Joint Meeting of the European Software Engineering Conference and the ACM SIGSOFT Symposium on the Foundations of Software Engineering, ESEC/FSE 2013, pp. 59–69 (2013)
5. Rapps, S., Weyuker, E.: Selecting software test data using data flow information. IEEE Trans. Softw. Eng. **SE–11**, 367–375 (1985)
6. OMG: business process model and notation (BPMN). In: 20th ed.: Object Management Group (2011)
7. Horgan, J.R., London, S., Lyu, M.R.: Achieving software quality with testing coverage measures. Computer **27**, 60–69 (1994)
8. Weyuker, E.: The cost of data flow testing: an empirical study. IEEE Trans. Softw. Eng. **16**, 121–128 (1990)
9. Lyu, M., Huang, Z., Sze, S., Cai, X.: An empirical study on testing and fault tolerance for software reliability engineering. In: 14th International Symposium on Software Reliability Engineering, pp. 119–130 (2003)
10. Cai, X., Lyu, M.R.: The effect of code coverage on fault detection under different testing profiles. SIGSOFT Softw. Eng. Notes **30**, 1–7 (2005)
11. Falcioni, D., Polini, A., Polzonetti, A., Re, B.: Direct verification of BPMN processes through an optimized unfolding technique. In: 12th International Conference on Quality Software (QSIC), pp. 179–188 (2012)
12. Drools, J.: Drools fusion: complex event processor. http://www.jboss.org/drools/drools-fusion.html
13. Learn PAd project: model-based social learning for public administrations project. http://www.learnpad.eu/
14. Thönssen, B., Hinkelmann, K., Witschel, F.: Models for setting the wiki. In: Thönssen, B., Zhang, C. (eds.) Deliverable D5.1 (The Learn PAd Consortium) (2015)
15. Koetter, F., Kochanowski, M.: A model-driven approach for event-based business process monitoring. In: Rosa, M., Soffer, P. (eds.) BPM Workshops 2012. LNBIP, vol. 132, pp. 378–389. Springer, Heidelberg (2013)
16. Lee, D., Netravali, A., Sabnani, K., Sugla, B., John, A.: Passive testing and applications to network management. In: Proceedings of International Conference on Network Protocols, pp. 113–122 (1997)
17. Yang, Q., Li, J.J., Weiss, D.M.: A survey of coverage-based testing tools. Comput. J. **52**, 589–597 (2009)
18. Ali, L., Hatala, M., Gašević, D., Jovanović, J.: A qualitative evaluation of evolution of a learning analytics tool. Comput. Edu. **58**, 470–489 (2012)

An Experience on Applying Process Mining Techniques to the Tuscan Port Community System

Giorgio O. Spagnolo[1,2](✉), Eda Marchetti[1](✉), Alessandro Coco[1],
Paolo Scarpellini[3], Antonella Querci[3], Fabrizio Fabbrini[1], and Stefania Gnesi[1]

[1] ISTI CNR, Pisa, Italy
{spagnolo,eda.marchetti,alessandro.coco,fabrizio.fabbrini,
stefania.gnesi}@isti.cnr.it
[2] Department of Information Engineering, University of Florence, Florence, Italy
[3] Livorno Port Authority, Livorno, Italy
{scarpellini,a.querci}@porto.livorno.it

Abstract. [Context & Motivation] The Business Process Management is an important and widespread adopted proposal for modelling process specifications and developing an executable framework for the management of the process itself. In particular the monitoring facilities associated to the on-line process execution provide an important means to the control of process evolution and quality. In this context, this paper provides an experience on the application of business process modelling techniques and process mining techniques to the TPCS, Tuscan Port Community System. This is a web-services based platform with multi-level access control and data recovery facilities, developed for supporting and strengthening the Motorways of the Sea and Italian regulations. The paper describes a storytelling approach applied to derive the TPCS business process model and the conformance checking techniques used to validate it and improve the overall TPCS software quality.

Keywords: Business process modelling · Storytelling · Process mining

1 Introduction

In recent years in many industrial contexts and application domains, the Business Process Management has increased its spread. The success of this approach is mainly due to the possibility to easily model process specifications, to provide concise definitions and taxonomies, and to develop an executable framework for the management of the process itself. Indeed, the business process modeling has been recognized as an effective means for creating meaningful representations of knowledge and formalized definitions of the various activities. It can be also exploited for monitoring and controlling the on-line process execution and/or evolution [1].

The generic and adaptable nature of this methodology makes easy its application in many different environments, from the clinical one, managing the patient

D. Winkler et al. (Eds.): SWQD 2016, LNBIP 238, pp. 49–60, 2016.
DOI: 10.1007/978-3-319-27033-3_4

treatment and diagnosing, to the financial one ruling the bank processes. In all these environments the data collected during the business process execution are a precious source of information for quality analysis and for demonstrating the compliance to the specifications.

Usually Business Process Management relies on a Business Process Model (BPM), specified by using one of the available Business Process Modeling Notation (BPMN) [2]. BPM represents the steps that can be performed by the different participants (people, teams or distributed organizations or IT systems) during the process execution. The data collection is demanded to monitor and log facilities that can be associated or integrated to the business process [3,4] execution framework. These facilities exploit the formal specification of a BPM and allow the logging of the activities evolution and information exchange and let a posterior verification of the conformance of the implementation. The offline analysis of the data collected can provide a precious means for discovering weaknesses between the specification and the implementation of the BPM.

In this paper we report an experience in the application of business process modelling and process mining in a real word context. Thus the main purpose of the BPM data analysis has been to find commonalities and discrepancies between the modeled behaviour (Business Process Model) and the observed behaviour (Logs) of the real implemented system. For this a storytelling approach has been used to create the business process model for the Tuscan Port Community System (TPCS), which is a web-services based on platform for supporting Motorways of the Sea and the customs clearance process. Event logger has been integrated into TPCS code system in order to monitor the information exchange into the platform and between the different web-services, and to collect data useful to assess the TPCS conformance to the BPM specification. In particular conformance checking techniques have been used to relate events in the event log to activities in the process model and compare them.

The experience highlights important challenges in the application of process mining techniques and lets the detection of inconsistencies in the process execution promptly corrected during the current experience reports. In particular the mining activity confirm to be an useful means both for quality assurance and control of software in operation. However, this experiment reveals also that the identification of the BPM elements can be a key factor for the final results. In particular the identification of the rules, the policies, the roles, the responsibilities, as well as the interactions between users and platform represent the main criticalities both to derive a precise business processes model and to correctly manage it.

In the following, an overview about the Business Process Management main concepts and an introduction of the Port Community are provided. Subsequently, the description of the process adopted in this paper for the Business Process Model definition and the implemented monitoring activity are described. In Sect. 5 the conformance checking results are presented and discussed while in Sect. 6 related work are listed. Finally, the conclusions (Sect. 7) close the paper.

2   Background

2.1   Business Process Management

Usually Business Process (BP) refers to any structured collection of related activities or tasks that are carried out to accomplish the intended objectives of an organization. Tasks within a business process may represent steps that can be performed manually by a human or automatically by an IT system [5]. Thus Business Process Management consists of different phases, such as analysis, design, implementation, deployment, monitoring, and evaluation. The main focus is therefore in creating an abstract but meaningful representation of the real business domains and sharing a formalized definition so to improve expressiveness and networked enterprises [6]. Usually in the industrial context the process followed during the analysis and design phases of the Business Process Model, that is known as externalization [7], involves direct requirements elicitation from employees by means of meetings where the participants develop group stories [8]. The collected information are then translated into Business Model by using one of the available Business Process Modeling Languages (BPML) [9]. The Business Process Model and Notation (BPMN) [2] is the formalism chosen to represent business models, which is the *de facto* standard for process modeling. It's indeed a rich and expressive but also complex language to be used for the tasks associated with process modeling [10]. The model derived during the design phase represents a formal means for capturing a significant portion of requirements and specific knowledge and improving common understanding. During the subsequent implementation and deployment phases the business model is executed in an existing environment in order to control the business process evolution and collect important data.

2.2   Port Community

The TPCS, Tuscan Port Community System, is a web-services based platform with multilevel access control and data recovery facilities, realized with the aim of developing technological tools for supporting and strengthening Motorways of the Sea and Italian regulations. TPCS is designed by the Livorno Port Authority as the institution in charge of managing and controlling the activities of the port involved in the voyages of ships, goods arriving and departing from Livorno (Italian City). TPCS processes a huge amount of information allowing a reduction in costs and streamlining bureaucratic procedures. TPCS provides the complete management of the connected applications for handling Cargo Manifests, involving all the actors interested in the information flow related to import/export operations like shipping agencies, custom forwarders, freight forwarders, terminals, hauliers and, for checking purposes, Control Authorities.

In particular, during the export operations the users can generate and manage Cargo Manifests, while during the import operations users can generate and manage Unloading Lists. In both those operations the users can also interact with the platform in order to know the status of goods (e.g. loaded or unloaded,

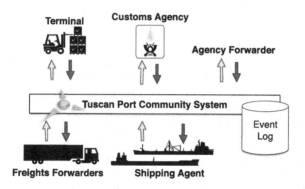

Fig. 1. Actors of the Tuscan Port Community System

cleared for customs etc.). The users can request and receive goods checking certificates and authorizations (e.g. phytosanitary authorization) for dangerous goods by the SUD (Sportello Unico Doganale - Customs Single Window) interface. Figure 1 summarizes the actors involved in the TPCS and interact the among them.

3 Create the Model

In this section we explain the method used to derive the Business Process Models of the TPCS platform.

In order to provide models of the TPCS we applied the storytelling methodology [11,12] based on collected stories of the Domain Experts using natural language. The stories describe the critical activities for the management of the ship voyages for the import and the export of the goods.

The method is summarized in Fig. 2, where three main stakeholders are in charge of carrying out the tasks proposed by the storytelling methodology: the *Tellers*, the *Facilitator* and the *Modelers*. The tellers are the individuals who participate in the process and have therefore domain knowledge. They are asked to describe their activities explicitly through a story. The facilitator is an experienced professional in the application domain who provides support to story tellers for producing coherent stories and the first abstraction of the models. The modelers are process analysts who refine the graphical model developed based on abstractions extracted from the stories.

The method follows three phases, each one involving all the roles with the purpose of transforming stories into models.

In the first phase meetings targeting the definition of the useful context of the story are planned. This in order to guide the storytellers, and let them to describe the activities for the management of the ship voyages. The meeting team was composed by three *Modelers*, three *Tellers* and one *Facilitator*. Modelers were five researchers from the ISTI (an institute of the Italian National Research Council (CNR)) with strong background in BP modeling and software engineering; tellers were Domain Expert of the Port Community; the facilitator was the Project manager of the Tuscan Port Community System of the Livorno Port Authority. During the first phase, three meetings of two hours have been necessary. To the end of this phase the stories were collected.

In the second phase the process elements are identified from the collected stories. The examination of the stories produces activities, flow, events, business rules, in order to extract the models elements of the process. In this phase, two meetings of two hours have been necessary.

Finally, in the third phase, the elements of the identified processes have been converted into BPMN models. The models have been presented to the participants in order to consolidate them, to implement necessary corrections and generate a final version. Therefore the quality assessment of the BPMN model has been manually performed by domain experts. Also in this phase two meetings of two hours have been necessary.

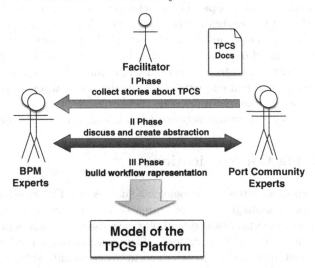

Fig. 2. Methodology to create the model

We have produced two high-level models that describe the processes of Import and Export of the TPCS platform and two lower level models that describe the sub-processes tasks "Packing List" and "Outward Cargo Manifest" of the Export process. For space limitations we report in Fig. 3 just one of the models created for the TPCS platform. This is the high-level model of the process representing the exportation of the goods from the port. The actors interact through the platform, according to the following procedure: (1) the agency forwarders insert the ship's data by an entry procedure (e.g. ship name, voyage, estimated time of arrival etc.); (2) the terminal confirms if ship's data entry operations are correct or not; (3) Freights Forwarders submit loading lists to the platform; (4) in parallel the shipping agents can begin to download the outward cargo manifest; (5) shipping agents transmit the data flow generated (called IRISP) in response to the TCPS; (6) the terminal sends confirmation of the completed loading operation (the list of the goods effectively loaded aboard called COARRI), after the ship sails.

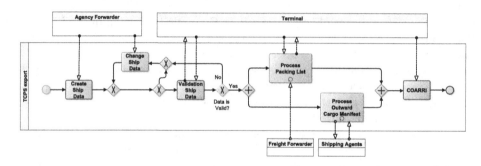

Fig. 3. Export high-level Model of TPCS

Lesson Learned in this Steps. The crucial point during the models creation was the definition of the context of the story, useful to properly guide the storytellers. An incremental approach in the storytelling, starting from a general description to a detailed one, has been the solution adopted. This allows all the critical aspects of the stories to be captured and reduces the possible inconsistencies. Nevertheless, since real contexts can have situations where several degrees of freedom can be possible, the models should abstract from not relevant details and aspects, thus a compromise between models and reality must be found.

4   Monitoring the Application

The development of web-based technologies, such as the TPCS, allows the port operators to better manage the procedures of the import and the export of the goods. These platforms are very complex because they involve many agents. Critical situation could be: What happens if the containers are not loaded on the ship? or if the containers are not discharged in the terminal? Who was wrong in applying the import/export procedures (e.g. the terminal operators, the agency forwarders, the freights forwarders etc.)?

The log of the platform, like the one shown in this paper should answers to the previous questions. In particular this information will help in the case of disputes to identify which problems have prevented or delayed the movement of the goods.

The log is a set of information collected in chronological order. There are several log types that may be recorded: (1) message log: all messages at the transport layer; (2) debugging log: messages of debugger or messages of developer; (3) application log: the transaction about the business processes. The logs are further divided between structured logs and unstructured logs. The former have no restrictions on how the events should be recorded (usually 1 and 2 of the previous list). In structured logs, each event is reported according to a defined set of rules.

In this paper we refer to structured logs, in which each event refers to an activity (i.e., a well-defined step in some process) and is related to a particular case (i.e., a process instance). In particular each is established by means a "correlation key" that is a unique identifier or a set of unique identifier, informally in this experience the correlation key used is composed by the ship identifier number and the travel unique ID. The events belonging to a single case are ordered and they represent one "execution" of the process (often referred to as a trace of events). Event logs may store additional information such as the resource (i.e., person or device) executing or initiating the activity (lifecycle of the activity), the timestamp of the event, and data elements recorded with the event [13].

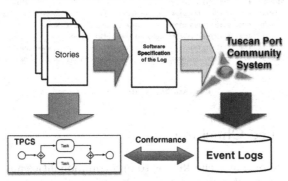

Fig. 4. Overview Software Specification of the Log

Log files were originally introduced in the TPCS platform as a means for the developers to monitor system operation and to trace back errors. These logs were essentially sequences of significant events which occurred in the system, listed in chronological order. Successively the platform has been equipped with a structured log to uniquely identify all system activities. The specification of the log was extracted by the storytelling collected during the modelling of the TPCS (see Fig. 4), according to the business models already derived. Then TPCS has been enriched with a monitor facility that records significant events in a database of the platform.

Figure 5 reports an extract of the log which details in each column the following info respectively: (1) the "case ID" that is the unique identifier of the record; (2) "IMO" (International Maritime Organization numbers) that is a unique ship identification number; (3) "Travel" that is a unique number of ship travel; (4) "Time-stamp" that is data and hour when the event is registered; (5) "Activity Name" that is the event that generated the record; (6) "Lifecycle" that is the status of the activity that generated the record; (7) "Resource" that is the person or system that generated the event. To identify the process instance we have used the correlation key descrited above in this section, i.e. the ship number and the travel number (*IMO+Travel*).

Lesson Learned in this Step. The important aspect of this phase was the quality of the event logs because it influenced the quality of the process mining. Therefore, event logs should be treated as a mandatory requirement for the information systems supporting the processes to be analyzed. Moreover a further critical aspect, strictly connected with the event logs, is the definition of the correlation keys to identify the process instance.

Case id	IMO	Travel	Timestamp	Activity	Lifecycle	Resource
1	9 9873	3 3	23/12/ 13 18:19:25:203	C ATE SHIP DATA	st	Delt n.c.
2	9 2872	4 6	23/12 13 18:19:25:635	C ATE SHIP DATA	sta	Nat oup
3	9372872	4576	23/12/2013 18:19:26:032	CREATE SHIP DATA	complete	Nat Group
4	9169873	3423	23/12/2013 18:19:27:266	CREATE SHIP DATA	complete	Delta s.n.c.
5	9372872	4576	23/12/2013 18:19:28:231	VALIDATION SHIP DATA	start	TerBlu Snc
6	9169873	3423	23/12/2013 18:19:29:103	VALIDATION SHIP DATA	start	Alpha s.r.l.
7	9372872	4576	23/12/2013 18:20:45:213	VALIDATION SHIP DATA	complete	TerBlu Snc
8	9169873	3423	23/12/2013 18:22:29:166	VALIDATION SHIP DATA	complete	Alpha s.r.l.
9	9372872	4576	23/12/2013 18:25:38:128	RECEIVE PACKAGE LIST	start	Ship s.p.a.
10	9169873	3423	23/12/2013 18:29:21:623	RECEIVE PACKAGE LIST	start	Beta s.p.a.
11	9372872	4576	23/12/2013 18:29:45:243	RECEIVE PACKAGE LIST	complete	Ship s.p.a.
12	9169873	3423	23/12/2013 18:30:21:748	RECEIVE PACKAGE LIST	complete	Beta s.p.a.
13	9372872	4576	23/12/2013 18:30:33:321	SEND OUTWARD CARGO MANIFEST	start	Ben s.r.l.
14	9169873	3423	23/12/2013 18:31:21:795	SEND OUTWARD CARGO MANIFEST	start	Gamma srl
15	9372872	4576	23/12/2013 18:32:42:633	SEND OUTWARD CARGO MANIFEST	complete	Ben s.r.l.
16	9169873	3423	23/12/2013 18:32:53:842	SEND OUTWARD CARGO MANIFEST	complete	Gamma srl

Fig. 5. Structured Log

5   Conformance Checking

The goal in the conformance checking is to find commonalities and discrepancies between the modeled behaviour (Business Model) and the observed behaviour (Logs) [14]. Conformance checking relates events in the log to activities in the process model and compares both.

In order to apply the conformance checking techniques we have used the most popular process mining framework ProM[1] [14,15]. The ProM framework provides many process mining plugins using XES as input format to the logs [16,17]. The logs extracted on the platform are in the CSV format, and to translate CSV-files into XES logs we have used the *"KeyValue"* ProM plugins [18]. In particular by using the "Activity Name" (as column 5 of Fig. 5) each event log has been associated with the corresponding activity of the BPMN model, with same name.

For performing the conformance checking, we have selected *"PNetReplayer"* [19,20], a plugin from ProM framework. This plugin is based on *"Alignments approach"*: an alignment between a recorded process execution and a process model is a pairwise comparison between the executed activities and the activities allowed by the model. Such sequences of pairs are called movement sequences. The movement sequences are: moves on log only, moves on model only, and moves on both (synchronous moves) are considered as legal moves. A movement sequence is a legal movement sequence if it contains only legal moves [20].

The metrics used in this work for conformance checking is the fitness. Fitness measures the extent to which process models can reproduce the traces recorded in the log. Many approaches in literature are related to this particular dimension, for this work we have selected *Cost-based fitness metric* [21].

---

[1] ProM is an extensible framework that provides a comprehensive set of tools/plugins for the discovery and analysis of process models from event logs. See www.processmining.org for more information and to download ProM.

The plugin operates on a Petri Nets. A Petri net or P/T net is a directed bipartite graph, in which the nodes represent transitions (events that may occur) and places (i.e. conditions). A Petri net are used because it's one of several mathematical modeling languages for the description of distributed systems.

To translate BPMN into Petri nets we have used the *"BPMNtoPN"* plugins that use the mapping presented in Dijkman et al. [22] to translate BPMN models into Petri nets extended with the translation of BPMN task, for which we generate a net with two transitions, to model the lifecycle of the activites [23].

Table 1. Log statistics

Time slot	#Instances	#Events	#Originators	#Event classes
Feb unfiltered	70	14888	83	12
Feb filtered	45	8930	78	12

Here we show the results produced by the analysis of the high-level model, that describe the export process of the TPCS platform, shown in Fig. 3 and the data collected to TPCS execution as shown in Fig. 5 shows as an extract.

We decided to analyse the log data considering a week as a unit of time so to reduce the number of the events logged and to make easy the (manual) inspection in the case of serious conformance problems.

The log used for the conformance analysis on the Export high-level Model of TPCS refers to the period from 16 to 27 February 2015 and it's divided in unfiltered and filtered logs. The unfiltered log is the original log of TPCS plaform, whereas in filtered log events of original log are filtered to extract only the instances that started in the time-slot selected. The Unfiltered log is composed of 12 events classes by 14888 events for a total of 70 process instances, generated from 83 originators, whereas the filtered log is composed of 12 events classes by 8930 events for a total of 45 process instances, generated from 78 originators, (see Table 1). The filtered log is ~60 % of the unfiltered log.

Table 2. Conformance statistics

Log	Alignment without penalize completion statistics			Alignment with penalize completion statistics		
Time slot	Average fitness trace	Min fitness trace	#Max fitness trace	Average fitness trace	Min fitness trace	#Max fitness trace
Feb unfiltered	0,971	0,60	38	0,951	0,77	7
Feb filtered	0,998	0,97	38	0,957	0,82	7

In Table 2 the results of the conformance analysis performed by the ProM plugin are presented. The analysis is based on two algorithms to measure fitness that differ from each other for the penalty considered for the completion of a trace, if are present or not all event classes in the process instance. The table shows for any log and for algorithms the average and the minimum fitness trace and the number of trace that have the maximum fitness trace, that is one.

Table 2 reports the data collected: (1) there are six complete process instances in both logs that fully conform to the model; (2) there are 31 incomplete process instances in the logs that fully conform to the model. Finally seven process instances in the log are the non-conformance instances, these were manually investigated to explain the causes of non-conformance.

In order to investigate the non-conformances found, meetings have been scheduled with *Tellers* and *Facilitator* (see Sect. 3). The detailed analysis highlighted problems in the practices put in place by the actors of the process. For example some *"Terminal"* send the COARRI into different parts instead of a unique document. Indeed the COARRI has been modeled in the BPM by a single activity, but in the platform it is possible to upload it in separated parts, because the platform does not know the number of the elements of COARRI.

Lesson Learned in this Step. A critical aspect using the process mining techniques is that it requires high-quality event data logs, see Sect. 4. In order to analyse and inspect the results of conformance analysis the *process miner* must know the model very well. A further critical aspect is that the real world is usually to complex to be faithfully represented by models therefore a certain level of abstraction is necessary.

6 Related Work

Process mining has been successfully applied in a set of business areas such as healthcare [24,25], insurance [26], auditing [27], tourism industry [28]. In this paper we present a case study from a different application area, Port Community System platform. The goal here was to understand, model and validate the information flow and the actions performed by all the stakeholders of this business domain, using process mining techniques. Due to the complexity of this kind of system, we used the storytelling approach [7,29,30] of transmitting knowledge. An evaluation of this approach is provided in [11] where the authors emphasize, through experiments, the beneficial effects to collective knowledge recall by means of group storytelling approach, comparing this technique to the more traditional approach based on interviews.

The goal in our research was to validate the process model derived from the storytelling approach. The structured logs provided us the main elements of information to support the ProM analysis for the validation of the business model. The opposite point of view was adopted in Rubin et al. [28] where they start analysing the log to discovery the model of the touristic domain.

7 Conclusion and Future Works

In this paper, we presented an experience on applying conformance checking techniques to the Tuscan Port Community System.

We started with storytelling techniques to derive the business process of the TPCS platform and then the platform has been equipped with the activity process log. Next using process mining techniques on the log of the platform with the process model derived we have performed the conformance analysis. The results obtained were used to investigate the behaviour of the platform and validate the process model.

For some sections we provided the lessons learned. As we expected the storytelling approach helped in identifying flows, activities, events and business rules allowing all the stakeholders to use natural language without any specific competence in business process modelling. The most significant difficulties faced in deriving the business process result from the complexity of the platform, from the non homogeneous actors involved and from the too many detailed aspects not relevant to the process, open issue remain to establish the granularity in order of the data to be collected.

This work is a contribution to the industrial application of formal techniques for the monitoring of the business processes.

Future research aims to apply performance analysis to measure execution time, waiting time and synchronization time between activities to detect bottlenecks in the process model.

References

1. vom Brocke, J., Rosemann, M.: Handbook on Business Process Management 1: Introduction, Methods, and Information Systems. Springer, Berlin (2010)
2. Object Management Group (OMG): Business Process Model and Notation (BPMN) Version 2.0. Technical report (2011)
3. Koetter, F., Kochanowski, M.: A model-driven approach for event-based business process monitoring. Inf. Sys. E Bus. Manag. **13**(1), 5–36 (2015)
4. Bertolino, A., Calabrò, A., Lonetti, F., Di Marco, A., Sabetta, A.: Towards a model-driven infrastructure for runtime monitoring. In: Troubitsyna, E.A. (ed.) SERENE 2011. LNCS, vol. 6968, pp. 130–144. Springer, Heidelberg (2011)
5. Gerth, C.: Introduction. In: Gerth, C. (ed.) Business Process Models (Dissertation). LNCS, vol. 7849, pp. 1–12. Springer, Heidelberg (2013)
6. Jeston, J., Nelis, J.: Business Process Management. Routledge, London (2014)
7. Perret, R., Borges, M.R.S., Santoro, F.M.: Applying group storytelling in knowledge management. In: de Vreede, G.-J., Guerrero, L.A., Marín Raventós, G. (eds.) CRIWG 2004. LNCS, vol. 3198, pp. 34–41. Springer, Heidelberg (2004)
8. Carminatti, N., Borges, M.R.S., Gomes, J.O.: Analyzing approaches to collective knowledge recall. Comput. Artif. Intell. **25**(6), 547–570 (2006)
9. van der Aalst, W.M.P., ter Hofstede, A.H.M., Weske, M.: Business process management: a survey. In: van der Aalst, W.M.P., ter Hofstede, A.H.M., Weske, M. (eds.) BPM 2003. LNCS, vol. 2678, pp. 1–12. Springer, Heidelberg (2003)
10. Recker, J.C.: Opportunities and constraints: the current struggle with BPMN. Bus. Process Manag. J. **16**(1), 181–201 (2010)
11. Santoro, F.M., Borges, M.R.S., Pino, J.A.: Acquiring knowledge on business processes from stakeholders' stories. Adv. Eng. Inform. **24**(2), 138–148 (2010)
12. de A. R. Gonçalves, J.C., Santoro, F.M., Baião, F.A.: Business process mining from group stories. In: CSCWD, pp. 161–166. IEEE (2009)

13. van der Aalst, W.M.P.: Mediating between modeled and observed behavior: The quest for the "right" process: keynote. In: Research Challenges Information Science. IEEE (2013)

14. van der Aalst, W.: Process Mining: Discovery, Conformance and Enhancement of Business Processes. Springer, Heidelberg (2011)

15. Verbeek, H., Buijs, J., Dongen, B.V., Aalst, W.M.P.V.D.: ProM 6: the process mining toolkit. In: BPM Demonstration Track, vol. 615, pp. 34–39 (2010)

16. Gnther, C.W., Verbeek, H.M.W.: XES Standard Definition. Technical report BPM-14-09, Eindhoven University of Technology (2014)

17. Verbeek, H.M.W., Buijs, J.C.A.M., van Dongen, B.F., van der Aalst, W.M.P.: XES, XESame, and ProM 6. In: Soffer, P., Proper, E. (eds.) CAiSE Forum 2010. LNBIP, vol. 72, pp. 60–75. Springer, Heidelberg (2011)

18. Westergaard, M.: KeyValue, ProM Plugins. Technical report, Eindhoven University of Technology (2014)

19. van der Aalst, W., Adriansyah, A., van Dongen, B.: Replaying history on process models for conformance checking and performance analysis. Wiley Int. Rev. Data Min. Knowl. Disc. **2**(2), 182–192 (2012)

20. Adriansyah, A.: Aligning observed and modeled behavior. Master thesis, Eindhoven University of Technology (2014)

21. Adriansyah, A., van Dongen, B.F., van der Aalst, W.M.P.: Conformance checking using cost-based fitness analysis. In: EDOC, pp. 55–64. IEEE (2011)

22. Dijkman, R.M., Dumas, M., Ouyang, C.: Semantics and analysis of business process models in BPMN. Inf. Softw. Technol. **50**(12), 1281–1294 (2008)

23. Bruni, R., Corradini, A., Ferrari, G., Flagella, T., Guanciale, R., Spagnolo, G.: Applying process analysis to the italian egovernment enterprise architecture. In: Carbone, M., Petit, J.-M. (eds.) WS-FM 2011. LNCS, vol. 7176, pp. 111–127. Springer, Heidelberg (2012)

24. Mans, R., Schonenberg, M., Song, M., van der Aalst, W., Bakker, P.: Application of process mining in healthcare – A case study in a dutch hospital. In: Fred, A., Filipe, J., Gamboa, H. (eds.) Biomedical Engineering Systems and Technologies. CCSI, vol. 25, pp. 425–438. Springer, Heidelberg (2009)

25. Rebuge, A., Ferreira, D.R.: Business process analysis in healthcare environments: a methodology based on process mining. Inf. Syst. **37**(2), 99–116 (2012)

26. Suriadi, S., Wynn, M.T., Ouyang, C., ter Hofstede, A.H.M., van Dijk, N.J.: Understanding process behaviours in a large insurance company in australia: a case study. In: Salinesi, C., Norrie, M.C., Pastor, Ó. (eds.) CAiSE 2013. LNCS, vol. 7908, pp. 449–464. Springer, Heidelberg (2013)

27. Jans, M., Alles, M., Vasarhelyi, M.: The case for process mining in auditing: sources of value added and areas of application. Int. J. Account. Inf. Syst. **14**(1), 1–20 (2013)

28. Rubin, V., Mitsyuk, A., Lomazova, I., van der Aalst, W.M.P.: Process mining can be applied to software too! In: Empirical Software Engineering and Measurement. ACM (2014)

29. Schäfer, L., Valle, C., Prinz, W.: Group storytelling for team awareness and entertainment. In: Nordic Conference on Human-computer Interaction, pp. 441–444. ACM, New York (2004)

30. Valle, C., Prinz, W., Borges, M.: Generation of group storytelling in post-decision implementation process. In: Computer Supported Cooperative Work in Design, pp. 361–367 (2002)

Requirements Engineering

Preventing Incomplete/Hidden Requirements: Reflections on Survey Data from Austria and Brazil

Marcos Kalinowski[1(✉)], Michael Felderer[2], Tayana Conte[3],
Rodrigo Spínola[4], Rafael Prikladnicki[5], Dietmar Winkler[6],
Daniel Méndez Fernández[7], and Stefan Wagner[8]

[1] Computing Institute, Universidade Federal Fluminense,
Av. Milton Tavares de Souza s/n, Campus Praia Vermelha,
Niterói 24210-346, Brazil
kalinowski@ic.uff.br
[2] Institute of Computer Science, University of Innsbruck,
Technikerstr. 21a, 6020 Innsbruck, Austria
michael.felderer@uibk.ac.at
[3] Computing Institute, Universidade Federal do Amazonas,
Av. Rodrigo Otávio 6200, Campus Universitário Senador Arthur Virgílio Filho,
Manaus 69077-000, Brazil
tayana@icomp.ufam.edu.br
[4] Systems and Computing Graduate Programm, Universidade Salvador,
Alameda das Espatódias 912, Salvador 41.820-460, Brazil
rodrigo.spinola@pro.unifacs.br
[5] Computer Science Graduate Programm, Pontifícia Universidade Católica do
Rio Grande do Sul, Av. Ipiranga 6681, Porto Alegre 90619-900, Brazil
rafael.prikladnicki@pucrs.br
[6] Institute of Software Technology and Interactive Systems,
Vienna University of Technology, Favoritenstr. 9/188, 1040 Vienna, Austria
dietmar.winkler@tuwien.ac.at
[7] Institut für Informatik, Technische Universität München,
Boltzmannstr. 3, 85748 Garching, Germany
daniel.mendez@tum.de
[8] Institut für Softwaretechnologie, University of Stuttgart,
Universitätsstraße 38, 70569 Stuttgart, Germany
stefan.wagner@informatik.uni-stuttgart.de

Abstract. [Context] Many software projects fail due to problems in requirements engineering (RE). [Goal] The goal of this paper is analyzing a specific and relevant RE problem in detail: incomplete/hidden requirements. [Method] We replicated a global family of RE surveys with representatives of software organizations in Austria and Brazil. We used the data to (a) characterize the criticality of the selected RE problem, and to (b) analyze the reported main causes and mitigation actions. Based on the analysis, we discuss how to prevent the problem. [Results] The survey includes 14 different organizations in Austria and 74 in Brazil, including small, medium and large sized companies, conducting both, plan-driven and agile development processes. Respondents from both countries cited the incomplete/hidden requirements problem as one of the

© Springer International Publishing Switzerland 2016
D. Winkler et al. (Eds.): SWQD 2016, LNBIP 238, pp. 63–78, 2016.
DOI: 10.1007/978-3-319-27033-3_5

most critical RE problems. We identified and graphically represented the main causes and documented solution options to address these causes. Further, we compiled a list of reported mitigation actions. [Conclusions] From a practical point of view, this paper provides further insights into common causes of incomplete/hidden requirements and on how to prevent this problem.

Keywords: Survey · Requirements engineering · NaPiRE · Incomplete requirements · Hidden requirements · Implicit requirements · Causal analysis · Defect prevention

1   Introduction

The importance of high-quality requirements engineering (RE) has been widely accepted and well documented. RE constitutes a holistic key to successful development projects [1]. However, industry is still struggling to apply high-quality RE practices [2] and getting a further understanding on common RE problems and their causes is of great interest to both, industry and academy.

Many researchers have addressed identifying and analyzing RE problems faced by industry [3, 4]. More recently, a project called NaPiRE (**Na**ming the **P**ain in **R**equirements **E**ngineering) comprises the design of a family of surveys on RE practice and problems, and it is conducted in joint collaboration with various researchers from different countries [5]. The main goal of this project is to provide an empirical foundation on the state of the practice in RE to allow steering future research in a problem-driven manner. The NaPiRE survey includes several countries around the globe.[1]

From the perspective of practitioners, information on RE problems could be particularly useful to discuss how to prevent the occurrence of such problems in their projects. An efficient means for preventing RE problems is the causal analysis [6], which involves identifying causes of problems to address them through concrete actions to prevent them in future projects. Kalinowski *et al.* [7] provide a comprehensive industrial experience report on conducting causal analysis on RE problems. One of the main difficulties reported during causal analysis sessions concerns the absence of a starting point for identifying potential causes [6], as there is no general documented and empirically grounded knowledge on common causes of critical RE problems usable as a starting point.

Data collected in the NaPiRE survey include information on critical RE problems and their causes. An initial effort to organize knowledge on common causes of critical RE problems has been recently undertaken based on NaPiRE data from the Brazilian replication [8]. In this paper, we extend this research by further analyzing a specific and critical selected RE problem: incomplete/hidden requirements, based on data from the NaPiRE replications conducted in Austria and Brazil. We use the data to (a) characterize the criticality of the selected RE problem, and to (b) analyze the main causes reported for the problem. Based on this industrial feedback, we discuss actions for

---

[1] NaPiRE: http://www.re-survey.org.

preventing the problem. As a result of the replications, we received complete answers from 14 different organizations in Austria and 74 in Brazil, including small, medium and very large sized companies, conducting both, plan-driven and agile development. Respondents from both countries cited the selected problem as one of the most critical RE problems. We graphically represent the causes cited by the organizations and discuss solution options for addressing the most common reported causes.

The remainder of this paper is organized as follows. Section 2 describes the background on surveys on RE problems and on the NaPiRE project. Section 3 describes the NaPiRE survey replication in Austria and in Brazil. Section 4 presents the survey results on the criticality of RE problems in both countries. Section 5 contains the analysis of the selected problem including its main reported causes and the discussion on solution options for addressing them. Finally, Sect. 6 presents the concluding remarks and future work.

2   Background

As background for this paper, we describe related work on surveys on RE problems and the required information on the NaPiRE project.

2.1   RE Surveys

A well-known survey on causes for project failure is the Chaos Report of the Standish Group on cross-company root causes for project failures. While most of these causes are related to RE, the survey has serious design flaws and the validity of its results is questionable [9]. Additionally, it exclusively investigated failed projects and general causes at the level of overall software projects. Thus, unfortunately it does not directly support the investigation of RE problems in industry.

Some surveys have been focusing specifically on RE problems in industry. These surveys include the one conducted by Hall *et al.* [3] in twelve software organizations. Their findings, among others, suggest that most RE problems are organizational rather than technical. Some country-specific RE problem investigations include the surveys conducted by Solemon *et al.* [10] and Liu *et al.* [11], with Malaysian and Chinese organizations, respectively. Khankaew and Riddle [12], report on a survey with focus on more recently conducted semi-structured interviews with organizations from Thailand. These investigations provide valuable insights into industrial environments. However, as each of them focuses on specific aspects in RE, their results are isolated and not generalizable. To address this issue, the NaPiRE project was launched in a joint collaboration with researchers from different countries [5].

2.2   The NaPiRE Project

The NaPiRE project resulted in the design of a global family of surveys to overcome the problem of isolated investigations in RE that are not representative [5]. Thus, a long-term goal of the project is to establish an empirically sound basis for understanding trends and problems in RE [13]. Currently several surveys are going to be replicated in several countries around the globe.

The design of the survey is aligned to a well-thought theory and its instruments have been extensively reviewed by several researchers [5, 13]. In summary, the NaPiRE survey contains 35 questions with focus on the following type of data from the responding organizations: (a) general information, (b) RE status quo, (c) RE improvement status quo, (d) RE problems faced in practice, and (e) RE problem manifestation (e.g., causes and impact). Further information on the project is available online1, including the target countries for survey replication and a sample of the questionnaire. Up to now, initial results from Germany have already been published [5, 13]. Currently, these initial results will now be updated by more recent trials in Germany and in other countries, such as Austria and Brazil.

3   Replicating the NaPiRE Survey in Austria and Brazil

This section describes the collected data in context of this paper based on the Austrian and Brazilian replication. Note that both replications apply the common design of the NaPiRE survey, including all relevant instruments (see [5] for details). Therefore, in this section we focus on the details on planning and execution aspects in both countries, i.e. in Austria and Brazil. To enable proper interpretations of the results, we include a description of the characterization of the responding organizations of both countries in this section.

3.1   Survey Replication in Austria

The Austrian NaPiRE survey replication was planned in two meetings with the general NaPiRE organizers from Germany. During these meetings, the online environment (EFS survey tool[2]) was introduced and some guidelines for conducting the survey were presented. For the survey in Austria, the questionnaire, applied in Germany, was duplicated and hosted on the same online environment.

As the goal of the survey was to gain high quality feedback on topics related to RE, the invitation to participate in the survey was sent – in coordination with the general NaPiRE organizers – to selected experts in requirements and software quality engineering of representative organizations in Austria. The organizations covered development of embedded as well as information systems in different domains.

Invitation letters, including a link to the online survey and a password, were sent to the list of experts via e-mail in June 2014 and July 2014. In total, 22 of 25 invited experts logged into the online survey and provided answers between June and September 2014. Out of these, we received 14 completed surveys; 8 experts dropped the survey before completion. The median duration for completing the survey was about 30 min.

---

[2] EFS survey tool: www.unipark.com/en.

3.2 Survey Replication in Brazil

The planning of the survey replication in Brazil also involved two meetings with the NaPiRE general organizers (see Footnote 1). Again, during these meetings, the online environment (EFS survey tool (see Footnote 2)) was presented and some general guidelines for conducting the survey were provided. For this replication we decided to translate all instruments to Portuguese, the participants' native language.

Given the geographic dimensions of Brazil, to reach organizations from different regions and to collect representative data, the first author assembled a team of industry-focused researchers spread across the country. The strategy consisted of having researchers from the four main industry intensive regions of the country involved. The resulting NaPiRE Brazil team (see Footnote 1) comprises a researcher from the South of the country, one from the Southeast, one from the North and one from the Northeast. Additionally, we contacted Softex,[3] the association responsible for the most widely adopted software process improvement reference model in Brazil, the MPS-SW[4] [14], with over 600 assessments in Brazil. They promptly trusted us contacts of 254 organizations with currently valid MPS-SW assessments so that they could be invited to take part in the survey. Including a set of 80 additional relevant industry contacts from the authors (20 contacts per author on average), we created a list with contacts of representatives from 334 software organizations. We believe this set to be representative for the Brazilian software industry. Given the size of this industry (thousands of software organizations [15]), an extensive survey to reach all of them would be almost impossible. We then configured the environment and sent the invitations with a link and password to the online survey to the list of contacts by e-mail. The survey was sent in December 2014, with reminders in January 2015 and February 2015. In total, 118 of the 334 invited organization representatives logged into answer the survey. Out of these, we received 74 completed questionnaires (9 only read the initial instructions, 18 dropped at the first page of the questionnaire, and 17 dropped the survey later without completing the questionnaire). The median time to answer the survey completely was 29 min.

3.3 Characterization

To provide a summary of the characterization of the responding organizations in Austria and Brazil, we will present information on their company size, used process models, and RE standards. We will also present the roles of the participants within the organizations and their experience in this role. While the data from Austria is more representative to the European context and relies on carefully selected experts in requirements and software quality engineering, we believe that the large data set from Brazil serves as an interesting complement to enable further understanding the investigated phenomena. Concerning size, in Table 1 presents the data from Austria and Table 2 presents the data from Brazil. It is possible to observe that, while in both

---

[3] Softex: http://www.softex.br.

[4] MPS-SW: http://www.softex.br/mpsbr.

Table 1. Size of the organizations surveyed in Austria

Size[a]	No. of answers	Share [%]
1–10 employees	2	16.68 %
11–50 employees	1	8.33 %
51–250 employees	1	8.33 %
251–500 employees	4	33.33 %
501–1000 employees	0	0.00 %
1001–2000 employees	1	8.33 %
More than 2000 employees	3	25.00 %
Invalid (missing) answers	2	n/a
Valid responses:	12	100.00 %

[a] Size including software and other areas

Table 2. Size of the organizations surveyed in Brazil

Size[a]	No. of answers	Share [%]
1–10 employees	11	15.49 %
11–50 employees	15	21.13 %
51–250 employees	17	23.94 %
251–500 employees	5	7.04 %
501–1000 employees	3	4.23 %
1001–2000 employees	5	7.04 %
More than 2000 employees	15	21.13 %
Invalid (missing) answers	3	n/a
Valid responses:	71	100.00 %

[a] Size including software and other areas

countries we have small and large organizations, in the Austrian set the medium-sized organizations also play a relevant role representing 33 % (cf. 251–500 employees) of the valid answers.

Regarding the process model, Tables 3 and 4 shows that most of the surveyed organization adopt agile (mainly Scrum-based) process models, followed by iterative and incremental process models and the traditional waterfall model. Note that the respondents could nominate more than one process model typically applied in their organization. A slight difference is that apparently the V-Model XT is more popular in Austria (mentioned by 20.00 % of the organizations) than in Brazil (mentioned by 5.41 % of the organizations). It is noteworthy that some organizations reported to use more than one process model to handle different types of projects. One explanation for changing process models is that organizations might have to follow a waterfall like model during a bidding procedure while adopting Scrum after formal project assignment.

Tables 5 and 6 presents the application of RE standards reported by the Austrian and Brazilian respondents. We can observe that in Austria most organizations adopt self-defined standards and few of them base their standards on external regulations and/or software reference models. In Brazil, on the other hand, most of the surveyed

Table 3. Process models used in Austria

Process model	No. of answers	Share [%]
Scrum	6	40.00 %
Waterfall	4	26.67 %
V-Model XT	3	20.00 %
Rational Unified Process (RUP)	1	6.67 %
Extreme Programming (XP)	0	0.00 %
Others[a]	4	26.67 %
Organizations (multiple answers possible):	14	100.00 %

[a] Others includes project or customer dependent process (2), and other process models based on agile (1) or plan-driven methods (1)

Table 4. Process models used in Brazil

Process model	No. of answers	Share [%]
Scrum	45	60.81 %
Waterfall	22	29.73 %
Rational Unified Process (RUP)	19	25.68 %
Extreme Programming (XP)	7	9.46 %
V-Model XT	4	5.41 %
Others[a]	11	14.86 %
Organizations (multiple answers possible):	74	100.00 %

[a] Others includes self-adapted process models (4), other iterative and incremental development process models (4) and other process models based on agile methods (3)

organizations follow regulation/reference-model-based standards. This, of course, may have been influenced by the strategy of also distributing the survey to the organizations with valid MPS-SW assessments. Nevertheless, many organizations answered that they follow the standards of the adopted development process and their own standards.

To characterize the participants, the NaPiRE survey collects their roles in the organization and their experience. The roles in Austria and Brazil are shown in

Table 5. RE Standards used in Austria

RE standard	No. of answers	Share [%]
Self-defined (including artefacts and templates)	7	50.00 %
Self-defined (including a process with roles and responsibilities)	6	42.86 %
Adopted development process (e.g., RUP, Scrum)	4	28.57 %
Self-defined (including a process with deliverables, milestones and phases)	4	28.57 %
Regulation (e.g., ITIL) /SW ref. model (e.g., CMMI-Dev)	2	14.29 %
None	0	0.00 %
Others[a]	1	7.14 %
Organizations (multiple answers possible):	14	100.00 %

[a] Others includes project or customer dependent standards (1)

Table 6. RE standards used in Brazil

RE standard	No. of answers	Share [%]
Regulation (e.g. ITIL) /SW ref. model (e.g., CMMI-Dev, MPS-SW)	39	52.70 %
Adopted development process (e.g., RUP, Scrum)	25	33.78 %
Self-defined (including a process with deliverables, milestones and phases)	19	25.68 %
Self-defined (including a process with roles and responsibilities)	18	24.32 %
Self-defined (including artefacts and templates)	18	24.32 %
None	1	1.35 %
Organizations (multiple answers possible):	74	100.00 %

Tables 7 and 8. It can be seen that participants in both countries are mainly project managers and business analysts. The main difference is that in Austria the answers are more evenly distributed between the roles, while in Brazil about half of the answers were provided by project managers.

Table 7. Roles of the participants in Austria

Role	No. of answers	Share [%]
Business analyst	3	25.00 %
Project manager	2	16.67 %
Requirements engineer	2	16.67 %
Test Manager/Tester	2	16.67 %
Architect	1	8.32 %
Others[a]	2	16.67 %
Invalid (missing) answers	2	n/a
Valid responses:	12	100.00 %

[a] Others include trainer and test manager (1), and quality assurance (1)

Table 8. Roles of the participants in Brazil

Role	No. of Answers	Share [%]
Project manager	32	45.07 %
Business analyst	8	11.27 %
Developer	4	5.63 %
Software architect	4	5.63 %
Test Manager/Tester	3	4.23 %
Requirements engineer	2	2.82 %
Others[a]	18	25.35 %
Invalid (missing)	3	n/a
Valid responses:	71	100.00 %

[a] Other informed values include development directors, program managers and portfolio managers (7), quality assurance analysts (7), and people from the software engineering process group (4)

Table 9. Experience of the participants in Austria

Experience	No. of Answers	Share [%]
Expert (more than 3 years)	9	81.82 %
Experienced (1 to 3 years)	2	18.18 %
Novice (up to 1 year)	0	0.00 %
Invalid (missing)	3	n/a
Valid responses:	11	100.00 %

Table 10. Experience of the participants in Brazil

Experience	No. of Answers	Share [%]
Expert (more than 3 years)	52	73.24 %
Experienced (1 to 3 years)	15	21.13 %
Novice (up to 1 year)	4	5.63 %
Invalid (missing)	3	n/a
Valid responses:	71	100.00 %

Finally, Tables 9 and 10 show that participants of both countries are highly experienced in their roles, with the majority having more than 3 years of experience.

4 Criticality of RE Problems in Austria and Brazil

During the NaPiRE survey, based on a set of 21 precompiled general RE problems listed in the NaPiRE questionnaire [5], participants were asked – according to their expertise – to rank the five most critical requirement issues. The outcomes in Austria and Brazil are shown in Tables 11 and 12. In these tables, we present all issues that were cited among the five most critical requirements issues by at least 20 % of the participants. We also show how often each problem was cited and how often it was ranked as the most critical. For instance, Table 11 shows that problem *incomplete/ hidden requirements* was cited as one of the five most critical by 9 of the 14 Austrian participants (64.28 %) and this issues has been listed as the most critical one by five of them (35.71 %).

It is possible to observe that in both countries the most critical reported RE problems are related *incomplete/hidden requirements, underspecified requirements, communication flaws between the project team and the customer,* and *communication flaws within the project team*. Besides these problems, both tables also share the *moving targets* and *time boxing* problems. We believe that this very similar reported problem profile might be due to using similar process models (mainly Scrum-based, cf. Tables 3 and 4). Differences in the criticality were observed in the *"stakeholders with difficulties in separating requirements from previously known solution designs problem"*, which was cited by more than 20 % of the participants in Austria, but not in Brazil. On the other hand, the problems *"insufficient support by customer"* and *"inconsistent requirements"* were cited by more than 20 % of the participants in Brazil, but not in Austria.

Table 11. Most critical RE problems in Austria

#	RE problems and issues	Cited[a]		Ranked #1[a]	
		No.	%	No.	%
1	**Incomplete and/or hidden requirements**	**9**	**64.28 %**	**5**	35.71 %
2	Underspecified requirements that are too abstract and allow for various interpretations	4	26.67 %	1	7.14 %
3	Communication flaws within the project team	4	26.67 %	1	7.14 %
4	Communication flaws between the project team and the customer	3	21.42 %	1	7.14 %
4	Moving targets (changing goals, business processes and/or req.)	3	21.42 %	1	7.14 %
4	Stakeholders with difficulties in separating reqs from previously known solution designs	3	21.42 %	3	21.43 %
4	Time boxing /Not enough time in general	3	21.42 %	1	7.14 %

[a] The probabilities were calculated based on the overall amount of 14 participants

Table 12. Most critical RE problems in Brazil

#	RE problems and issues	Cited[a]		Ranked #1[a]	
		No	%	No	%
1	Communication flaws between the project team and the customer	32	43.24 %	9	12.16 %
2	**Incomplete and/or hidden requirements**	**31**	**41.89 %**	**12**	16.22 %
2	Underspecified requirements that are too abstract and allow for various interpretations	31	41.89 %	3	4.05 %
4	Communication flaws within the project team	26	35.14 %	5	6.67 %
5	Insufficient support by customer	21	28.38 %	5	6.76 %
6	Inconsistent requirements	18	24.32 %	2	2.70 %
7	Time boxing /Not enough time in general	17	22.97 %	1	1.35 %
8	Moving targets (changing goals, business processes and/or req.)	15	20.27 %	5	6.67 %

[a] The probabilities were calculated based on the overall amount of 74 participants

In this paper, we focus on the specific problem of *incomplete/hidden requirements*. According to Tables 11 and 12 this issue is highly relevant for both contexts, being the most cited problem in Austria and the second most cited problem in Brazil. Moreover, the majority of respondents have cited this issue as the most critical one in both countries (see the last columns of Tables 11 and 12).

5 Analyzing the Incomplete/Hidden Requirements Problem

Considering the specific problem of incomplete/hidden requirements, Tables 13 and 14 show how survey respondents from Austria and Brazil judge its applicability to their own projects (participants were asked to judge the applicability of all the precompiled

Table 13. Applicability/relevance of incomplete and hidden requirements to projects of Austrian respondents

Problem	Disagree	Partially disagree	Neutral	Partially agree	Agree	Valid responses
Incomplete	0 (0.00 %)	1 (7.69 %)	2 (15.38 %)	7 (53.85 %)	3 (23.08 %)	13 (100 %)
Hidden requirements	0 (0.00 %)	0 (0.00 %)	2 (15.38 %)	6 (46.15 %)	5 (38.46 %)	13 (100 %)

Table 14. Applicability/relevance of incomplete and hidden requirements to projects of Brazilian respondents

Problem	Disagree	Partially disagree	Neutral	Partially agree	Agree	Valid responses
Incomplete	8 (11.94 %)	2 (2.99 %)	12 (17.91 %)	17 (25.37 %)	28 (41.79 %)	67 (100 %)
Hidden requirements	7 (10.45 %)	0 (0.00 %)	14 (20.90 %)	18 (26.87 %)	28 (41.79 %)	67 (100 %)

RE problems). In this question, *incomplete* and *hidden* requirements were analyzed separately, which would not make sense for the question to rank the most critical ones discussed in the previous section, as these problems are often similar (requirements are often incomplete because there are hidden requirements which were not specified) and should therefore not be counted twice in a ranking.

It can be observed that in both countries most of the respondents consider the problem applicable/relevant to their own projects, with more than 75 % and 65 % agreeing or partially agreeing on its relevance in Austria and in Brazil, respectively. In fact, the judgements for both items, *incomplete* and *hidden*, were almost similar in each of the countries, which reinforces the decision of analyzing them together as *incomplete/hidden requirements* when discussing the most relevant problems and their causes.

After selecting the five most critical RE problems, respondents were asked to provide what they believe of being the main causes for each of the problems. They provided the causes in an open question format, with one open question for each of the previously selected RE problems.

Six of the nine respondents from Austria that reported *incomplete/hidden requirements* among the most critical ones also listed causes for this problem. We analyzed their textual cause descriptions, using the coding terms used for the German NaPiRE trial as a starting point and decided to add new terms only when strictly needed. As a result, we identified 7 causes (each one cited once) and no new coding terms were needed. Then, we represented these causes in a cause-effect diagram [16], using the categories suggested in [6]: *input, method, organization, people,* and *tools*. The resulting cause-effect diagram is shown in Fig. 1.

We repeated the same process for the Brazilian data, in which 27 out of the 31 that reported incomplete/hidden requirements among the most critical ones also listed causes for this problem. We identified 18 different causes in the textual descriptions (in this case, the coding terms were slightly extended – adding four new terms – due to

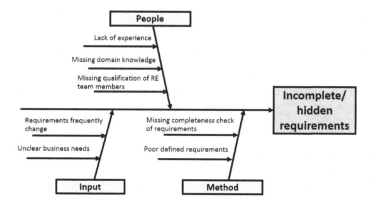

Fig. 1. Austrian cause-effect diagram for incomplete/hidden requirements.

textual descriptions that could not be mapped to the previously provided terms). Given the size of this data set, we also counted the frequency in which each cause was cited (at all we had 35 cause citations).

With this additional information on the frequency, we were able to build a probabilistic cause-effect diagram [17, 18], which enables identifying the most common causes based on probabilistic percentages (in this case, their frequencies). Figure 2 extends the traditional cause-effect diagram [16] by (a) showing the probabilities for

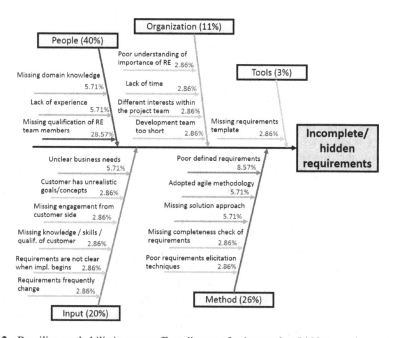

Fig. 2. Brazilian probabilistic cause-effect diagram for incomplete/hidden requirements.

each possible cause to lead to the analyzed problem, and (b) representing the causes using grey tones, where causes with higher probability are shown closer to the center and in darker tones. The resulting probabilistic cause-effect diagram is shown in Fig. 2. We believe that this representation complements the information on causes reported for the problem in Austria. In fact, the causes reported in Austria are contained in the causes reported in Brazil, with additional causes and information on their frequency based on a larger sample. In fact, most of the most frequently cited causes in Brazil shown in Fig. 2 were also identified in the results of the Austrian survey. According to the survey responses we highlight the *missing qualification of RE team members, lack of experience, missing domain knowledge, unclear business needs* and *poor defined requirements* as the main causes.

To address the first three of these causes, related to the *people* category, aiming prevention, we recommend training on best RE practices, selecting highly experienced requirements analysts and involving domain experts and/or providing appropriate training on the application domain. For cases were the lack of domain knowledge plays a significant role, we also recommend some specific domain immersive elicitation techniques, such as ethnography. *Unclear business needs* can be addressed by applying business case analysis that helps fostering discussions and clarifying business objectives and values and by facilitating a stronger involvement and clear communications of the customer. In context of RE joint RE workshops in collaboration with the customer might help to precisely identify the real business needs. Finally, the *poor defined requirements* could be addressed by providing a detailed requirements specification template and conducting peer reviews with appropriate inspection methods (e.g., checklists or reading techniques), ideally involving different stakeholders (e.g., users, designers, and testers) in the verification and validation process. These counter measures represent a set of initial strategies based on the experience of the study team, i.e., the authors.

However, during the NaPiRE survey, candidate measures to address these issues have been collected from survey participants. Tables 15 and 16 presents an overview on risk and RE issue mitigation actions, reported by the participants in Austria and Brazil. These mitigation action can serve as an additional input (from industry projects) to investigate best practices to prevent the incomplete/hidden requirements problem. However, more detailed analysis is required to investigate (a) which mitigation actions are most promising to improve the incomplete/hidden requirements problem and (b) how to support engineers in better addressing these issues.

Table 15. Mitigation actions for incomplete/hidden requirements reported in Austria

Mitigation cctions for incomplete/hidden requirements
Having testers testing requirements
Increased efforts during the review process
After project retrospective with project team
Checklists for requirements

Table 16. Mitigation actions for incomplete/hidden requirements reported in Brazil

Mitigation actions for incomplete/hidden requirements
Improve the documentation and conduct more meetings with the developers to detect analysis defects
Hire or specialize a requirements analyst
Creating templates
Creation of a DoR (Definition of Readiness) for the team
Invest more time in requirements specification, using scenarios and prototypes to gather requirements more completely
Peer reviews involving testes
Invest more effort in requirements validation using prototypes
Peer reviews involving developers
Provide training to the RE team
Process models
Avoiding including incomplete requirements, when already known to be incomplete, in development sprints
Prototyping; technical reviews and consensus meetings
Improve the analysis to be more detailed
More frequent meetings with the customer to align expectations
Requirements reviews and frequent releases
Improving the quality of the requirements documentation, or improving elicitation methods
Developing requirements according to suggestions of the MPS-SW reference model
Improvement of the artefacts; adoption of software inspections
Standardizing the requirements specifications, using a validation checklist and peer reviews
Training, mentoring, selecting professionals with an adequate profile, a highly skilled team
Provide training to the RE team
Reviewing the RE processes
The customer should have a better understanding of the problem; requirements verification with all stakeholders (applying Perspective-Based Reading)

6   Concluding Remarks

Many projects fail due to problems in RE. In this paper, we further analyzed a specific and relevant RE problem: *incomplete/hidden requirements*. Therefore, we used the data of the NaPiRE survey replications we conducted in Austria and Brazil. We provided the basic characterization of the responding organizations (14 in Austria and 74 in Brazil), which include small, medium and large sized companies, conducting both, plan-driven and agile development. Thereafter, we characterized the criticality of the selected RE problem. Results showed that in both countries the survey respondents considered it one of the most critical RE problems (#1 in Austria and #2 in Brazil) and reported that it is applicable and relevant to their projects.

To provide further knowledge on the causes of this problem, we compiled all the causes reported in Austria into a cause-effect diagram and the causes reported in the large Brazilian sample into a probabilistic cause-effect diagram. Most commonly reported causes were *missing qualification of RE team members, lack of experience, missing domain knowledge, unclear business needs* and *poor defined requirements.*

Based on these causes, we discussed solution options on how to address them in order to prevent incomplete/hidden requirements in future projects. Furthermore, we compiled the lists of mitigation actions cited by the survey respondents from Austria and Brazil, which may serve as additional input for preventing the problem.

We believe that, from a practical point of view, this paper provides further insights into common causes of incomplete/hidden requirements and on how to prevent this problem.

Future work includes a more detailed analysis of NaPiRE Austria and NaPiRE Brazil surveys with regard to other RE problems, and to triangulate our results with data from other countries where NaPiRE was performed to increase the validity and reliability of the results achieved.

Acknowledgments. The authors would like to thank the NaPiRE community for their support. Thanks also to the Brazilian research council (CNPq) for financial support (grant #460627/2014-7). Part of this work was also supported by the Christian Doppler Forschungsgesellschaft, the Federal Ministry of Economy, Family and Youth, and the National Foundation for Research, Technology and Development, Austria.

References

1. Broy, M.: Requirements engineering as a key to holistic software quality. In: Levi, A., Savaş, E., Yenigün, H., Balcısoy, S., Saygın, Y. (eds.) ISCIS 2006. LNCS, vol. 4263, pp. 24–34. Springer, Heidelberg (2006)
2. Méndez Fernández, D., Wagner, S., Lochmann, K., Baumann, A., de Carne, H.: Field study on requirements engineering: investigation of artefacts, project parameters, and execution strategies. Inf. Softw. Technol. **54**, 162–178 (2012)
3. Hall, T., Beecham, S., Rainer, A.: Requirements problems in twelve software companies: an empirical analysis. Empirical Softw. Eng. **8**, 7–42 (2003)
4. Khankaew, S., Riddle, S.: A review of practice and problems in requirements engineering in small and medium software enterprises in Thailand. In: International Workshop on Empirical Requirements Engineering (EmpiRE), pp.1–8 (2014)
5. Méndez Fernández, D., Wagner, S.: Naming the pain in requirements engineering: a design for a global family of surveys and first results from Germany. Inf. Softw. Technol. **57**, 616–643 (2015)
6. Kalinowski, M., Card, D.N., Travassos, G.H.: Evidence-based guidelines to defect causal analysis. IEEE Softw. **29**(4), 16–18 (2012)
7. Kalinowski, M., Mendes, E., Travassos, G.H.: An industry ready defect causal analysis approach exploring bayesian networks. In: Winkler, D., Biffl, S., Bergsmann, J. (eds.) SWQD 2014. LNBIP, vol. 166, pp. 12–33. Springer, Heidelberg (2014)
8. Kalinowski, M., Spínola, R.O., Conte, T., Prickladnicki, R., Méndez Fernández, D., Wagner, S.: Towards building knowledge on causes of critical requirements engineering problems. In: International Conference on Software Engineering and Knowledge Engineering (SEKE), p. 6 (2015, accepted for publication)

9. Eveleens, J., Verhoef, T.: The rise and fall of the chaos report figures. IEEE Softw. **27**, 30–36 (2010)
10. Solemon, B., Sahibuddin, S., Ghani, A.A.A.: Requirements engineering problems and practices in software companies: an industrial survey. In: Ślęzak, D., Kim, T.-h., Kiumi, A., Jiang, T., Verner, J., Abrahão, S. (eds.) ASEA 2009. CCIS, vol. 59, pp. 70–77. Springer, Heidelberg (2009)
11. Liu, L., Li, T., Peng, F.: Why requirements engineering fails: a survey report from China. In: International Conference on Requirements Engineering (RE), pp. 317–322 (2010)
12. Khankaew, S., Riddle, S.: A review of practice and problems in requirements engineering in small and medium software enterprises in Thailand. In: International Workshop on Empirical Requirements Engineering (EmpiRE), pp.1–8 (2014)
13. Méndez Fernández, D., Wagner, S.: Naming the pain in requirements engineering: design of a global family of surveys and first results from Germany. In: International Conference on Evaluation and Assessment in Software Engineering (EASE), pp. 183–194 (2013)
14. Kalinowski, M., Weber, K., Franco, N., Duarte, V., Santos, G., Travassos, G.: Results of 10 years of software process improvement in Brazil based on the MPS-SW Model. In: International Conference on the Quality in Information and Communications Technology (QUATIC), pp.28–37 (2014)
15. Softex: Software e Serviços de TI: A Indústria Brasileira em Perspectiva. Observatório Softex (ISSN 1984-6797), vol. 2 (2012)
16. Ishikawa, K.: Guide to Quality Control. Asian Productivity Organization, Tokyo (1976)
17. Kalinowski, M., Travassos, G.H., Card, D.N.: Towards a defect prevention based process improvement approach. In: Euromicro Conference on Software Engineering and Advanced Applications (SEAA), pp. 199–206 (2008)
18. Kalinowski, M., Mendes, E., Travassos, G.H.: Automating and evaluating the use of probabilistic cause-effect diagrams to improve defect causal analysis. In: Caivano, D., Oivo, M., Baldassarre, M.T., Visaggio, G. (eds.) International Conference on Product Focused Software Development and Process Improvement (PROFES). Lecture Notes in Computer Science, vol. 6759, pp. 232–246. Springer, Heidelberg (2011)

An Expert-Based Requirements Effort
Estimation Model Using Bayesian Networks

Emilia Mendes[1,2(✉)], Veronica Taquete Vaz[3],
and Fernando Muradas[4]

[1] BTH – Blekinge Institute of Technology,
37179 Karlskrona, Sweden
emilia.mendes@bth.se
[2] University of Oulu, Oulu, Finland
[3] UFRJ – Federal University of Rio de Janeiro,
P.O. Box 68511, Rio de Janeiro, Brazil
veronica@cos.ufrj.br
[4] Naval Systems Analysis Centre, San Diego 20091000, Brazil
muradas@casnav.mar.mil.br

Abstract. [Motivation]: There are numerous software companies worldwide
that split the software development life cycle into at least two separate projects –
an initial project where a requirements specification document is prepared; and a
follow-up project where the previously prepared requirements document is used
as input to developing a software application. These follow-up projects can also
be delegated to a third party, as occurs in numerous global software development scenarios. Effort estimation is one of the cornerstones of any type of
project management; however, a systematic literature review on requirements
effort estimation found hardly any empirical study investigating this topic.
[Objective]: The goal of this paper is to describe an industrial case study where
an expert-based requirements effort estimation model was built and validated for
the Brazilian Navy. [Method]: A knowledge engineering of Bayesian networks
process was employed to build the requirements effort estimation model.
[Results]: The expert-based requirements effort estimation model was built with
the participation of seven software requirements analysts and project managers,
leading to 28 prediction factors and 30+ relationships. The model was validated
based on real data from 11 large requirements specification projects. The model
was incorporated into the Brazilian navy's quality assurance process to be used
by their software requirements analysts and managers. [Conclusion]: This paper
details a case study where an expert-based requirements effort estimation model
based solely on knowledge from requirements analysts and project managers
was successfully built to help the Brazilian Navy estimate the requirements
effort for their projects.

Keywords: Requirements effort estimation · Bayesian networks · Requirements engineering · Cost estimation · Industrial case study

D. Winkler et al. (Eds.): SWQD 2016, LNBIP 238, pp. 79–93, 2015.
DOI: 10.1007/978-3-319-27033-3_6

1 Introduction

Reliable software effort estimates are the basis for project scheduling, cost estimation[1] and sound resource allocation, thus contributing strongly to projects being completed on time and within budget. Most studies in software effort estimation (e.g. [1, 7]) focus on software development effort, rather than on effort estimation relating to only specific phases of a software life cycle (e.g. requirements specification, testing). Therefore, their estimation techniques take as input some measure(s) of software size and cost drivers that relate to estimating the effort for the entire software development process, rather than for a specific activity part of this process.

However, in practice there are also several software companies worldwide that consider the specification of software requirements as a separate project, for which effort also needs to be estimated. Some of the contexts within which such scenario may likely occur are as follows:

- Companies who provide a detailed requirements specification document as part of contracting out (outsource) the development of software applications to other services suppliers. In such distributed projects, communication tends to be less frequent and less effective, increasing the need to provide an explicit and complete software requirements specification to support software development (e.g. [4, 5, 13]).
- Companies working with fixed price and scope projects. In this scenario it is important to have a detailed understanding of requirements prior to project budget and schedule agreements, as the company will be committed to a fixed scope from the beginning. In this case, companies usually run a preliminary project to further analyze and specify the requirements prior to developing the software.

When we focus upon the scenarios abovementioned, and relate them to the effort estimation process, it is clear that the prediction factors that need to be taken into account should only represent factors deemed relevant within the context of a requirements specification process. In addition, we cannot assume that effort prediction factors that have been proposed in the literature targeting at the entire software development process can be readily applied to estimating effort for a requirements specification activity. Therefore, the investigation of which factors are relevant to estimate effort for a software requirements specification activity is a legitimate research agenda.

Recently, Vaz and Travassos conducted a systematic literature review (SLR) on the state of the art in software requirements specification's effort estimation [16]. This SLR based its evidence on searches executed in three databases: EI Compendex[2], IEEEX-plore[3] and Scopus[4]. A total of 559 papers were screened; however only 10 primary studies were selected. Despite the practical need to estimate effort for the requirements

---

[1] Project costs may include hardware costs, environment costs etc., but it is mostly influenced by the cost of human resources. For this reason the majority of researchers in this field use the terms cost and effort interchangeably [7].

[2] http://www.engineeringvillage2.org/.

[3] http://ieeexplore.ieee.org/.

[4] http://www.scopus.com/.

specification phase, one of the main findings from this SLR was the lack of effort estimation models specifically targeted at that phase. Only one primary study investigated software requirements effort estimation [8]. In this study, Mao et al. propose an artificial neural network model for predicting the effort spent on requirements changes during the later stages of the software development (design, coding, testing, and maintenance). This model uses a set of factors (representing some project characteristics) as input and the output is the effort in person-days needed to tackle the requirements changes. In addition, it only targets at the effort needed to handle future changes in the specification of the requirements, and not the effort involved in eliciting, analyzing and building the initial requirements specification.

Therefore, the goals and main contributions of this paper are twofold: (i) to detail an industrial case study where Bayesian networks (BN) was used to build and validate a requirements effort estimation model with the participation of seven requirements analysts and project managers from a technology center part of the Brazilian Navy; (ii) to present a set of requirements effort estimation predictors and their causal relationships that not only add to the existing body of knowledge in software effort estimation, but also may be useful by other practitioners who estimate effort for the requirements specification phase. BN was chosen because it has been previously used successfully by the first author to build expert-based software effort estimation models for a diverse range of companies [11].

The case study was conducted at a center part of the Brazilian Navy. This center is called Centre for the Analysis of Naval Systems (CASNAV). The CASNAV is recognized as a Brazilian Navy institution for Science and Technology with expertise in the areas of Information Technology, Operational Research and Cryptology. It employs around 350 employees, among military and civilians. The case study took place at CASNAV's Systems Engineering Department (SED), where close to 200 employees work. This department is responsible for CASNAV's target activities and its productivity has presented a continuous increase in serving all areas in the Navy and, as much as possible, also to third party customers. One of the main activities carried out in SED is to manage a large set of requirements specification projects. Their need to treat requirements as a separate project with its own effort estimates, is motivated by two of their current scenarios: (i) a range of projects that have their development outsourced to other companies; (ii) other projects that follow a waterfall process model, which means that the requirements phase needs to be completed prior to estimating development effort.

SED estimates their requirements specification projects based on both project managers' experience and on comparisons with previous similar projects. In addition, in order to obtain budget approval, project managers also need to provide their line managers with a detailed rationale explaining how estimations are obtained; however, this has been a very difficult issue for SED as estimations were often decided upon via subjective means. Their need to improve their current requirements effort estimation process prompted them to participate in this case study.

The remainder of this paper is structured as follows: Sect. 2 provides an overview of BNs, followed by the description, in Sect. 3, of the general process used to build and validate BNs. Section 4 details this process within the context of the model described herein, followed by a discussion of the results & threats to validity in Sect. 5, and finally conclusions in Sect. 6.

2 Introduction to Bayesian Networks

A Bayesian Network (BN) is a model that supports reasoning with uncertainty due to the way in which it incorporates existing knowledge of a complex domain [12]. This knowledge is represented using two parts. The first, the qualitative part, represents the structure of a BN as depicted by a directed acyclic graph (digraph) (see Fig. 1). The digraph's nodes represent the relevant variables (factors) in the domain being modeled. The digraph's arcs represent the causal relationships between variables, where relationships are quantified probabilistically [12].

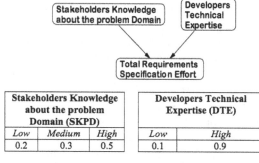

Stakeholders Knowledge about the problem Domain (SKPD)			Developers Technical Expertise (DTE)	
Low	*Medium*	*High*	*Low*	*High*
0.2	0.3	0.5	0.1	0.9

Total Requirements Specification Effort (Low, Medium, High)				
SKPD	**DTE**	*Low*	*Medium*	*High*
Low	*Low*	0.7	0.2	0.1
Low	*High*	0.2	0.6	0.2
Medium	*Low*	0.1	0.7	0.2
Medium	*High*	0	0.5	0.5
High	*Low*	0.2	0.6	0.2
High	*High*	0	0.1	0.9

Fig. 1. Example bayesian network

The second, the quantitative part, associates a conditional probability table (CPT) to each node, its probability distribution. A parent node's CPT describes the relative probability of each state (value) (Fig. 1, nodes 'Stakeholders Knowledge about the problem Domain' and 'Developers Technical Expertise'); a child node's CPT describes the relative probability of each state conditional on every combination of states of its parents (Fig. 1, node 'Total Requirements Specification Effort'). So, for example, the relative probability of 'Total Requirements Specification Effort' being 'Low' conditional on 'Stakeholders Knowledge about the problem Domain' and 'Developers Technical Expertise' being both 'Low' is 0.7. Each row in a CPT represents a conditional probability distribution and therefore its values sum up to 1 [12].

Once a BN is specified, evidence (e.g. values) can be entered into any node, and probabilities for the remaining nodes automatically calculated using Bayes' rule [12]. Therefore BNs can be used for different types of reasoning, such as predictive, diagnostic, and "what-if" analyses to investigate the impact that changes on some nodes have on others.

3 Knowledge Engineering of Expert-Based Bayesian Network Process

The BN model presented herein was built and validated using a process model called the Knowledge Engineering of Expert-based Bayesian Network (EKEBN) process [10] (see Fig. 2). In Fig. 2 arrows represent flows through the different processes, depicted by rectangles. The three main steps within the EKEBN process are the Structure Building, Uncertainty Quantification, and Model Validation. This process iterates over these steps until a complete BN is built and validated. Each of these three steps is detailed in the next Sub-sections.

Structure Building: This step represents the qualitative component of a BN, which results in a graphical structure comprised of, in our case, the factors and causal

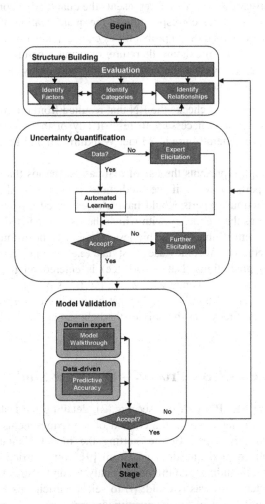

Fig. 2. EKEBN process

relationships identified as fundamental for requirements specification effort estimation. In addition to identifying variables and causal relationships, this step also comprises the identification of the states (values) that each variable should take. The BN's structure is refined through an iterative process. This structure construction process has been validated in previous studies (e.g. [11]) and uses the principles of problem solving employed in data modeling and software development [14]. As will be detailed later, knowledge from the domain experts were employed to elicit the BN's structure. Throughout this step the BN's structure was also evaluated to check whether variables and their values had a clear meaning; all relevant variables have been included; variables are named conveniently; all states are appropriate (exhaustive and exclusive). Sometimes a BN's structure may also need to be optimized to reduce the number of probabilities that need to be elicited or learnt for the network. As will be detailed later, this was the case herein.

Uncertainty Quantification: This step represents the quantitative component of a BN, where conditional probabilities corresponding to the quantification of the relationships between variables are obtained. Such probabilities can be attained via expert elicitation, automatically from data, from existing literature, or using a combination of these. As will be explained later on, within the context of this case study, all the probabilities were obtained via expert elicitation.

Model Validation: This step checks the BN that resulted from the two previous steps, and determines whether it is necessary to re-visit any of those steps. Two different validation methods are generally used - Model Walkthrough and Predictive Accuracy.

Model walkthrough represents the use of real case scenarios that are prepared and used by domain experts to assess if the predictions provided by the BN model correspond to the predictions experts would have chosen based on their own expertise. Success is measured as the frequency with which the BN's predicted value for a target variable (e.g. quality, effort) that has the highest probability corresponds to the experts' own assessment. Predictive Accuracy uses past data (e.g. past project data), rather than scenarios, to obtain predictions. Data (evidence) is entered on the BN model, and success is measured as the frequency with which the BN's predicted value for a target variable (e.g. quality, effort) that has the highest probability corresponds to the actual past data. Prediction accuracy was the only method chosen by CASNAV to validate the model.

4   Revisiting the EKEBN Process – Our Case Study

Herein we revisit the EKEBN process (see Fig. 2), detailing the tasks carried out for each of the three main steps, within the context of the requirements effort estimation BN model focus of this paper. Before starting the model elicitation, preliminary interviews, using an adapted questionnaire from [9], were carried out with several company members, including requirements analysts and project managers. The objective of such interviews was twofold: (i) to select participants for the study; and (ii) to identify the initial set of factors identified as relevant for requirements effort

Table 1. Effort involved in the EKEBN process

Phase	Effort (person hours)
Structure building	114
Uncertainty quantification	136
Model validation	16
Total	266

estimation. This initial set of factors was used as input during the knowledge elicitation meetings, since our previous experience eliciting BNs in other domains (e.g. ecology) suggested that it was best to start the elicitation with a few factors, rather than to use a "blank canvas" as a starting point. We interviewed a total of 10 requirements analysts and five project managers. Each interview was conducted individually, with one company member and the first author. All interviews started with an explanation about the interview's objective, followed by open-ended questions aimed to identify the factors the interviewee believed to drive the effort needed during a requirements elicitation process. Once all the interviews were carried out we selected five requirements analysts and two project managers to take part in the model elicitation and validation. Selection was based on subjects' expertise and experience with requirements analysis, effort estimation, project management and availability to participate. The requirements analysts and the project managers had respectively 4 and 8 years of experience on average. Table 1 details the effort involved in each phase of the EKEBN process. Every session lasted for three hours.

Detailed Structure Building and Uncertainty Quantification: In order to identify the initial set of factors considered important by the requirements analysts and project managers when estimating requirements effort, the second author analyzed the interviews using principles from Grounded Theory (GT) [14] method, in which she has a lot of experience. The GT method provides a viable way of conducting qualitative research, whether with the intention of generating a basic theory or simply to make a conceptual classification [2]. Following the principles defined by Strauss and Corbin [14], this method is based on coding – the analytic processes through which data are fractured, conceptualized, and integrated, and in addition contains three data analysis steps: open coding, where concepts are identified, categorized, and their properties and dimensions are discovered in the data; axial coding, where connections between the categories (and sub-categories) are identified; and selective coding, where the core category (that integrates the theory) is identified and described.

In the context of this case study we only executed the open coding activities as they were sufficient to provide us with the initial set of factors needed as a starting point for the EKEBN process.

Details on the Open Coding: The data analysis began with the open coding of the transcribed interviews. The objective of the open coding activity was to analyze the data collected and allocate codes to the text. We did not use "seed categories" (an initial set of codes); rather, started coding directly from the text, creating in-vivo codes. The open coding procedures stimulate the constant creation of new codes and merging of

Table 2. Results from initial interviews.

Category	Requirements Effort Influence Factor
Solution Domain	Solution size and complexity (**SD1**)
Problem Domain	Processes followed within the Stakeholders' organization are documented (**PD1**)
	Stability of the business environment (**PD2**)
	Discrepancies between documented procedures and actual processes (**PD3**)
	The need to adhere strictly to existing standards (defined by an external entity) that are subject to audit (**PD4**)
Environment for RE	Existence of tools to support the specification (**ERE1**)
Technical Team	CASNAV's requirements team's knowledge about the problem domain (**TT1**)
	CASNAV's requirements team knowledge of requirements engineering (**TT2**)
	Turnover in requirements team (**TT3**)
Stakeholders	Stakeholders knowledge about the problem domain (**ST1**)
	Stakeholders' availability to work in activities related to the project (**ST2**)
	Existence of divergences or conflicts of interest between the information received from various stakeholders (**ST3**)
	Stakeholders' understanding about requirements specification notations (**ST4**)
	Number of stakeholders participating in the project (**ST5**)
	Hierarchical differences between stakeholders (**ST6**)
	Stakeholders turnover (**ST7**)
	Percentage of key stakeholders involved in the project (**ST8**)
Interaction between Stakeholders and Technical Team	Geographical distance between stakeholders and CASNAV's requirements team (**IST1**)
Effort involved in requirements activities	Requirements elicitation effort (**ERA1**)
	Requirements specification effort (**ERA2**)
	Requirements validation effort (**ERA3**)
	Requirements maintenance effort

existing codes as new evidence and interpretations emerge. Whenever two or more interviewees were talking about the same influence factor we combined them into a single code representing both statements. This is the process described by the methodology as the incident-incident comparison [2]. The final step in the open coding phase is to group codes into categories. Categories are clusters of concepts joined in a higher degree of abstraction. They are useful to reduce the number of units the researcher will work with and to make the results easier to visualize. As Banks et al. [3] (see Strauss and Corbin 1990, p. 67) note, categories have to be analytically developed by the researcher. Table 2 presents the categories identified and the complete results of the coding from the preliminary interviews. Each row also presents an identifier (e.g. SD1), which is used to relate the Factor to the set of factors that were ultimately included in the BN model (see Table 3). Note that within the context of this work the different types of Customers are identified jointly as Stakeholders; a Representative is a Stakeholder who interfaces between CASNAV and the other Stakeholders.

Each code represented a factor to be used as part of the Structure building step. All the factors were displayed in a white board, and explained to the participants. The next step was to remove all the factors considered irrelevant to the requirements analysts and project managers participating in the model elicitation, followed by adding to the white board any additional factors deemed relevant. We also documented descriptions for each of the factors suggested. Next, we identified the states that each factor would take, i.e., how each factor was to be measured. All states were discrete. Whenever a factor represented a measure of effort (e.g. Total Requirements Effort), we also documented the effort range corresponding to each state, to avoid any future ambiguity. For example, 'low' Total Requirements Effort corresponded to 0 + to 180 person hours, etc.

Table 3. Results from initial interviews.

Factor (*How it is shown in the BN*)	Categories (*How it is shown in the BN*)	Description
Hierarchical differences between the Representative and other Stakeholders	One rank, two+ ranks	Indicates the existence of differences in military rank between the Representative and other stakeholders
Representative's participatory style	Authoritarian, Good coordination capability, limited coordination capability	Indicates whether the Representative wants to be the sole provider of the requirements, or to also share the elicitation of requirements with other stakeholders.
Stakeholders' and Representative's availability (**ST2**)	Low, High	Stakeholders' and Representative's availability to discuss the project
Stakeholders' level of commitment	Negative, Low, Medium, High	Stakeholders' level of commitment towards project success
Hierarchical differences between Stakeholders (**ST6**)	One rank, 2+ ranks	The highest rank difference between Stakeholders
Number of Stakeholders (**ST5**)	Up to 4, from 5 to 8, 9+	Number of Stakeholders participating in the project
Number of Military Sectors and Organizations	1 sector in 1 MO, N sectors in 1 MO, 2+ MOs	The number of military organizations (MO) and sectors (sub-division within a MO) that have Stakeholders who are participating in the project
Representative's commitment to the project	Negative, Low, Medium, High	The Representative's level of commitment to project success
Stakeholders and Representative turnover (**ST7**)	Low, Medium, High	The number of Stakeholders who leave the project within a period of one year
System type	Operative, Administrative	Indicates whether the system under specification will support operational or administrative activities
Stakeholders' and Representative's knowledge about the problem domain (**ST1**)	None, Basic, Average, Good, Expert	The amount of knowledge/experience that Stakeholders and Representative have regarding the problem domain
Amount of divergences or conflicts of interest amongst the requirements elicited from various Stakeholders (**ST3**)	Low, Medium, High	The amount of divergences and/or conflicts of interest relating to the requirements that were elicited amongst all the Stakeholders, including the Representative.
Representative's Personality factors	Easy going, Slightly Difficult, Very Difficult	The degree of difficulty in dealing with the Representative due to their personality
Stakeholders' understanding about requirements specification notations (**ST4**)	None, Conversant, High	Level of familiarity of Stakeholders with requirements specification notations (e.g. use case descriptions)
Geographical distance between the Stakeholders and CASNAV's requirements team (**IST1**)	Within the same military district, requires a car, requires an airplane but videoconference is also available, requires an airplane and videoconference is not available	Rough indicator of the geographical distance between the Stakeholders and CASNAV's Requirements team
Hierarchical differences between the Representative and CASNAV's Representative	One rank, 2+ ranks	The difference in military rank between the Representative and those representing CASNAV in the project
Stakeholders' MO processes (**PD1+PD3**)	Not documented, documented but not followed, documented and followed	Identifies the sort of processes followed within the Stakeholders' Military organization(s)
Problem domain's complexity	Low, Medium, High	The degree of complexity of the problem domain, as perceived by CASNAV's requirements team
The need to adhere strictly to existing standards (**PD4**)	Yes, No	The need to adhere strictly to existing standards (defined by an external entity) that are subject to audit (e.g. accessibility standards)

(*Continued*)

Table 3. (*Continued*)

Requirements Elicitation Effort **(ERA1)**	Low (0+ a 60) Medium (60+ a 120) High (120+)	Effort in person hours spent by CASNAV on requirements elicitation activities
Requirements' Approval Effort **(ERA3)**	Low (0+ a 60) Medium (60+ a 120) High (120+)	Effort in person hours needed to obtain the approval and the required signatures within CASNAV and also at the Stakeholders' organization(s)
Total requirements Effort	Low (0+ a 180) Medium (180+ a 400) High (400+)	Total effort spent by CASNAV's requirements team on requirements activities
Requirements specification and modelling Effort **(ERA2)**	Low (0+ a 60) Medium (60+ a 160) High (160+)	Effort spent by the CASNAV's requirements team on requirements specification and modelling activities
CASNAV's requirements team's knowledge about the problem domain **(TT1)**	None, Basic, Average, Good, Expert	The level of knowledge/experience that the CASNAV's requirements team has regarding the problem domain
CASNAV's requirements team knowledge of requirements engineering **(TT2)**	None, Basic, Average, Good	The level of knowledge that the CASNAV's requirements team has relating to requirements engineering techniques
Stakeholders' Degree of participation	None, Low, Medium, High	The overall level of commitment with and availability for the project by all Stakeholders
Complexity of the Stakeholders' MO(s)	Low, Medium, High	A subjective measure of how complex CASNAV's requirements team perceives the Stakeholders' Military organization(s) to be
Problem Solution's complexity **(SD1)**	Low, Medium High	The perceived complexity of the solution, as perceived by CASNAV's requirements team
Suitability of CASNAV's requirements team to the project at hand	None, Low, Medium, High	The level of appropriateness of CASNAV's requirements team to the project's needs
Clients Interaction Effort	Low, Medium, High, Very High	Amount of effort required to interact with Clients

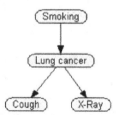

Fig. 3. A simple medical example from (Jensen, 1996)

Once all states were identified and documented, it was time to elicit the cause and effect relationships. As a starting point to this task we used the same example used in Mendes et al. [10] - a simple medical example from [6] (see Fig. 3).

This example introduces one of the most important points to consider when identifying cause and effect relationships – timeline of events. If smoking is to be a cause of lung cancer, it is important that the cause precedes the effect. This may sound obvious with regard to the example used; however, it is our view that the use of this simple example significantly helped the project managers and requirements analysts understand the notion of cause and effect, and how this related to requirements effort estimation and the BN being elicited.

Once the cause and effect relationships were identified, and after some minor changes to the original structure, the final Requirements Effort BN's causal structure

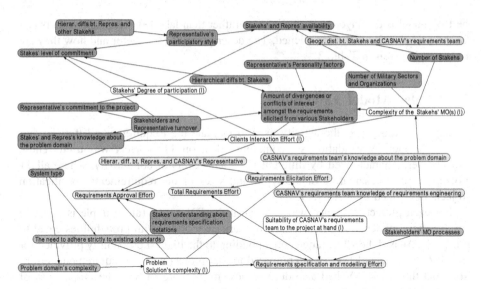

Fig. 4. Final BN structure of the requirements effort estimation model

was as follows (see Fig. 4). Note that Fig. 4 is not a BN based directly on Table 2. Some of the factors in Fig. 4 have a '(I)' at the end of their names; this means that these factors were artificially introduced (I) in order to reduce the amount of probabilities to be elicited. The final version of the BN, including its probabilities, is shown in Fig. 5;

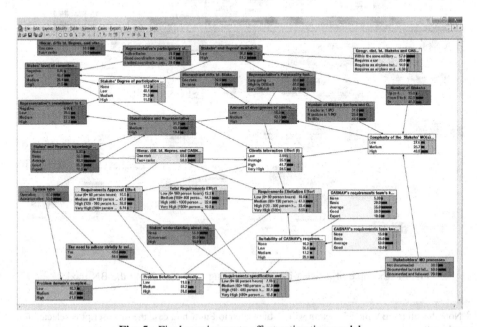

Fig. 5. Final requirements effort estimation model

the BN model is displayed using belief bars rather than labelled factors, so readers can see the probabilities that were elicited. The description of each factor and how they are measured is given in Table 3.[5]

5 Detailed Model Validation

Predictive accuracy was the activity used to validate the Requirements Effort Prediction BN model. A validation set containing data on 11 projects was used. These projects were characterized by different sizes and levels of complexity, where all 11 projects were representative of the types and sizes of the requirements specification projects developed by CASNAV.

For each project, evidence was entered in the BN model (an example is given in Fig. 6, where evidence is characterized by dark grey nodes with probabilities equal to 100 % (1...)), and the effort range corresponding to the highest probability provided for 'Total Requirements Effort' was compared to that project's actual requirements effort. Note that the CASNAV had also defined how to measure each of the factors part of their model. Whenever actual effort did not fall within the effort range associated with the category with the highest probability, there was a mismatch; this meant that some

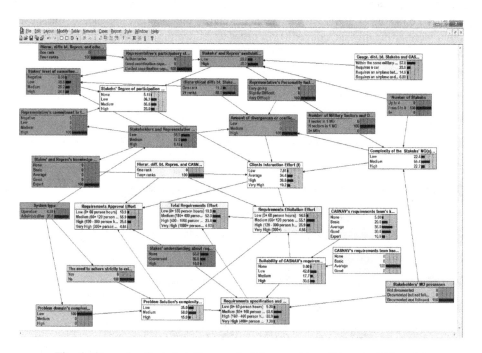

Fig. 6. Example of a 'what-if' scenario being used to validate the BN model

---

[5] Note that all the BN models herein will be translated to English in case the manuscript is selected for publication.

probabilities needed to be adjusted. In order to know which nodes to target first we used a Sensitivity Analysis report, which provided the effect of each parent node upon a given query node. Within our context, the query node was 'Total Requirements Effort'. Whenever probabilities were adjusted, we re-entered the evidence for each of the projects in the validation set that had already been used in the validation step to ensure that the calibration already carried out had not affected. This was done to ensure that each calibration would always be an improved upon the previous one.

Within the context of this work, some calibration was needed; in addition, the requirements project managers decided that all the factors related to effort should have an additional category, and also that the model could be simplified further. This resulted in the model shown in Fig. 5.

The changes to the model are detailed in Table 4 below.

Table 4. New/modified factors, categories and descriptions.

Factor	Categories	Description
Requirements Elicitation Effort	Low (0+ to/a 60) Medium (60+ to/a 120) High (120+ to/a 300) Very High (300+)	Already part of original BN model (see Table III)
Requirements' Approval Effort	Low (0+ to/a 60) Medium (60+ to/a 120) High (120+ to/a 300) Very High (300+)	Already part of original BN model (see Table III)
Total requirements effort	Low (0+ to/a 180) Medium (180+ to/a 400) High (400+ to/a 1000) Very High (1000+)	Already part of original BN model (see Table III)
Requirements specification and modelling effort	Low (0+ to/a 60) Medium (60+ to/a 160) High (160+ to/a 400) Very High (400+)	Already part of original BN model (see Table III)
Level of Complexity dealing with Stakeholders (Replaced Stakeholders' Degree of participation)	Low, Medium, High, Very High	Level of complexity dealing with the Stakeholders, as perceived by CASNAV's requirements team

All probabilities were created from scratch, and the probabilities elicitation, considering the original and the revisited model, took 136 h (the three authors and one requirements analyst).

6 Discussion

In terms of the use of this BN model, CASNAV's main goal is to use the model via its 'what'if' scenarios to support their decision-making relating to estimating effort for all of their requirements projects.

The second round of validations was finalized early 2014, and was carried out using the same 11 projects used in the first validation phase. The model was presented to the entire SED department in April 2014, as part of CASNAV's plan to incorporate it into SED's requirements projects. The third author is managing CASNAV's quality control Sector, and was the person responsible to lead the uptake of the BN model into SED.

The changes that took place as the result of developing the BN model are as follows:

- Introduction and Detailing of the model to the entire SED Department;
- All the estimations provided by any of the requirements analysts and project managers would start to be based on the factors that are part of the BN model. This means that they will use the factors that have been elicited, as well as the BN model, as basis for decision-making during their requirements effort estimation sessions.
- Whenever there are changes to the types of projects been managed, the BN model will be revisited.
- With regard to lessons learned we believe that the successful development of this Requirements Effort estimation BN model was greatly influenced by a number of factors, such as:
- CASNAV's commitment to providing their time and expertise.
- The use of a process where project managers' and requirements analysts' participation was fundamental. This approach was seen as extremely positive by CASNAV as they could implicitly understand the value from building a model that was totally geared towards their needs.

The project managers' and requirement analysts' experience in managing and estimating effort for SED's requirements specification projects.

7   Conclusions

This paper has presented a case study where a Bayesian Model for requirements specification effort estimation was built using solely knowledge of five requirements analysts and two project managers from the Systems Engineering Department from the Brazilian Navy's Centre for the Analysis of Naval Systems (CASNAV). This model was developed using the expert knowledge engineering for Bayesian Networks process (see Fig. 2). Each session with the project managers and requirements analysts lasted for 3 h. The final BN model was calibrated using data on 11 past projects. These projects represented typical projects developed by CASNAV, and believed by the experts to provide enough data for model calibration.

The model is about to be adopted by SED, and the entire process used to build and validate the BN model took 266 person hours.

As part of our future work, we plan to compare our model to that from other related research using BNs within the context of software effort estimation.

References

1. Azhar, D., Mendes, E., Riddle, P.: A systematic review of web resource estimation. In: Proceedings of the 8th Promise Conference, pp. 49–58 (2012)

2. Bandeira-de-Mello, R., Cunha, C.J.: "Operationalizing the Grounded Theory methodology in strategy research: Techniques and analysis procedures with support of the Atlas/IT Tool" (original title: "Operacionalizando o método da Grounded Theory nas pesquisas em estratégia: técnicas e procedimento de análise com apoio do software Atlas/TI"), I Encontro de Estudos em Estratégia (2003)

3. Banks, S., Louie, E., Einerson, M.: Constructing personal identities in holiday letters. J. Soc. Pers. Relat. **17**(3), 299–327 (2000)

4. Cusumano, M.A.: Managing software development in globally distributed teams. Commun. ACM **51**(2), 15–17 (2008)

5. Herbsleb, J.D.: Global software engineering: the future of socio-technical coordination. In: Future of Software Engineering, FOSE 2007, pp. 188–198 (2007)

6. Jensen, F.V.: An introduction to Bayesian networks. UCL Press, London (1996)

7. Jorgensen, M., Shepperd, M.: A systematic review of software development cost estimation studies. IEEE Trans. Softw. Eng. **33**, 33–53 (2007)

8. Mao, C., Lu, Y.S., Wang, X.: A study on the distribution and cost prediction of requirements changes in the software life-cycle. In: Li, M., Boehm, B., Osterweil, L.J. (eds.) SPW 2005. LNCS, vol. 3840, pp. 136–150. Springer, Heidelberg (2006)

9. Matos, O., Fortaleza, l., Conte, T., Mendes, E.: Realising web effort estimation: a qualitative investigation. In: Proceedings of the 17th EASE Conference, pp. 12–23 (2013)

10. Mendes, E., Polino, C., Mosley, N.: Building an expert-based web effort estimation model using bayesian networks. In: Proceedings of the 13th International Conference on Evaluation & Assessment in Software Engineering, pp. 41–50 (2009)

11. Mendes, E.: Using knowledge elicitation to improve Web effort estimation: Lessons from six industrial case studies. In: Proceedings of ICSE 2012, pp. 1112–1121 (2012)

12. Pearl, J.: Probabilistic Reasoning in Intelligent Systems. Morgan Kaufmann, San Mateo (1988)

13. Prikladnicki, R., Audy, J.L.N., Evaristo, R.: Global software development in practice lessons learned. Softw. Process Improv. Pract. **8**(4), 267–281 (2004). doi:10.1002/spip.188

14. Strauss, A., Corbin, J.: Basics of Qualitative Research: Techniques and Procedures for Developing Grounded Theory, 2nd edn. SAGE Publications, London (1998)

15. Studer, R., Benjamins, V.R., Fensel, D.: Knowledge engineering: principles and methods. Data Knowl. Eng. **25**, 161–197 (1998)

16. Vaz, V.T.: Effort estimation in software requirements specification projects. MSc thesis COPPE/UFRJ (2013)

Software Architecture

Experiences from Monitoring Effects of Architectural Changes

Ulf Asklund[✉], Martin Höst, and Krzysztof Wnuk

Department of Computer Science, Lund University, Lund, Sweden
{ulf.asklund,martin.host,krzysztof.wnuk}@cs.lth.se

Abstract. A common situation is that an initial architecture has been sufficient in the initial phases of a project, but when the size and complexity of the product increases the architecture must be changed. In this paper experiences are presented from changing an architecture into independent units, providing basic reuse of main functionality although giving higher priority to independence than reuse. An objective was also to introduce metrics in order to monitor the architectural changes. The change was studied in a case-study through weekly meetings with the team, collected metrics, and questionnaires. The new architecture was well received by the development team, who found it to be less fragile. Concerning the metrics for monitoring it was concluded that a high abstraction level was useful for the purpose.

Keywords: Software architecture · Software metrics

1 Introduction

Architectural changes are often introduced to improve some aspects of a software product or a software development project. The selection of changes and their introduction need to be systematic and well planned [1], followed by a follow-up analysis if the applied changes resulted in the desired improvements. Software metrics can support both change planning and evaluation [2]. These metrics need to accurately describe the principles behind the changes and the main objects of these changes.

Developing software products via prototyping is nowadays widely used. The first prototype version is usually rather small, and then the product and the number of included functions grow. However, during such incremental development a problem can occur that the changes made to the product affect many parts of the product, resulting in that changes can result in unpredictable software faults. This is typically the effect of an immature architecture for the purpose and/or because of a development process with insufficient quality assurance practices. The result is a suboptimal architecture that needs refactoring to bring its quality to an acceptable level. However, architecture changes can not be carried out in isolation. There is a relationship between the business, the architecture, the process, and the organization, as described by the BAPO model, e.g. [3], and

© Springer International Publishing Switzerland 2016
D. Winkler et al. (Eds.): SWQD 2016, LNBIP 238, pp. 97–108, 2016.
DOI: 10.1007/978-3-319-27033-3_7

currently further analyzed in the ITEA project SCALARE.[1] This means that, for example, the development process and the organization also might need to be changed at the same time as the architecture.

This paper presents a case study where requirements changes and a more large scale usage of the product triggered an architectural change. The introduction of the architecture change and a related process change is monitored with a set of object oriented design metrics, inspired by Martin [4]. Versions of these metrics are available in several metrics collection tools, and the objectives of this study include evaluating to what extent they can be useful in the context of an architectural change.

2   Related Work

Software refactoring is an integral and important part of software maintenance and evolution and often associated with restructuring [5]. It is a way to restore quality after frequent changes [6], improve extensibility, modularity, reusability, complexity, maintainability and efficiency [6] or transform centralized software components into distributed [7]. Software restructuring is a form of "perfective maintenance" with the goal to modify the structure of the source code and facilitate correctly previously undetected errors [8]. Moreover, it is rather straightforward to estimate the payoffs of restructuring in terms of time and money saved, and shorter development cycles [9]. Refactoring can be achieved with the help of assertions (pre-conditions, post-conditions and invariants), graph transformations, model transformations with semantic annotations [10], aspect oriented concepts [11]. However, these methods are rarely empirically evaluated.

Several authors focused on software architecture stability. Among them, Aversano et al. proposed a set of instability metrics combined with thresholds when the architecture can be considered fully stable, leveling, improving, fully unstable [12]. Tony et al. suggested a metric-based approach for evaluating architecture stability based on: growth rate, change rate, cohesion and coupling and evaluated them on several open source projects [13]. Interestingly, Bahsoon and Wolfgand suggested using real options theory for evaluating architectural stability and estimating volatility, exemplified on ten architectural changes [14]. Figueiredo et al. focused on design stability of software product lines in terms of modularity, change propagation and feature dependency identifying a number of positive and negative scenarios [15]. However, they analyzed two small product lines with 10 KLOC and 3 KLOC.

3   Case Description

3.1   Overall Architecture

The case system is a client system for server software, intermediate software, specifically developed hardware, and other units. The system architecture is depicted in Fig. 1.

---

[1] http://scalare.org.

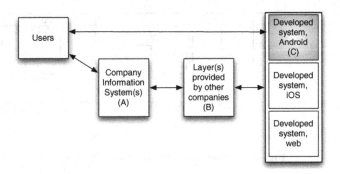

Fig. 1. High level architecture of the whole system

The overall project is managed by Company A and includes a large customer base. Company A has a number of Information Systems (marked A in Fig. 2) in order to manage the customer and user data. Other companies, marked as B in Fig. 2 access this data in different ways in their applications. The customers receive a number of functions for observing, and taking actions upon the data in the Company Information System (A). The application is developed in three versions, one for iOS, one for the web and one for Android. We studied the Android application in this paper, further called "developed system" in this paper (C). Other companies (B) can influence and extend the functionality provided by the system using the benefits of the layered design. Often, the new functionality development is done in both layers.

The layered design combined with the interaction between the development company and other companies impose several requirements and constraints. Firstly, many companies are involved in the project with some significantly influencing the project scope (Company A). Secondly, the division of the work to be done between the layers is not always straightforward. Thirdly, development cycles should be short since users expect new functionality frequently delivered. Fourthly, reliability requirements are high due to a large amount of users. Finally, the company wants to keep the current maintainability and lead-time levels. The result of high release frequency is limited functionality and complexity of the early versions. Therefore, the case company does not see the initial architecture of the developed system as good as it should be and they are trying to obtain a better architecture which will provide better maintainability.

3.2 Organization and Process at the Case Company

On average, 2–3 developers work full time on the system. About the same number of developers work on the web version and the iOS version of the developed system, and the development must of course be synchronized. Since the project has existed for rather long time there has been some change of personnel, which also puts requirements on maintainability.

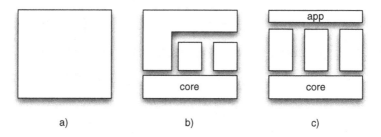

Fig. 2. Architecture change of application

The project followed an agile approach, mainly based on Scrum with collective code ownership where the developers assign the tasks to themselves to the next task independent of what it is and what part of the system it affects.

There were two main reasons for the company to make a change. There was a negative trend of quality issues like old bugs being re-introduced and too many errors found late in testing. There were also several future development activities planned in a near future, including new usage scenarios, targeting new market segments, and developing new business models.

Based on the overall system architecture, the development time requirements remained high and considered together with the business drivers (Extended functionality). The detailed analysis of the change drivers revealed that the developers spend too much time browsing, for them uninteresting, files and documents. Moreover, the developers struggled to find the relevant parts of the system to add new functionality. Finally, extensive dependencies make the developed product quite fragile, i.e. a change to one part of the system has non intuitive dependencies to other parts, which are not always considered by the developers.

3.3   Introduced Architectural Changes to the Developed System

The architecture was designed with focus on reuse, i.e. when new functionality is added, existing classes are reused as much as possible. Extensive reuse may lead to an architecture with many dependencies resulting in a, more or less, monolithic system. This was identified as the major reason to the problems mentioned above, and in order to better structure the dependencies and make the design less fragile, the architecture was divided into modules. Each module implemented one specific function provided to the user, implemented as separate projects in the development environment (Eclipse). Functional decoupling allowed the developers to make corrections or updates of existing functions, e.g. only the code valid for the function was browsed, understood, and updated, which makes the change fast and with high quality. It also allowed for parallel updates of different functions, and new functionality can be added independent of the existing.

The architecture guidelines were changed to focus on independent modules and how to manage them individually. Previously, all developers worked on the whole code base when changes were implemented, which often required changes to a large part of the system. The new process allows developers to avoid change request in modules they have not yet know - but also to deliberately choose to work in a module for the first time in order to increase system knowledge. From an organizational perspective, the new architecture makes it is easier to scale, letting new developers joining the project to start work on one function in one module, learning the system function-by-function.

The drawback of the new architecture is less reuse and more double-maintenance of "similar" code in different modules. However, the case company believed that changes in the new architecture can be limited to one module and therefore better fulfill the architecture maintainability requirements. Both architectural and process changes were gradually introduced by the case company. This was done by adding one module after another to the initial codebase. This means that there were different versions of the system during the research project.

The gradual changes that were made to the application architecture are sketched in Fig. 2. In the beginning, there was a monolithic architecture (Fig. 2.a). The objective of the changes was to achieve an architecture with separate modules and a limited of common functionality, as shown in Fig. 2.c. The main common layer in Fig. 2.c is marked "core" and handles parts of the product that is common to all modules. It also serves as the interface to layers provided by other companies (B). There is also a small common part marked "app" which is the Android application, which, for example, is responsible for configuring and launching the modules. The other parts of the architecture is made up of separate and independent modules. The current situation is that a bottom layer has been formed, and a few independent modules introduced as described above (Fig. 2.b). In the current version of the architecture there are still parts of the old architecture remaining.

3.4 Selected Metrics for Monitoring the Changes

Several metrics are available in the literature for monitoring stability and abstractness of a design. Martin has presented a number of metrics based on the coupling between classes and packages (code categories) (e.g. [4,16]) as described below. One aspect that is of interest for a package is to what extent it depends on other packages. The fewer other packages it depends on, the more stable it is (does not break due to changes outside the package). Martin [4,16] defines a metric for efferent coupling (C_e) as the number of classes in a package that depend on classes outside the package. We make an alternative definition of efferent coupling of a code segment as the number of other code segments that it depends on, where a code segment can be a package or a project. This level we found sufficient for our purpose in order to measure how dependent a code segment is of other code segments. It can also be noticed that it is the same definition of efferent coupling as is used in the JDepend metrics tool[2] for analysis of coupling between java packages.

---

[2] http://clarkware.com/software/JDepend.html.

Another aspect that is of interest for a package is its responsibility. The more other packages are dependent on it the more responsible it is, and the more responsible it is the more stable it is forced to be. Martin [4, 16] defines a measure of afferent coupling (C_a) as the number of classes outside the package that depend on classes inside the package. In this study we define this metric as the number of code segments outside a code segment that depend on the code segment, where a code segment can be a java package or a project in Eclipse.

We use Martin's [4, 16] definition of instability $I = C_e/(C_a + C_e)$, but with our definition of C_e and C_a. $I = 0$ indicates a maximally stable segment, and $I=1$ indicates a maximally unstable segment. I.e. instability, I, can be seen as a measure of to what extent changes that are made in other parts of the code affects the code and to what extent it is likely to be changed based on new requirements, etc.

An interesting question to discuss is on what abstraction level the metrics for coupling and instability should be collected on. This can either be between classes, between packages, or between projects in Eclipse. Since the goal of the organization in the study was to get independent "pipes", which are implemented as projects in Eclipse we choose to measure the coupling between projects. However, this means that the metrics can only be collected for the latest version where a division into different projects has been made.

4   Research Methodology

The research methodology follows a case study approach (e.g. [17]), i.e. it is a flexible research approach [18] where some detailed are left undecided before all data collection is performed. The high-level goal of the research was to understand how to monitor the architectural transformation and to be able to provide objective evidence regarding the positive impact of the suggested changes. The main research questions are:

1. What are the motivations for introducing the changes described in Sect. 3.3, and what are the experiences of introducing them?
2. What are the experiences of using the set of metrics as described in Sect. 3.4 for the purpose of monitoring (and keeping) this kind of change?

4.1   Data Collection

The data collection steps are outlined in Fig. 3. The data was continuously collected during the architectural changes. To the left of Fig. 3, the "normal improvement work" of the case company is shown, i.e. how the company goes from an initial version of the architecture to a "final version", i.e. the last version during this case study. The data collection started when the change process had been initiated and some changes were already introduced. Thus, the authors were not involved in the decisions or selecting the goals of the architectural transformations. During the data collection, information that is the basis for

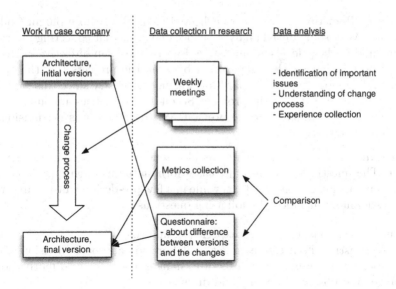

Fig. 3. Main steps of data collection and analysis

understanding the background, the type of changes and the introduced changes as presented in Sects. 3.1, 3.2 and 3.3 were gathered.

Weekly Meetings. The researchers held approximately every week, or at least bi-weekly, meetings with a case company contact person of the project. The objectives of the meetings were to understand what happened in the project and what decisions are taken at different points in time. The meetings were also held in order to understand more about why different decisions were taken. During the meetings questions about the business, architecture, process, and organization were asked. The meetings were informal and held either in the company premises or over skype/telephone. The following list of questions were used to guide the meetings:

- What has happened since the last meeting?
- What important events or decisions have been taken, with respect to (i) business, (ii) architecture, (iii) process, (iv) organization?
- What are your plans, with respect to (i) business, (ii) architecture, (iii) process, (iv) organization?

Since the meetings were held informal, not all questions were asked every time. However, they were used to ensure that no important dimension was missed but the discussions always covered these aspects. During the meetings, notes were taken by the researchers. No audio recordings were carried out. There were also a few meetings with the person in charge of collecting the metrics at the company where different metrics were discussed. This is further discussed in Sect. 3.4.

Metrics Collection. Metrics were collected using the Eclipse plugin CodePro AnalytiX.[3] After some initial analysis, it became clear that collecting metrics on the class and package levels is unfeasible. Firstly, the main objective of the case company was to have a clear separation between the projects (i.e. the "pipes" in Fig. 2). Therefore, package separation was not necessary since this would not show the difference between the projects. Secondly, the metrics are only collected for the latest version, since in the previous versions there was no division into projects in this way.

Questionnaires. A questionnaire was also sent to developers in the Android project. The questions were in most cases formulated as open questions where the participants answers in free-text, while in a few pre-decided answer questions. The questionnaire included the following questions:

1. General questions, e.g. name, experience, and role
2. Characteristics about the team, e.g. collaboration approach, division of tasks
3. Questions concerning the architecture changes, e.g. perceived motivation for change, and observed benefits and drawbacks
4. Questions concerning the development process, with sub-questions about noticed change in product quality, noticed change in how easily the code can be browsed and searched, and perceived change regarding how much code a developer must be able to work with
5. Questions about testing, e.g. how the architectural change affected test-case selection and the number of faults found
6. Question about how changes negatively affect other parts of the system, before and after the architectural change
7. Question about how the amount of duplicate code has changed after the architectural change.

Analysis. The metrics analysis was carried out by collecting the metrics on the last available version of the system and analyzing them, see Sect. 5.1. Qualitative data analysis included summarizing the answers to each major question category.

5   Results

5.1   Metrics Collection

Since the study focused on the relations between the different projects, the metrics were collected on the higher abstraction looking at the separation of projects. The results are presented in Table 1. The calculation of C_e was based on the number of the referenced projects. Figure 4 extends the general sketch in Fig. 2.b with some more details. The figure consists of a number of parts:

---

[3] https://marketplace.eclipse.org/content/codepro-analytix.

Table 1. Metrics results

Project	Referenced projects	C_e	Referencing projects	C_a	I
P1	P2, P4, P6	33	P2, P4, P6	3	0.5
P2	P1, P3	2	P1	1	0.67
P3	–	0	P2, P4, P5, P6	4	0
P4	P1, P3	2	P1	2	0.5
P5	P3	1	–	0	1
P6	P1, P3	2	P1	1	0.67

- P1: This part denotes the "original project", i.e. the architecture according to Fig. 2.a. This part has evolved by breaking out some of the functionality of the large architecture in Fig. 2.a when developing other parts, and it has been improved in general.
- P3: This part denotes the "core" functionality that is intended to be used by the other projects. It is intended to be stable, which is also reflected in the value of $I = 0$.
- P2, P4, P5, P6: These parts are individual "pipes" which are dependent on P3, but not on each other. Since they are dependent on P3 they are not stable in respect to I.

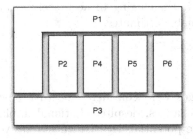

Fig. 4. Architecture of the current version

5.2   Interviews/Questionnaires

The questionnaire was answered by five persons with different types of roles. The answers to the questions can be summarized as follows:

1. Two developers, one architect, are customer representative and one manager (core reviewer) answered the survey. Their experience in the project was between 4 and 19 months (median 8) and industrial experience between 1 and 10 years (median 9).

2. The team consisted of 6–7 persons working as a cohesive team and physically in the same location. The development methodology is agile and based on Scrum with work allocation performed by the developers. Developers worked together with the same feature, i.e. they take a feature "together" and work with that until it was done. The feature work is divided into tasks that take 1–8 h to develop. Sometimes, front-end and back-end development efforts are split.

3. The studied architectural change is considered as an improvement. The understanding of the necessity and the detailed of the changes among the participants is high. The benefits of the changes include that changes will not spread to other parts of the code, it is easier to get an overview, which means that the maintainability is better, and unit test is easier. One participant also highlighted better discussions about the code and the architecture as a benefit. The drawbacks that are seen include that some code may be duplicated since the focus is so much on independent architectural parts. One person also thought that the setup process of the projects were more complicated.

4. The developed code consists fewer faults and it is easier to find what changes have been made to the code.

5. The participants think that it is easier to formulate the right tests. This may however be due to an overall code improvements.

6. Some of the introduced changes may actually negatively impact other parts of the software. The participants think that this problem has decreased in the current version.

7. The participants admitted that the amount of duplicate code has increased, however they found it challenging to accurately estimate the amount of it due to the lack of reliable estimates.

6   Discussion

The architectural changes were considered positive since no participant was clearly negative to the changes, despite additional duplicate code. One explanation could be that the potential negative effects are yet to be discovered. It can also be that this type of project is suitable for this kind of architectural changes and therefore no negative effects occur. The studied code focuses on providing outputs based on input without complicated algorithms, which may be one reason the solution is suitable.

The organizational set up in this case made it possible to move the logic to the server (implemented in decoupled "modules") and focus on thin clients, allowing for decoupled implementation of new features. The clients got thicker than needed, which also may be the reason there is still different teams for iOS and Android, something that can be avoided by having a pure feature oriented organization cross different OS. This fits well the studied context, see B in Fig. 1, since different companies are responsible for client applications and the server layers. Moreover, canonical data forced the client code to process data not valid for them. To summarize, other contexts can also benefit from this type of architectural changes, e.g. in a telecom service provider (corresponding to company A) with customers who have outsourced information systems management to other companies (corresponding to layers here).

The used metrics were suitable for a rather high level of abstraction (between Eclipse projects and not on one specific project). They successfully measured if the architectural changes were achieved. Once in place, these metrics can also serve as continuous verification of the quality of the architecture.

Validity can, for example, be discussed with the respect to construct validity, internal validity, external validity, and reliability, e.g. [17]. Construct validity was strengthened by having a long time contact with weekly meetings, which can reduce the risk of misunderstandings. Internal validity threats in terms of other factors affecting the values of the architectural measures were minimized by studying the whole change and trying to understand what was actually changed, e.g. the way of working was changed somewhat at the same time. However, a risk remains that the changes were made as a result of positive attitude and just because the participants were not happy with the old architecture. Moreover, the study was conducted with a rather small team for an Android application threatening external validity. Thus, further replications are needed for this type of projects, and if other types of projects are consider additional research is probably needed. Finally, we address reliability threats by having regular meetings with the team and recording all research steps in the case study protocol.

7 Conclusions

Concerning the motivation for introducing the changes described in Sect. 3.3, the main motivations are that it can decrease the risk of making changes that negatively affect other parts of the system, and that it makes it possible to divide the work between different people in natural way. There was also a need to refactor the architecture since the software has grown and future anticipated requirements include further growth of the software and increased differentiation between customer segments. The experiences of introducing the changes are in general positive, which indicates that it in this case was correct to prioritize modularization over the avoidance of code duplication. If the same change is made in another project, conclusions from this study may be relevant if the project is similar in e.g. size and the type of code (e.g. with respect to how complicated algorithms etc. it involves).

One conclusion that can be drawn concerns the level of abstraction of the metrics. Even if this is only one study it seems like it is reasonable to study the metric on a high level of abstraction, since the focus is on the whole project and not on a specific part when this change is made.

Acknowledgement. This work was funded by Vinnova in the ITEA2 project 12018 SCALARE.

References

1. Bergman, B., Klevsjö, B.: Quality, from Customer Needs to Customer Satisfaction, 3rd edn. Studentlitteratur, Lund (2010)
2. Fenton, N., Pfleeger, S.L.: Software Metrics, a Rigorous and Practical Approach, 2nd edn. PWS Publishing Company, Boston (1997)
3. Betz, S., Wohlin, C.: Alignment of business, architecture, process, and organisation in a software development context. In: Proceedings of the International Symposium on Empirical Software Engineering and Measurement (ESEM), pp. 239–242 (2012)
4. Martin, R.C.: Agile Software Development Principles, Patterns, and Practices, 2nd edn. Prentice-Hall, Upper Saddle River (2003)
5. Chikofsky, E., Cross II, J.H.: Reverse engineering and design recovery: a taxonomy. IEEE Softw. **7**(1), 13–17 (1990)
6. Mens, T., Tourwé, T.: A survey of software refactoring. IEEE Trans. Softw. Eng. **30**(2), 126–139 (2004)
7. Seriai, A., Bastide, G., Oussalah, M.: Transformation of centralized software components into distributed ones by code refactoring. In: Eliassen, F., Montresor, A. (eds.) DAIS 2006. LNCS, vol. 4025, pp. 332–346. Springer, Heidelberg (2006)
8. Eloff, J.: Software restructuring: implementing a code abstraction transformation. In: Proceedings of the 2002 Annual Research Conference of the South African Institute of Computer Scientists and Information Technologists on Enablement Through Technology, SAICSIT 2002, Republic of South Africa, pp. 83–92 (2002)
9. Arnold, R.: Software restructuring. IEEE Softw. **77**(4), 607–617 (1989)
10. Ivkovic, I., Kontogiannis, K.: A framework for software architecture refactoring using model transformations and semantic annotations. In: 10th European Conference on Software Maintenance and Reengineering (CSMR), March 2006
11. Rizvi, S., Khanam, Z.: A methodology for refactoring legacy code. In: International Conference on Electronics Computer Technology (ICECT 2011), pp. 198–200 (2011)
12. Aversano, L., Molfetta, M., Tortorella, M.: Evaluating architecture stability of software projects. In: Working Conference on Reverse Engineering, pp. 417–424 (2013)
13. Tonu, S.A., Ashkan, A., Tahvildari, L.: Evaluating architectural stability using a metric-based approach. In: Proceedings of the European Conference on Software Maintenance and Reengineering, (CSMR), Bari, Italy, pp. 261–270 (2006)
14. Bahsoon, R., Emmerich, W.: Evaluating architectural stability with real options theory. In: IEEE International Conference on Software Maintenance, ICSM, Chicago, IL, United States, pp. 443–447 (2004)
15. Figueiredo, E., Cacho, N., Garcia, A., Ferrari, F., Khan, S., Sant'Anna, C., Monteiro, M., Soares, S., Filho, F.C., Kulesza, U., Dantas, F.: Evolving software product lines with aspects: an empirical study on design stability. In: International Conference on Software Engineering, Leipzig, Germany, pp. 261–270 (2008)
16. Martin, R.C.: OO design quality metrics. Technical report, Object Mentor (1994)
17. Runeson, P., Höst, M., Rainer, A., Regnell, B.: Case Study Research in Software Engineering - Guidelines and Examples. Wiley, Hoboken (2012)
18. Robson, C.: Real World Research, 2nd edn. Blackwell, Oxford (2002)

Making the Case for Centralized Software Architecture Management

Georg Buchgeher[1]([✉]), Rainer Weinreich[2], and Thomas Kriechbaum[3]

[1] Software Competence Center Hagenberg, Hagenberg im Mühlkreis, Austria
`georg.buchgeher@scch.at`
[2] Johannes Kepler University, Linz, Austria
`rainer.weinreich@jku.at`
[3] Racon Software GmbH, Linz, Austria
`thomas.kriechbaum@racon.at`

Abstract. Architectural knowledge is an important artifact for many software development and quality control activities. Examples for quality control activities based on architectural information are architecture reviews, dependency analyses, and conformance analyses. Architecture is also an important artifact for understanding, reuse, evolution, and maintenance. Unfortunately, in many projects architectural knowledge often remains implicit and is not available for a particular system stakeholder or outdated when it is actually needed. To address this problem, we propose to manage semi-formal software architecture knowledge in a central repository, where it is accessible to all stakeholders and where it can be automatically and continuously updated and analyzed by different tools. In this paper we discuss important elements and use cases of such an approach, and present an example for an architecture knowledge and information repository in the context of an enterprise service-oriented architecture (SOA).

Keywords: Software architecture management · Software architecture knowledge management · Software architecture information repositories · Software architecture as a service · Software architecture models · Software architecture views · Software architecture use cases

1 Motivation

Architectural knowledge is required for a variety of activities in the software development process by many different stakeholders [1]. Stakeholders have different concerns and require different kinds of knowledge [2]. Despite much progress in software architecture research in areas like software architecture documentation and software architecture knowledge management (SAKM) during the last few years, making architectural knowledge explicit, and having it available, when and where it is actually needed, remains a fundamental problem [3].

The unavailability of correct and up-to-date architectural information is also the root cause of many other problems in software development. Examples include costly architecture evaluations that require architecture knowledge

© Springer International Publishing Switzerland 2016
D. Winkler et al. (Eds.): SWQD 2016, LNBIP 238, pp. 109–121, 2016.
DOI: 10.1007/978-3-319-27033-3_8

to be documented or recovered [4], higher maintenance and system evolution costs resulting from the high resource demand required for understanding a system's architecture [5], architecture erosion [6], redundant development of already existing functionality/components because developers are not aware of existing assets, missing reuse of architecture knowledge across projects, and last but not least architectural knowledge vaporization - the loss of architectural knowledge over time [7].

But even if software architecture knowledge is made explicit, it is often hidden in documents and artifacts that are not accessible for all stakeholders, or it is scattered over multiple different documents [3]. This situation is unsatisfying, especially when looking into other areas of software engineering. For example, in requirements-, bug and issue-, test-, source-code-, and project-management it has become industrial practice to store information in central repositories, where it can be easily accessed by stakeholders and automatically processed by development tools like quality dashboards, test tools, static code analysis tools, build tools, and configuration tools. For architectural knowledge, such repositories have not yet found their way into mainstream software development (except for isolated use cases) and are still missing.

We propose such a central repository and associated services for managing structured and semi-formally defined architectural knowledge. Aside from supporting different stakeholders with a central access point but different views on architectural information, it is important that architectural information can be integrated with different tools in a continuous build and development process, and also synchronized with other information resources.

The main contributions of this paper are (1) the presentation of main elements, use cases, and benefits of a central architecture information repository (AIR), and (2) an example for such a repository that is currently being established in the context of an enterprise service-oriented architecture (SOA).

The remainder of this paper is organized as follows: In Sect. 2 we characterize the concept of architecture information repositories. Section 3 discusses use cases, benefits, and perspectives of establishing an AIR. In Sect. 4 we present views, knowledge types, and tools of an AIR for an enterprise SOA and reflect on its development history. Related work is discussed in Sect. 5. The paper is concluded in Sect. 6 with a summary and an outlook of future work.

2   Architecture Information Repository (AIR)

In the following we discuss some consequences of providing architecture information in a central repository and give an overview of the different types of architectural knowledge such a repository may contain.

Central Access and Management. By managing architectural knowledge in a central repository and providing central access through networked connections, all stakeholders and tools operate on the same data, which eliminates problems like scattered information sources, redundant definition of data, and inconsistencies between models. The repository also lays the foundation for stakeholder collaboration and provides means for versioning architectural knowledge.

Support of different stakeholders and multiple views. Architectural knowledge contained in the repository can be accessed by different stakeholders via different clients and views as proposed by ISO/IEC/IEEE 42010:2011 [2].

Integration and synchronization with other information sources. An AIR can also be integrated with existing information sources constituting a project infrastructure (e.g., code repositories, requirements, bug, and issue management systems, etc.). For example, architecture structures contained in the system implementation can be extracted from code repositories, and architecturally significant requirements (ASRs) can be synchronized with requirement management systems.

Integration with processes and automatic processing. Knowledge contained in the AIR is not only accessed by stakeholders but also used by automated tools. Such tools casn perform different kinds of analysis and synchronize (import, export, transform) architectural information with other information sources. Automated processing keeps architectural information up-to-date and helps to support other development and management activities based on current architecture information (e.g., test and service governance activities).

Types of Knowledge. Architectural knowledge managed in an AIR can be project-specific and project-generic [8]. Aside from architectural structures on different abstraction levels (class, component, system), an AIR may contain design decisions and their rationale, ASRs (used for evaluation), generic knowledge (e.g., patterns, styles, and reference architectures), constraints representing company-wide restrictions on an architecture, and process data representing results of already performed architecture analyses and evaluations. Storing all information in one place also enables extensive tracing between the different knowledge entities.

3 Use Cases, Benefits and Perspectives

An AIR provides the foundation for a variety of architecture knowledge management (AKM) activities not only in the software architecture life cycle [9], but also beyond. In the following, we present common examples of how architecture knowledge may be produced and consumed by different stakeholders and tools in the software architecture life cycle.

Design Support. Software architects store architecture solution structures including their rationale in the repository, which serves as a blueprint for developers. They can search the repository for architecture styles and reference architectures related to their project including references to other projects where styles and reference architectures have been applied.

Development Support. Architecture solution structures can be used for generating (parts of) the system implementation by means of model-driven development

(MDD). Code and component solution structures can be automatically analyzed for conformance with the system implementation. Developers can be immediately informed about deviations between planned and implemented architecture preventing architectural drift and erosion [6].

Quality Control. Reviewers can evaluate architecture design models located in the AIR for conformance to ASRs. Further architectural knowledge in the AIR can be subject to automated quality control. For example, architecture models can be analyzed for model completeness and consistency, and for compatibility with reference architectures, architectural styles, and patterns. Architecture metrics can also be calculated from the architectural knowledge contained in the AIR. Results of architecture evaluations and analyses can be stored in the AIR and are accessible to software architects, quality managers, and developers. Quality managers can view aggregated quality data along with other quality data in quality dashboards, where they can perform trend analyses and plan countermeasures in the case of quality problems.

Test Support. Since the AIR supports versioning of architectural knowledge, testers can detect modified system parts that need to be considered during system testing. Evolution analysis permits focusing the testing process on new and modified system parts as well as on system parts using the modified parts.

Maintenance Support. Maintainers can browse architecture models created by software architects in the AIR to become familiar with the system under maintenance. They can trace where a requirement to be modified is currently addressed in architecture design and implementation, and determine which requirements might be affected when modifying a system. They can perform change impact analysis and virtual refactoring [10] before actually modifying a system's architecture and/or implementation.

Governance Support. System governance activities can be planned, analyzed, and monitored based on architecture models stored in the repository, provided the stored models resemble the currently implemented architecture.

Reuse Support. Architectural knowledge can be reused across project boundaries. Architecture designs and also review results can act as reference and input for new architecture designs. Reusable system components and libraries can be identified.

In addition to software architecture life-cycle-related activities, AIRs will also open new perspectives on AKM activities. For example, the widespread use of AIRs could lead to establishing AIR mining as a new research field. Mining architecture knowledge repositories would provide valuable feedback on how AKM is performed in practice. Potential use cases are the analysis of how architectural knowledge evolves over time, the analysis of the kinds of architectural knowledge that are actually used/documented, and the analysis of the kinds of architectural knowledge that are consumed and produced by specific stakeholders.

4   An AIR for an Enterprise SOA

In this section we report on our experiences on establishing an AIR (LISA AIR) in a company in the banking domain [11]. Figure 1 provides an overview of the approach, including the supported stakeholders, the provided (sub)models and views, and the currently developed/used tools working on the repository and related data sources. The elements shown in the figure are described in more detail in the following subsections.

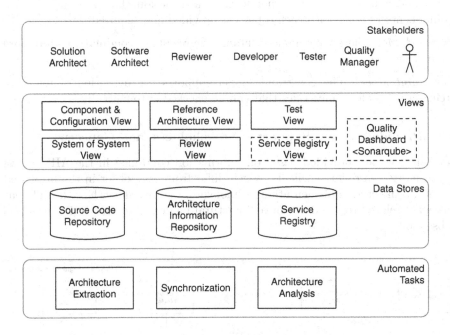

Fig. 1. LISA AIR overview

4.1   Supported Types of Architectural Knowledge

The different types of architectural knowledge provided by our approach are represented by different integrated submodels of a general architecture information model in the AIR. The models are integrated to eliminate redundancies, prevent inconsistencies, and enable cross-model traceability. Therefore, views may be based on several different submodels (see Fig. 2), which can be accessed through one general model API. The main models are the *code model*, the *component and configuration model*, the *review model*, and the *constraint model*. Elements of the models can be provided to external clients and tools though the provided service API. Additional models can be contributed as needed.

Code Model. The code model reflects the system implementation in terms of implementation artifacts (i.e., classes, methods, functions, fields), their organization (i.e., namespaces), and their dependencies. This model not only permits dependency analysis and management at the code level, but is also used for extracting architectural information from the system implementation, which is then used to derive the component model (see [12]).

Component and Configuration Model. The component and configuration model describes a system as a configuration of components (providing and using services) and connectors at a higher level of abstraction than the code model. Components interact with each other via provided and required ports.

Review Model. The review model contains the results of conducted architecture evaluations.

Constraint Model. The constraint model supports the definition of reference architecture conformance rules that can be checked automatically.

4.2   Provided Views, Supported Stakeholders, and Concerns

Several views are provided based on information contained in the AIR. Views are visualized in different clients, which differ from each other in the presented views and the used implementation technologies. Figure 2 shows how the different views are related to the different architectural models described in the previous subsection.

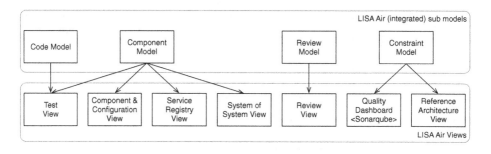

Fig. 2. Model - view relationships

Component and Configuration View. The component view visualizes the architecture of SOA subsystems at the component/service abstraction level. This view provides a higher abstraction level than code views. Main use cases are architecture/implementation conformance analyses performed during the development process (developers) and as part of quality gate reviews (reviewers, software architects), impact analysis during system evolution (solution architects, software architects), as well as impact analysis during system integration testing (testers).

System View. The system view provides an overview of the complete enterprise SOA consisting of different kinds of SOA subsystems (i.e., service modules, clients, backend services) and their dependencies. This view is also used for impact analysis during system evolution (solution architects, software architects), for architecture evaluations (reviewers, software architects), as well as for impact analysis across SOA subsystem boundaries during system integration testing (testers).

Reference Architecture View. The reference architecture view supports the definition and checking of company-wide reference architecture rules (see [13]). Reference architecture rules are defined and analyzed by the software architect as part of quality control activities.

Review View. The review view is used for performing architecture evaluations (reviewers) that are performed as part of quality gate reviews. It is also possible to define reusable questionnaires (software architect) that need to be answered during evaluations. During an evaluation the review view is typically used along with the component and system view.

Test View. The test view provides a dedicated view for the test team for system integration testing. This view provides specific information relevant for the testing process. This includes 'hot spots' in terms of performance and scalability, system components/services that have been modified since the last release, and components/services that are affected by a modification. The test view assists the test team in focusing their testing efforts.

Quality Dashboard View. The quality dashboard is a gathering place for all kinds of quality data. In addition to information on code quality the dashboard also contains information about architecture quality. In our case we extend an existing quality dashboard (Sonarqube[1]) and integrate information about violations of reference architecture rules. This view is used by the quality manager as well as by developers for assessing the quality of the enterprise SOA.

Service Registry View. The service registry view contains information about the provided services of a SOA subsystem as well as current service usage dependencies. The service registry plays an essential role for SOA governance activities along the entire system life cycle and is used by solution architects, developers, and testers. The service registry is not directly connected with the AIR, but uses its own repository data. However, information between the AIR and the service registry is automatically synchronized.

4.3   Tools for Automation

In addition to the provided architectural views used for stakeholder interaction (see above), a set of automated tools also operates on the AIR. In the following we provide an overview of the currently used tools:

---

[1] http://www.sonarqube.org.

Architecture Extraction. This tool extracts architecture models (i.e., code and component models) from the system implementation and stores them in the AIR.

Synchronization. This tool updates the service registry with information from the AIR to keep the service registry up-to-date and to eliminate the redundant maintenance of the service registry.

Reference Architecture Analysis. This tool automatically analyzes architecture models for compatibility with defined company-wide reference architectures.

All aforementioned tools can either be invoked manually or as part of a continuous build process to completely automate the process of updating architectural knowledge in the AIR.

4.4   Development History and Experiences

The establishment of an AIR is the result of years of research on software architecture management and analysis, and particularly a long-term research cooperation with our current industrial partner. We started with developing tools for software architecture visualization and analysis. Originally these tools were intended for individual stakeholders, particularly developers and architects within a small development team. For this reason, the tools were originally integrated within an IDE (Eclipse) and we focused on keeping architecture representation and implementation in sync, particularly in a continuous software development setting. The available tools supported mainly a code (module) view and a component view and were eventually merged to one integrated, still tool-based solution [9]. Aside from architecture/implementation conformance we supported dependency analysis as provided by architecture management tools like Lattix [14] and Structure 101 [15]. We further extended the toolset by supporting different component models and by integrating features for AKM [16], tracing [17], aspect-oriented programming, feature management and variability management [18] over the following years.

Continuous synchronization of architecture and implementation required continuous extraction of architecture from code, which was one of the main reasons for entering a long-term research collaboration with our current industrial partner. When working with our partner it became evident that architectural knowledge was required by different stakeholders and that there was also a need to synchronize this information with other information resources within the enterprise. For this reason we completely reengineered our approach and moved to a repository-based solution.[2]

Stakeholders now include software architects, solution architects, test managers, developers, reviewers, and quality managers. Our efforts initially focused on software architecture knowledge that can be extracted from the system implementation (see [12]). It is possible to keep this kind of architectural knowledge

---

[2] We should note that we were not able to move all features we had implemented in the original toolset to the reengineered version. For example, currently feature and design decision management are not part of the repository-based solution.

(i.e., module dependencies, components, configurations) up-to-date over time nearly automatically. Humans are only required for enriching the system implementation with a small set of metadata to facilitate the extraction of the components and configurations. This pays off, because the component and system view are central views that are used by many different stakeholders since they represent the system at the abstraction level where system design, analysis, and evolution are discussed.

The automatic analysis of reference architecture compatibility rules (see [13]) and the synchronization with the service registry are based on the component and configuration model. This means that the complete process of extracting the code, component, and system models from the system implementation, analyzing these models for compatibility with reference architectures, and updating information in the service registry can be performed automatically.

Architecture reviews and reference architecture rules are currently the only types of architectural knowledge stored in the repository that need to be defined manually. Dealing with architecture reviews is still in an early stage. The decision to add the results of architecture reviews to the AIR was made to raise the awareness of review results - especially with regard to detected problems. Storing review results along with other architecture models facilitates bidirectional tracing between review comments and affected model elements. For example, a solution architect also sees all review remarks when selecting a component in the component view. In the long term, we plan to analyze the evolution (detection and resolution) of issues in the enterprise SOA.

A major advantage of the central AIR is that it facilitates architecture knowledge sharing - not only between different stakeholders within a project team but also across project boundaries. For example, at our industrial partner different SOA subsystems are developed by different project teams that are also geographically distributed. Services developed by other teams are typically black boxes for the project team. A global system view on services and service dependencies is an important information for evolution, testing, and deployment. Testers can determine clients affected by a service change that need to be retested. In the future, we also plan to augment the repository with runtime information so that developers and testers can analyze how expensive services are in terms of runtime performance.

5   Related Work

Application lifecycle management (ALM) tools share the central characteristics of managing architectural information in a central repository, i.e., the central management of development artifacts, support for different stakeholders, integration and synchronization with other information sources, and integration with processes and tools. While ALM tools provide support for many development activities (i.e., project planning and controlling, issue management, test execution, source code versioning, code quality analysis, and collaboration), support for AKM processes has been neglected so far. Most tools provide no explicit support for AKM at all, although some provide support for UML modeling. Explicit support for multiple architectural views and stakeholder concerns is typically not provided. However, ALM tools are typically extensible, which permits the integration of architectural models, views, and tools with ALM platforms.

Wikis are a common way for managing architectural knowledge in companies [19]. Wikis store architectural information on a central server where it can be accessed by all stakeholders via the web browser. Semantic wikis are an extension of the wiki concept where information can be put in relation to each other based on defined ontologies [20,21]. A major disadvantage of wikis is that information in them is informally defined, and thus needs to be created and maintained manually. This hinders the use of automated tools to support the development process.

SAKM tools often store architecture knowledge in a central repository. Examples are ADDSS [22], CADDMS [23], the Knowledge Architect [24], and PAKME [25,26]. However, the focus of these tools is often decisions and their rationale, as well as generic knowledge like patterns. They usually lack the management of solution structures and also typically do not provide explicit APIs for accessing the information from other tools.

In [27], Eloranta and Koskimies present an approach for creating topical documents from a central architecture knowledge base, which resembles the idea of different views for different stakeholders on architectural information. In [28] they argue for the need of a central place for storing and accessing architectural information in the context of agile software development, so that architectural information can be recorded immediately when it emerges. In the same article, they also mention the need for automatically populating the AIR.

Ghezzi and Gall [29] present a platform supporting software analysis as a service. Software analyses are offered as RESTful services that can be accessed over the Internet. Analysis services can be accessed by stakeholders through a software analysis catalog, where stakeholders can pick a specific analysis depending on their interests. The approach also supports the composition of analysis services through a dedicated UI and thus only for human users. A simple ad-hoc composition language for integrating analysis in programmatic work flow is listed as future work. The central idea of Ghezzi and Gall is similar to what is outlined in this paper, albeit restricted to software architecture analysis. The approach has not been developed to be a central hub for architectural knowledge within an enterprise and thus does not propose a central AIR as the basis for architecture-related services. Integration into a development landscape and processes through dedicated APIs is listed as future work.

6   Conclusion

In this paper we argued for central architecture management based on an AIR. We have established an AIR in the context of an enterprise SOA in the banking domain, which facilitates multiple views for different stakeholders, extracting architectural information from the system implementation, automatic analysis, and automatic synchronization with other information sources like a quality dashboard and a service registry.

Currently we are working specifically with the test team to provide them with architectural information that would allow them to create targeted tests, specifically for system parts that have been changed recently. Future work includes integrating runtime information as part of the repository and we are also working on restructuring the service itself towards a micro service architecture to individually develop different architecture management and analysis features based on the repository by different teams and based on different technologies.

Acknowledgements. The research reported in this paper has been partly supported by the Austrian Ministry for Transport, Innovation and Technology, the Federal Ministry of Science, Research and Economy, and the Province of Upper Austria in the frame of the COMET center SCCH.

The authors would like to thank Hermann Lischka from Racon Software GmbH for supporting the project, and Gernot Binder, and Heinz Huber (also Racon Software GmbH) for their cooperation.

References

1. van der Ven, J.S., Jansen, A., Avgeriou, P., Hammer, D.K.: Using architectural decisions. In: Hofmeister, C., Crnkovic, I., Reussner, R., Becker, S. (eds.) Perspectives in Software Architecture Quality, pp. 1–10. Universitaet Karlsruhe, Fakultaet fuer Informatik, Germany (2006)
2. ISO, IEC, IEEE: 42010:2011 systems and software engineering, architecture description. International Standard (2011)
3. Tang, A., Liang, P., van Vliet, H.: Software architecture documentation: the road ahead. In: Working IEEE/IFIP Conference on Software Architecture, pp. 252–255 (2011)
4. Maranzano, J.F., Rozsypal, S.A., Zimmerman, G.H., Warnken, G.W., Wirth, P.E., Weiss, D.M.: Architecture reviews: practice and experience. IEEE Softw. **22**(2), 34–43 (2005)
5. Glass, R.L.: Frequently forgotten fundamental facts about software engineering. IEEE Softw. **18**(3), 111–112 (2001)
6. Perry, D.E., Wolf, A.L.: Foundations for the study of software architecture. ACM SIGSOFT Softw. Eng. Notes **17**(4), 40–52 (1992)
7. Bosch, J.: Software architecture: the next step. In: Oquendo, F., Warboys, B.C., Morrison, R. (eds.) EWSA 2004. LNCS, vol. 3047, pp. 194–199. Springer, Heidelberg (2004)
8. Farenhorst, R., de Boer, R.C.: Knowledge management in software architecture: state of the art. In: Ali Babar, M., Dingsøyr, T., Lago, P., van Vliet, H. (eds.) Software Architecture Knowledge Management, pp. 21–38. Springer, Heidelberg (2009)
9. Weinreich, R., Buchgeher, G.: Towards supporting the software architecture life cycle. J. Syst. Softw. **85**(3), 546–561 (2012)
10. Merkle, B.: Stop the software architecture erosion. In: Proceedings of the ACM International Conference Companion on Object Oriented Programming Systems Languages and Applications Companion, SPLASH 2010, pp. 295–297. ACM, New York (2010)

11. Kriechbaum, T., Buchgeher, G., Weinreich, R.: Service development and architecture management for an enterprise SOA. In: Avgeriou, P., Zdun, U. (eds.) ECSA 2014. LNCS, vol. 8627, pp. 186–201. Springer, Heidelberg (2014)

12. Weinreich, R., Miesbauer, C., Buchgeher, G., Kriechbaum, T.: Extracting and facilitating architecture in service-oriented software systems. In: 2012 Joint Working IEEE/IFIP Conference on Software Architecture & European Conference on Software Architecture. IEEE (2012)

13. Weinreich, R., Buchgeher, G.: Automatic reference architecture conformance checking for SOA-based software systems. In: 11th Working IEEE/IFIP Conference on Software Architecture. IEEE Computer Society Press (2014)

14. Sangal, N., Jordan, E., Sinha, V., Jackson, D.: Using dependency models to manage complex software architecture. SIGPLAN Not. **40**(10), 167–176 (2005)

15. Sangwan, R.S., Vercellone-Smith, P., Laplante, P.A.: Structural epochs in the complexity of software over time. IEEE Softw. **25**(4), 66–73 (2008)

16. Weinreich, R., Buchgeher, G.: Integrating requirements and design decisions in architecture representation. In: Babar, M.A., Gorton, I. (eds.) ECSA 2010. LNCS, vol. 6285, pp. 86–101. Springer, Heidelberg (2010)

17. Buchgeher, G., Weinreich, R.: Automatic tracing of decisions to architecture and implementation. In: 2011 9th Working IEEE/IFIP Conference on Software Architecture, pp. 46–55 (2011)

18. Groher, I., Weinreich, R.: Supporting variability management in architecture design and implementation. In: 2013 46th Hawaii International Conference on System Sciences (HICSS), pp. 4995–5004, January 2013

19. Clerc, V., de Vries, E., Lago, P.: Using wikis to support architectural knowledge management in global software development. In: Proceedings of the 2010 ICSE Workshop on Sharing and Reusing Architectural Knowledge, SHARK 2010, pp. 37–43. ACM, New York (2010)

20. de Boer, R.C., van Vliet, H.: Experiences with semantic wikis for architectural knowledge management. In: 2011 Ninth Working IEEE/IFIP Conference on Software Architecture, pp. 32–41. IEEE (2011)

21. de Graaf, K.A., Tang, A., Liang, P., van Vliet, H.: Ontology-based software architecture documentation. In: 2012 Joint Working IEEE/IFIP Conference on Software Architecture and European Conference on Software Architecture, WICSA-ECSA 2012, pp. 121–130. IEEE Computer Society, Washington, DC (2012)

22. Capilla, R., Nava, F., Prez, S., Dueas, J.C.: A web-based tool for managing architectural design decisions. ACM SIGSOFT Softw. Eng. Notes **31**(5), 20–27 (2006)

23. Chen, L., Babar, M.A., Liang, H.: Model-centered customizable architectural design decisions management. In: Proceedings of the 2010 21st Australian Software Engineering Conference, ASWEC 2010, pp. 23–32. IEEE Computer Society, Washington, DC (2010)

24. Jansen, A., Avgeriou, P., van der Ven, J.S.: Enriching software architecture documentation. J. Syst. Softw. **82**(8), 1232–1248 (2009)

25. Babar, M.A., Wang, X., Gorton, I.: Pakme: a tool for capturing and using architecture design knowledge. In: IEEE INMIC 2005 9th International Multitopic Conference on Empirical Software Engineering. National ICT Australia Ltd., IEEE (2005)

26. Babar, M.A., Gorton, I.: A tool for managing software architecture knowledge. In: Proceedings of the Second Workshop on SHAring and Reusing architectural Knowledge Architecture, Rationale, and Design Intent, SHARK-ADI 2007, p. 11. IEEE Computer Society, Washington, DC (2007)

27. Eloranta, V.P.P., Hylli, O., Vepsalainen, T., Koskimies, K.: Topdocs: using software architecture knowledge base for generating topical documents. In: 2012 Joint Working IEEE/IFIP Conference on Software Architecture and European Conference on Software Architecture, pp. 191–195. IEEE (2012)
28. Eloranta, V.P., Koskimies, K.: Lightweight architecture knowledge management for agile software development. In: Babar, M.A.A., Brown, A.W., Mistrik, I. (eds.) Agile Software Architecture: Aligning Agile Processes and Software Architectures. Morgen Kaufmann (2013)
29. Ghezzi, G., Gall, H.C.: Sofas: a lightweight architecture for software analysis as a service. In: 9th Working IEEE/IFIP Conference on Software Architecture, pp. 93–102 (2011)

Software Estimation and Development

Preventing Composition Problems in Modular Java Applications

Kamil Jezek[1](✉), Lukas Holy[1], and Jakub Danek[2]

[1] NTIS – New Technologies for the Information Society, University of West Bohemia,
Univerzitni 8, 306 14 Pilsen, Czech Republic
{kjezek,lholy}@kiv.zcu.cz

[2] Department of Computer Science and Engineering, Faculty of Applied Sciences,
University of West Bohemia, Univerzitni 8, 306 14 Pilsen, Czech Republic
danekja@kiv.zcu.cz

Abstract. Java JAR files have become a common means to bring
reusability into Java programming. While they allow developers to easily share and use third-party libraries, they bring new challenges as well.
This paper addresses the problem of Linkage Errors that occur when
a type incompatibility or a missing dependency between two libraries
is detected at runtime. This is a direct impact of composing applications from pre-existing binary libraries as the problem would be normally detected during compilation. A problem may occur relatively easily
as rules of source and binary compatibility in Java differ and may be
counter-intuitive. To deal with this problem, we offer a set of tools that
analyse existing binaries and discover problems normally leading to runtime errors. The tools work automatically, may complement existing testing, and find problems effectively from the start of development. Their
additional features such as detection of redundant or duplicated libraries
are usually not provided by standard testing tools.

Keywords: Java · Linkage Errors · Libraries · Modules · Testing

1   Introduction

In the modern software development, not all of the code is written anew. Instead,
modules in the form of components, units, or libraries are used. Although they
increase the level of reusability, they also reveal the need to update development process as well. The reason is that functionality implementation is not the
only challenge anymore as correct composition of applications becomes more
and more challenging. In consequence, there is a need for innovative testing
approaches, focused not only on functional testing but also on application composition verification.

Correct composition is to date ensured by integration testing, oriented to
program invocation and validation of actual outputs against the expected ones.
This is typically implemented in the form of test cases where either humans
exercise the program, or automatic tests, which were prepared by humans in
advance.

© Springer International Publishing Switzerland 2016
D. Winkler et al. (Eds.): SWQD 2016, LNBIP 238, pp. 125–143, 2016.
DOI: 10.1007/978-3-319-27033-3_9

One of the less explored areas is analytical validation of software, which enables automation of the process and reduces human effort. Testing supported by analytic methods may complement current manually oriented human testing and perhaps decrease its amount.

This paper targets Java environment where modularisation is reached by JAR files, which represent third party reusable libraries. We propose early detection of incorrect composition of JAR files that normally results in runtime exceptions in the form of so called Java Linkage Errors[1]. Java produces them when its runtime, Java Virtual Machine, cannot instantiate a class, invoke a method, access a field, etc. because the respective element does not exist or is of a wrong type (e.g. a method is invoked with an incorrect signature).

The mentioned errors are a direct result of modularisation. If software is developed as a monolith, correctness and existence of all required types is assured by the compiler. In contrast, when compiled classes are re-used in another project, their mutual inconsistencies are discovered at runtime by the linker. We are motivated by problems of current Java, sometimes referred to as "JAR hell", where applications easily consist of thousands of libraries (JAR files) that may be potentially incompatible.

The Linkage Errors are dangerous because they may present themselves only under certain conditions, i.e. when a program flow reaches the problematic code. Existing integration testing may find them, but it highly depends on test coverage. When it proves insufficient, the errors leak to the production environment. However, they can be to some degree detected automatically by analysis of the whole software, which eliminates the possibility of undiscovered program flows.

This work proposes a set of tools that are able to detect the aforementioned Linkage Errors. The tools have a common core that reverse-engineers Java binaries into in-memory models and performs model checking to find possible inconsistent API usages. Tools may be attached to different phases of project life-cycle, most noticeably to the phases preceding the deployment and include several project roles such as tester, developer or designer. Our current experience shows that the tools may improve practice in software testing and detect possible failures early during development and testing.

The remainder of this paper is organised as follows: Sect. 2 shows related work, followed by wider introduction to the problem addressed in this paper in Sect. 3. Section 4 details our tools providing several innovative approaches to testing. It is followed by Sect. 5 that link our tools with typical project life-cycle. Before concluding, applicability of the approach is demonstrated on example in Sect. 6 while Sect. 7 discusses experience with the tools we have gained so far.

2   Related Work

There are several types of contracts collaborating software components have to comply with in order to collaborate successfully. Belguidoum et al. suggested the

---

[1] http://docs.oracle.com/javase/7/docs/api/java/lang/LinkageError.html (Jun 2015).

notions of horizontal and vertical compatibility [1]. This work focuses mainly on horizontal compatibility, i.e. the dependency of provided and required API of collaborating components.

Fluri [2] proposed a taxonomy of code changes to differentiate among types of changes and assess types of their impact on other source code entities. Consequently, it allows for deciding between functionality modifying or preserving changes. His work is useful for assessing backward compatibility of components but less relevant for API conformance of current application. Similar is work [3] by Kawrykow on detecting essential and non-essential changes of a Java source code. These works are important, because a full backward compatibility is difficult to assess if even possible. For that reason, it is meaningful to differentiate between dangerous and harmless changes. Ponomarenko [4] studied the backward compatibility of libraries by analysing signatures and type definitions obtained from C/C++ header files.

The notion of binary compatibility goes back to Forman et al. [5], who investigated this phenomenon in the context of IBM's SOM object model. In the context of Java, binary compatibility is defined in the Java Language Specification [6, Chap. 13]. Drossopoulou et al. [7] have proposed a formal model of binary compatibility. A comprehensive catalogue of binary compatibility problems in Java has been provided by des Rivières [8]. We extend his work by pointing at difference of source and binary compatibility. De Francesco et al. [9] proposed improved static analysis for Java interface types to avoid certain types of runtime errors, Kastner et al. [10] have used static analysis of modular applications in product lines to reduce the number of tests needed. These works analyse the system under development, but do not target problems of third-party libraries. Moreover, Rivières and Ponomarenko target only backwards compatibility.

Several authors have investigated the relationship between dynamic system updates and compatibility rules. For instance, Gregersen et al. [11] describes integration points for safe dynamic upgrades. They also proposed a framework for dynamic updates that guarantees both type and thread safety [12]. A similar approach is taken by JavAdaptor [13] enabling on-the-fly Java bytecode hotswaps. While their work may overcome shortcomings of the current Java Linker, we prefer to find similar bugs during the testing and keep the original byte-code.

There are many tools to check Java programs. For us, the most related are the tools that verify binary compatibility from reverse-engineered binaries. They include: Japitools[2], Clirr[3], or Java ACC[4]. These tools check backward compatibility of two given binaries (commonly JAR files). Another set of tools contains DepFinder[5] or Joops[6]. This set checks compositions of developed application. These tools are light-weighted and open-source, but usually simple or outdated. For instance, industry popular Clirr does not support Java generics as Clirr was

---

[2] http://sab39.netreach.com/Software/Japitools/42/.
[3] http://clirr.sourceforge.net/.
[4] http://ispras.linuxbase.org/index.php/Java_API_Compliance_Checker.
[5] http://depfind.sourceforge.net/.
[6] https://code.google.com/p/joops/.

developed before the generics were added to Java and newer versions were not released.

There have been attempts to deal with application composition in development tools. The modern approach is automatic dependency resolution, implemented for instance in Maven[7] or Gradle[8]. While they are widely adopted by industry, they have shortcomings as well, which we will demonstrate on Maven in this paper.

3   Problem Discussion and Examples

Incorrect application composition is usually a result of library evolution, where various versions of one library exist. In this environment, clients may use a wrong version that is not compatible with other libraries in their application, resulting in runtime linkage errors.

The selection of right libraries is not easy especially in situations when a library needs another library to work with. It creates an environment where a client must compose its application so that requirements of all libraries are fulfilled even if the libraries were developed by someone else.

Let us show Fig. 1. It depicts an example inspired by a popular Java open-source library for easy I/O operations, Apache Commons-IO[9]. This library used to provide the method **next** from **LineIterator** returning **Object**. Its new version, however, contains a method returning **String** as a result of adding generics to Java in version 1.5. Depending on other circumstances, this may or may not be a compatible change.

It is compatible when the client code is compiled directly against the library. Surprisingly, this is incompatible when a client is already compiled and the (binary) library is only switched in the target environment. This points to the less known feature of Java that the compiler performs type reasoning and generates correct method invocation when the types are not exactly the same as in the example but their conversion is possible. When the type reasoning is not possible, it produces a compilation error (for instance a String type cannot be converted to Number, while String can be converted to Object). On the other hand, the type reasoning is not performed by the Java Linker and exact type matching is required instead. As a consequence, the change from String to Object is not valid, i.e. binary compatible, and such a call results in a linkage error. In our previous work, we had discovered that these facts are unknown to developers [14] and thus may cause more problems when organisations use more pre-compiled libraries.

The situation may be difficult to handle when the number of libraries increases to tens or thousands, which is common in the current software. It is possible that two libraries within the application require two different versions of another library. This is shown in Fig. 2. Both Library-A and Library-B

---

[7] https://maven.apache.org/.

[8] https://gradle.org/.

[9] https://commons.apache.org/proper/commons-io/.

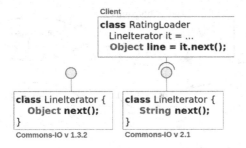

Fig. 1. Example: Commons-IO

work with Commons-IO, but they require different versions. These libraries were compiled against respective versions of Commons-IO. The problem arises when the application is complex and both libraries are used by the client. Then, the discrepancy between libraries may be missed and both accidentally included on the Java Classpath. Existing tools for automatic dependency resolution, such as Maven, produces these problems easily. Java will, in this situation, use sole class from one of the libraries. Even if the client notices the problem, the solution is not straightforward.

The natural way seems to use only the newest library, but it requires that they are backward compatible. We have, however, discovered that this is not a common practise [15]. The term backward compatibility may be also misunderstood. The presented libraries may be seen as backward compatible as a client compiling against the old one keeps compilable against the new one. The problem will arise when libraries are switched without recompilation due to mentioned inability of the Java Linker to convert types. From this point of view, the libraries are not backward compatible. To our best knowledge, the distinction between source and binary compatibility is not properly considered when libraries evolve. Although the solution of the issue is not trivial, at least tools to discover such problems should exist. We provide them in the next sections.

4   Our Tools for Linkage Errors Detections

This work summarises a set of tools that we have developed to assess composition of modular Java applications. The tools contain a common core that we call Java Compatibility Checker (JaCC) and a set of client tools on this core. Its main feature is reverse engineering of existing binaries into memory models and their checking. Figure 3 reveals the main idea. When the models are created and checked, detected problems are reported to the user. The following sections will overview fundamental ideas behind each step of this workflow and shows tools built on top of it.

There are several use-cases where the tools can be used. Generally speaking, they are useful in software development, testing or verification. Users may

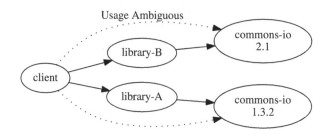

Fig. 2. Example: libraries composition

Fig. 3. Workflow

involve them in phases from design, through development and testing, to deployment. Some of the typical usages can be:

- Quality assurance – the tools may be used in any phases of software testing and quality assurance to detect inconsistencies in API usage. It includes verification of in-house developed modules as well as third-party ones.
- Integration projects – they usually involve a lot of third party code, whose internals are hidden. This makes testing cumbersome when API is not well documented and cross module dependencies are not known. In this situation, API may be reconstructed by the reverse-engineering and problematic parts discovered.
- Software certification – apart from incorrect API, software should not contain additional problems such as code smells or usage of discouraged, obsolete or prohibited API. In some domains, software may need to be certified as free of such problems. In this case, a certification authority may us the tools to reverse analyse the binaries and discover code flaws.

4.1   The Core Module

As mentioned, core part consists of a byte-code analyser and verifier. The input point of the analyser is a stream of byte-code from classes unpacked from JAR files. The byte-code is parsed by the ASM library[10] and API elements are reconstructed in the form resembling structure of Java classes from the original source-code. This process reconstructs provided and required elements in one walk-through of the byte-code.

Provided elements of the API are reconstructed by reading accessible classes with their accessible methods, constructors and fields included in the respective JAR file. Private parts are omitted because they cannot be accessed from the outside of a JAR file.

---

[10] http://asm.ow2.org/.

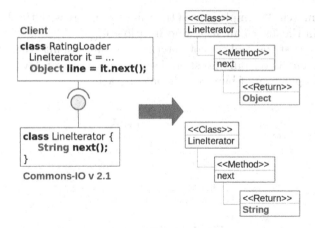

Fig. 4. Reverse engineering

On the other hand, the required elements are reconstructed by analysis of class and method bodies, including private ones. They are obtained from: (1) types used in generics, (2) super classes, (3) types of class fields, (4) types used in method signature (arguments, return types, type variable and declared exceptions), (5) types of implemented interfaces, (6) types of manipulated fields, (7) local variables including arrays, (8) types used in try-catch blocks.

The result of the analysis is illustrated by the Fig. 4. It shows the source-code only for the sake of clarity as we work with the byte-code. The bottom part of the illustration shows representation of real **LineIteration** class with its method returning the **String** type. The top part shows the actual invocation of this class and method. Since the method is invoked with the **Object** type, it is stored as Object in the memory data models. At the end, the analyser returns pairs of provided and required classes for each JAR file.

When the models are created, pairs representing provided and required classes are matched by name and their inner structure checked. Simplified illustration of the performed model checking is depicted in the Fig. 5. In general the tool detects situations when the types are mutated (incompatible types), generalised, specialised, or a type is missing, in sense of work by Brada [16]. We have described more details about this process in [17]. The verification is complex as the same rules enforced by the Java Linker, described in the Java Virtual Machine Specification [18], had to be implemented.

In addition, the analysis is able to assess if a type change is source compatible due to having information about generalised or specialised types. For instance, specialisation of method parameters is an allowed conversion. In such situations, discrepancy between binary and source compatibility can be detected and the user will be informed that the Linkage Error may be avoided by recompiling respective libraries (if the source code is available). This verification is not trivial. For instance, mentioned specialisation of method parameters is a valid conversion only when the method is not overridden as parameter of overridden methods must exactly match. We implemented the rules to comply with the Java compiler as described in the Java Language Specification [6].

Let us note that the tool cannot determine incompatibility that is not stored in the permanent byte-code. Most noticeably the usage of Java Reflection or on-the-fly manipulation of byte-code is out of reach.

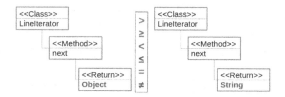

Fig. 5. Model checking

The tool does not construct only isolated required-provided pairs, but puts them into a graph of dependencies as introduced in [19]. This is a useful feature for the tools built on top of the core module giving them space for additional analysis. We had already presented detection of duplicated classes coming from various JAR files [20], which may cause problems when an unexpected version of a class is loaded by the Java Linker. Another application is a visualisation of program dependencies helping users comprehend complex systems. This will be shown later in this paper.

4.2 Modular Architecture

As it has been already revealed, the tool is designed as a set of modules. The Fig. 6 shows its architecture. The bottom part is the byte-code analyser while the middle part is the model checker. This paper describes mainly features related to verification of application composition, but the middle part is also able to assess backward compatibility of evolving libraries with respect to source and binary compatibility and usage scenario. In brief, we can decide if a library is backward compatible for extension (implementation of its interfaces and extension of its classes) or invocation only (invocation of methods, references to public fields) only.

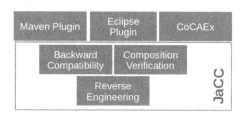

Fig. 6. Architecture

Two bottom layers are then used by a set of client tools shown on the top. We have developed integration with Maven, Eclipse IDE[11], our own visualisation tool CoCAEx and other ones may follow up. The next section provides an overview of our client tools and describes their involvement in typical project development life-cycle.

4.3 Maven Plugin

Maven is a popular build tool that uses declarative dependencies definition. This tool makes management of third-party libraries easier as users only have to define required libraries by the triplet: *groupId, artifactId* and *version* and Maven downloads libraries from the Internet. Additionally, Maven also fetches recursive dependencies of the directly defined libraries. A user needs to consider only the libraries he or she specifically works with and the rest of dependencies are managed automatically.

Since a lot of libraries are resolved and downloaded without direct involvement of user, the resulting Java Classpath may contain incompatible versions, duplicated and redundant libraries. In case this remains unnoticed by the developer, an incompatible library may be invoked at runtime and cause runtime Linkage Errors. We have already discovered that this problem exists on a set of open source projects and may lead to runtime failures [20].

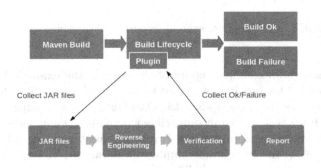

Fig. 7. Maven plugin

To deal with this problem, we have developed a Maven plugin. Its architecture is shown in Fig. 7. The top part refers to the standard Maven build process, where the build is started and several steps of project life-cycle are invoked. The build may be successful or fail when one of the phases fails. Standard phases include compilation, testing, packaging deployment and a few more. They are managed by built-in plugins and users may develop their own ones. Ours is depicted in the bottom part of the figure.

---

[11] https://eclipse.org/.

Plugin's main task is to collect all JAR files that are linked to the project under development. We hook to Maven dependency resolving process to fetch JARs. The next step is the verification by JaCC. The report is written to the Maven console and the plugin fails the build when a problem is detected. The collected libraries include recursive ones (i.e. transitive dependencies) and users may configure scope of collected libraries (e.g. compile, runtime, or test ones).

The plugin's basic feature is to find missing or incompatible elements (classes, methods, fields, ...). Since clashes of library versions are relatively frequent for Maven, the plugin can in addition detect situations where the project may be fixed simply by excluding one of the libraries.

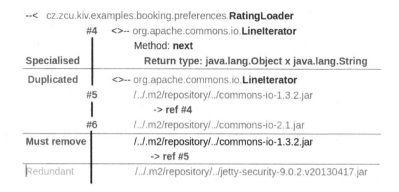

Fig. 8. Maven plugin, example report (Colour figure online)

Figure 8 shows an example report of the plugin (the example is simplified and colours added for brevity) produced to the console. First line shows a class RatingLoader that requires a class LineIterator. This example is based on the example from Sect. 3 with incompatible Commons-IO and shows mentioned specialisation of method return types. Errors are numbered (see #4) and linked from details below. In this example, duplicated libraries have been detected (see #5 and #6) and the incompatible library is referring to the particular problem by "ref #4". Since the other library is compatible, the incompatible one must be removed from the system as shown by the line starting with "must remove" and referring to the problematic library by "ref #5". Usually the outputs are long and this numbering and references help users investigate the report.

4.4 Eclipse Plugin

Another integration embeds JaCC into Eclipse, which allows developers transparently use verifications provided by JaCC directly from their IDE.

The plugin works similarly as the one for Maven shown in the previous section, but integrates the report directly into Eclipse views. The Fig. 9 illustrates the plugin on the example taken also from the previous section.

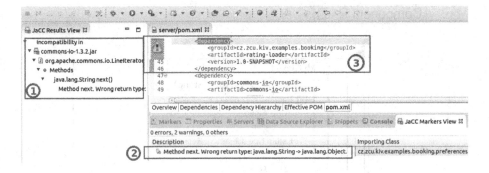

Fig. 9. Eclipse plugin, example report (Colour figure online)

The plugin provides two new Eclipse views, one shown on the left (1) and the other one at bottom (3) of the figure. When an incompatible library is detected, a warning marker (yellow triangle) is put to the editor (2) of pom.xml (Maven configuration) file and the two views show details. The bottom view shows an inline overview while the left side view shows a detail tree about the line selected from the bottom view.

4.5 CoCAEx

Besides showing results in the text form, we also provide a graphical output in a web application. We use the tool called CoCAEx, which is described in our previous papers [21,22]. It is primarily designed for exploring large software diagrams.

CoCAEx is able to show node-link graph of particular JAR files including incompatibilities among them. It is designed to handle large diagrams, which enables a user to quickly explore incompatibilities, even if the diagram contains many components and incompatibilities. It shows details on demand to explore particular incompatibilities and bundles dependencies between two JARs into one edge. All details are hidden and a red cross icon is shown on an incompatible edge. To further simplify the graph, we show only connections which contain a problem. Details of problems can be expanded in the tree structure from the classes down to the methods, fields, constructors, etc. Figure 10 shows problems that we can detect and draft of their visual look in CoCAEx. Following image visualises the problem drawn in previous sections as it looks directly in CoCAEx, see in Fig. 11.

Experimenting with our tools, we have discovered that the number of incompatibilities in real applications may be high. On the other hand, they often come from a few places. For instance, a library is refactored so that classes are moved into a different package. Then the text output may contain overwhelming number of incompatibilities, but deeper examination reveals only several problematic points, i.e. two or three packages. In such cases helps CoCAEx with its interactive

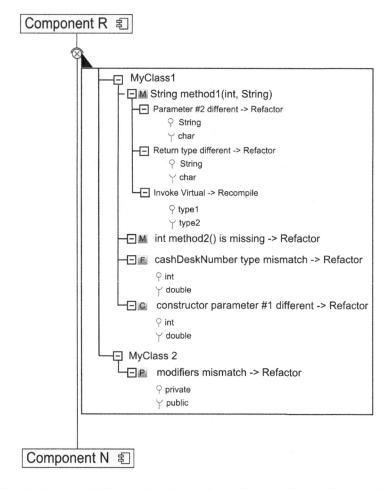

Fig. 10. Incompatibility exploration and visualization (Colour figure online)

approach and dependency bundling to comprehend incompatibility problems as they are bundled to edges and interactively discovered in tree structures.

5 Employment in Project Life-Cycle

Software quality can be monitored and improved at all phases of software development life-cycle, starting from requirements definition and management, through design, development, builds, testing itself to deployment, run and maintenance. In each phase a particular role uses various practices and tools for assuring quality. The roles are dependent on a methodology used in particular project, but in most of the projects a traditional set of software disciplines preserves its presence and order as in the traditional waterfall model [23], only the number and length of iterations (sprints or similar) varies.

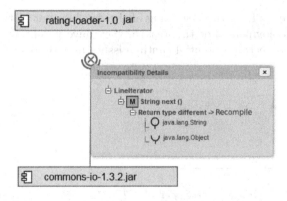

Fig. 11. Incompatibility visualization in CoCAEx (Colour figure online)

In this paper, we offer a solution for finding particular type of errors. These problems can be found in various phases of software development. Our solution is mostly useful in design, development, build, testing and release phases of the product development life-cycle. For each of these phases a particular role needs an appropriate tool implementing described problem detection.

We summarize a mapping among particular roles, project phases and appropriate variant of our tool in Fig. 12. We use particular roles representing appropriate phases of software development life-cycle for simplification. We can see that in earlier stages of the life-cycle, where the design and architecture is made by an architect or designer, the CoCAEx tool can be useful for choosing supporting libraries, analysing their dependencies and selecting correct versions. When it comes to the development phase, the Eclipse plugin can be used by the developer. The Maven plugin is mainly expected to be used by a tester, quality assurance engineer, release engineer and other roles involved in the later phases of software life-cycle. We expect that the plugin is integrated into modern integration tools such as open-source Jenkins[12] or proprietary uDeploy or uRelease[13]. Let us also point that the tools are loosely coupled to particular phase and therefore may be used in other phases as well. For instance, CoCAEx may be used by testers when they see it appropriate, and the Maven plugin may fit developers well.

In the worst case scenario, the problem is not detected before the actual deployment and is encountered by users at runtime. Generally, we need to find potential problems as soon as possible, because it is well known that the later we find a problem, the more effort needs to be wasted on producing potentially useless software product and more effort is spent on its fixing. The cost of fixing such defect is higher due to all necessary actions, communication overhead and usually a need to go through all of the phases of the software development life-cycle with a product modified only by the particular problem fix. The fact is illustrated by the blue curve in the top part of Fig. 12. As the image also shows,

---

[12] https://jenkins-ci.org/.

[13] https://developer.ibm.com/urbancode/products/urbancode-release/.

our tools cover areas from the beginning of the development to the later phases of release and deployment. For this reason, they have potential to cut price of development by detecting potential runtime issues in early phases of the cycle.

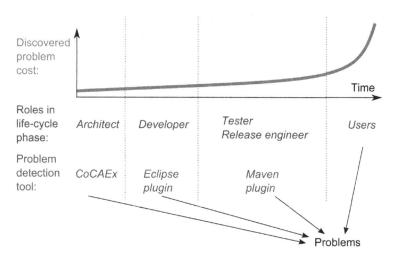

Fig. 12. Tools mapping to lifecycle phases with indicated cost of problems fixing (Colour figure online)

6   Practical Demonstration

The risk of problem caused by libraries from Sect. 3 is relatively high. There are 394 projects using Commons-IO 1.3.2 and 483 projects using Commons-IO 2.1 in the Maven Central Repository[14]. If a client combines any libraries from these two groups in an application, he or she may be in risk of encountering the problem described above.

We will demonstrate possible problem on a web application[15]. While the application is relatively simple, it shows a real problem with real libraries. The application is a simple web portal for accommodation booking. The application displays list of available booking options and for each item shows user rating of the place.

The implementation consists of a Java server and a JavaScript front-end. The server contains business logic and handles data persistence. Additionally, it exposes its functionality via web service API. The JavaScript front-end is implemented as a single-page application and fetches data from the server's web service API using AJAX calls.

---

[14] http://mvnrepository.com/artifact/org.apache.commons/commons-io (Jun 2015), http://mvnrepository.com/artifact/commons-io/commons-io (Jun 2015).

[15] https://github.com/kjezek/simple-booking-study.

The server part is modularised and uses two independent modules – one for the main application logic and web service endpoints (the *server* module) and the other one for management of customer ratings (the *ratings* module). The problem is that each module imports different version of the Apache Commons-IO, connected as shown in the Fig. 2 (Library-B as *server* and Library-A as *ratings*).

This particular issue would be detected if the developer discovered mismatch of the libraries and compiled the modules against the correct one. However, the problem is likely to remain undetected when *ratings* is a third-party library or developed by an independent team and the number of libraries is high. Therefore we believe that the current set-up does not lower the study's generality.

Due to the version conflict, the application does not function properly and users can see the value 0 % as rating of all accommodation offers. Figure 13 is provided to show the application when the bug occurs (see arrow 1). Whether the problem is discovered depends highly on preciseness of standard testing. The following paragraphs compare approaches developers can use to debug such issue using traditional methods and our tools.

Traditional Debug. Runtime nature of the problem makes it rather cumbersome to debug and locate the issue. Since the front-end application is separated from the server, the debug steps would look similar to:

(a) Debug JavaScript and network connection of the web application using Firebug, Chrome Developer Tools or similar. It is found that the ratings endpoint returns an error (see Fig. 13, arrow 2).
(b) Check server logs for errors (or use Java Debugger to trace the respective endpoint call) – java.lang.NoSuchMethodError is found (see Fig. 13, arrow 3).
(c) Find the conflicting libraries and replace them with a single working version.

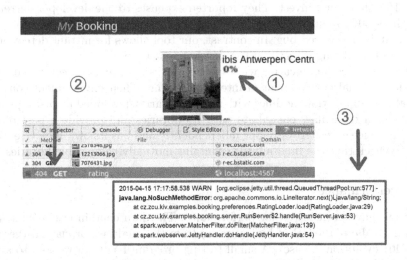

Fig. 13. Case study – accommodation booking application

The last step is not trivial in systems where number of modules and libraries grows to tens or hundreds. Finding a library version compatible with the application is trial and error process – even when the developer finds a version which works in the particular case, he or she can introduce new runtime errors into the application.

JaCC Based Tools. JaCC allows developers to reliably locate and remove the presented type of errors during the build process. When it is used in the form of either Maven or IDE plugin, JaCC would report the issue before deploying the application, thus preventing the error from being presented to the users. The Figs. 8 and 9 plus discussion above should already give an insight of this process. At this phase, we are able to show the users that the problem exists and provide a solution within the set of application libraries.

7 Evaluation

7.1 Implementation

We have already implemented a pilot project for our industry partner in automotive. They use the tool to verify third-party applications using their platform. Each time a new version of the platform is released, they may verify that no third-party application is negatively influenced. They also use the tool for internal development of the platform, which is composed of several independently developed modules.

According to their report, financial saving is high when they discover a bug early in the development. In particular, when the bug used to leak to production, they would invest approximately 2 h to locate the bug, 3 h to release a fix, 3 h to deliver a test application and 10 h to functional testing in the field. It sums up to 18 h they must invest. They reported expenses to one developer currently as high as 60€, requiring more than 1000€ to be approximately paid for each such a lately discovered bug. In contrast, our tool allows for instant detection of bugs and their fixing directly in the development time.

We are now communicating with another subject in the bank sector to use the tools for internal development of internet banking. Their environment contains several web application modules with shared libraries developed by distinguished teams. Each team may contribute with its libraries and provide a part of the banking. Since each part develops independently and has its own life-cycle, they need to check that the final mixture contains mutually compatible libraries.

7.2 Performance

The tools have been tested for performance. The data contain 661 open-source programs (about 120 GB of binary code) from the qualitas corpus [24] (version 20120401 evolution release). A small testing program has been written to automatically get JAR files from programs and run the JaCC core modules on them.

Other interactive tools built on top of the core were tested manually on subset of programs.

The machine for experiment was Intel Core i5 CPU, 1.90 GHz, 8 GB RAM laptop with Ubuntu 14.04. The time to verify all data oscillated from 40 to 50 min. However, the time to verify one project varied widely depending on its size. Bigger applications such as JBoss-5.1.0 (566 MB) needed about 2 min, netbeans-6.9.1 (1.2 GB) needed slightly above 30 s, compiere-330 (529 MB) needed almost 50 s. Other smaller applications required from several seconds up to 1/2 min each. These numbers gave us confidence that the time needed by the tools is acceptable.

Since the tools need to load all data representation into memory, we have detected high memory consumption. Almost all laptop memory was taken when evaluating JBoss. For other middle size applications (about 300 MB) the tools needed about 4 GB of Java heap. In this aspect, we see room for improvement. As current algorithm is based on memory models checking, memory reduction is not straightforward. We have profiled the tool and detected that millions of objects are loaded into the memory. Since each object is relatively small and their number cannot be easily decreased, there is no room for memory saving. For this reason, the only possible reduction is to load and verify data by parts. It may however slow down computation as some data must be repeatedly loaded. This must be considered and decided in the future. For that reason, our future work is to propose, implement and test an algorithm that allows processing the data by parts to save memory.

8   Conclusions

This paper has provided an overview of the set of tools that assess correct composition of current Java applications. The main feature is detection of incompatibilities that would normally lead to runtime Linkage Errors.

Since the tool builds on reverse-engineering of existing binaries, it fits into the current development where a lot of third-party libraries are used and the developers use them as black-boxes. The tool automatically builds representation of library dependencies and verifies its correctness. For this reason, its usage is cheap in sense of saving manual effort.

The proposed tools may complement current integration and functional testing. Since they analyse all libraries used in the project, they keep no room for untested parts. A feature that is not to our best knowledge provided by someone else is detection of duplicated classes, which have the same names but different content. This is especially dangerous as an existing integration test may pass on one class, while the other class is invoked at runtime.

We have already collected some feedback from our partners and extended client tools with a few features. We were for instance asked for a Sonar[16] plugin from several sources. In our future work, we would like to analyse yet more

---

[16] http://www.sonarqube.org/.

industry needs in sense of integration to development process and propose new or extend existing tools.

Our work is currently able to show a problem in an application and provide a solution within the set of application libraries. In the future, we would like to connect our tools to existing repositories to find a solution from the wider set of data. It will, however, require additional research as big repositories cannot be fully loaded into the memory as mentioned above.

Acknowledgement. This publication was supported by the project LO1506 of the Czech Ministry of Education, Youth and Sports, and by the UWB grant SGS-2013-029 Advanced Computer and Information Systems.

References

1. Belguidoum, M., Dagnat, F.: Formalization of component substitutability. Electron. Notes Theoret. Comput. Sci. **215**, 75–92 (2008)
2. Fluri, B., Gall, H.C.: Classifying change types for qualifying change couplings. In: Proceedings of the 14th IEEE International Conference on Program Comprehension, ICPC 2006, pp. 35–45. IEEE Computer Society, Washington, DC (2006)
3. Kawrykow, D., Robillard, M.P.: Non-essential changes in version histories. In: Proceedings of the 33rd International Conference on Software Engineering, ICSE 2011, pp. 351–360. ACM, New York (2011)
4. Ponomarenko, A., Rubanov, V.: Backward compatibility of software interfaces: steps towards automatic verification. Program. Comput. Softw. **38**(5), 257–267 (2012)
5. Forman, I.R., Conner, M.H., Danforth, S.H., Raper, L.K.: Release-to-release binary compatibility in SOM. In: Proceedings OOPSLA 1995, pp. 426–438. ACM, New York (1995)
6. Gosling, J., Joy, B., Steele, G., Bracha, G., Buckley, A.: The Java Language Specification, Java SE 7th edn. Addison-Wesley, USA (2012). (3rd edn. 2005)
7. Drossopoulou, S., Wragg, D., Eisenbach, S.: What is Java binary compatibility? In: ACM SIGPLAN Notices, vol. 33, pp. 341–361. ACM (1998)
8. des Rivières, J.: Evolving Java-based APIs (2007). http://wiki.eclipse.org/Evolving_Java-based_APIs. Accessed 1 December 2014
9. De Francesco, N., Lettieri, G., Martini, L.: Using abstract interpretation to add type checking for interfaces in java bytecode verification. Theor. Comput. Sci. **411**(22–24), 2174–2201 (2010)
10. Kästner, C., Apel, S., Thüm, T., Saake, G.: Type checking annotation-based product lines. ACM Trans. Softw. Eng. Methodol. **21**(3), 14:1–14:39 (2012)
11. Gregersen, A.R.: Implications of modular systems on dynamic updating. In: Proceedings of the 14th International ACM Sigsoft Symposium on Component Based Software Engineering, CBSE 2011, pp. 169–178. ACM, New York (2011)
12. Gregersen, A.R., Jørgensen, B.N.: Dynamic update of java applications-balancing change flexibility vs programming transparency. J. Softw. Maint. Evol. **21**(2), 81–112 (2009)
13. Pukall, M., Grebhahn, A., Schröter, R., Kästner, C., Cazzola, W., Götz, S.: JavAdaptor: unrestricted dynamic software updates for Java. In: Proceedings of the 33rd International Conference on Software Engineering, ICSE 2011, pp. 989–991. ACM, New York (2011)

14. Dietrich, J., Jezek, K., Brada, P.: What Java Developers Know About Compatibility. And Why This Matters, ArXiv e-prints, August 2014
15. Jezek, K., Dietrich, J., Brada, P.: How java apis break - an empirical study. J. IST **65**, 129–146 (2015)
16. Brada, P.: Enhanced type-based component compatibility using deployment context information. Electron. Notes Theor. Comput. Sci. **279**(2), 17–31 (2011)
17. Jezek, K., Holy, L., Slezacek, A., Brada, P.: Software components compatibility verification based on static byte-code analysis. In: SEAA, 39th EUROMICRO, pp. 145–152. IEEE Computer Society (2013)
18. Lindholm, T., Yellin, F., Bracha, G., Buckley, A.: The Java Virtual Machine Specification. Java SE 7 Edition. Oracle America Inc., California (2012)
19. Jezek, K., Ambroz, J.: Detecting incompatibilities concealed in duplicated software libraries. In: SEAA 2015 (2015) inprint
20. Jezek, K., Dietrich, J.: On the use of static analysis to safeguard recursive dependency resolution. In: SEAA 2014, pp. 166–173. IEEE Computer Society (2014)
21. Holy, L., Snajberk, J., Brada, P.: Visual clutter reduction for UML component diagrams: a tool presentation. In: 2012 IEEE Symposium on Visual Languages and Human-Centric Computing (VL/HCC), pp. 253–254, September 2012
22. Holy, L., Snajberk, J., Brada, P., Jezek, K.: A visualization tool for reverse engineering of complex component applications. In: 2013 29th IEEE International Conference on Software Maintenance (ICSM), pp. 500–503, September 2013
23. Petersen, K., Wohlin, C., Baca, D.: The waterfall model in large-scale development. In: Bomarius, F., Oivo, M., Jaring, P., Abrahamsson, P. (eds.) PROFES 2009. LNBIP, vol. 32, pp. 386–400. Springer, Heidelberg (2009)
24. Tempero, E., Anslow, C., Dietrich, J., Han, T., Li, J., Lumpe, M., Melton, H., Noble, J.: The qualitas corpus: a curated collection of Java code for empirical studies. In: Proceedings APSEC 2010, pp. 336–345. IEEE (2010)

Deriving Extract Method Refactoring Suggestions for Long Methods

Roman Haas[1]([✉]) and Benjamin Hummel[2]

[1] Technical University of Munich, Munich, Germany
haas@in.tum.de
[2] CQSE GmbH, Garching near Munich, Germany
hummel@cqse.eu

Abstract. The extract method is a common way to shorten long methods in software development. Before developers can use tools that support the extract method, they need to invest time in identifying a suitable refactoring candidate. This paper addresses the problem of finding the most appropriate refactoring candidate for long methods written in Java. The approach determines valid refactoring candidates and ranks them using a scoring function that aims to improve readability and reduce code complexity. We use length and nesting reduction as complexity indicators. The number of parameters needed by the candidate influences the score. To suggest candidates that are consistent with the structure of the code, information such as comments and blank lines are also considered by the scoring function. We evaluate our approach to three open source systems using a user study with ten experienced developers. Our results show that they would actually apply 86 % of suggestions for an extract method refactoring.

Keywords: Refactoring suggestion · Long method · Extract method

1 Introduction

Long methods are a bad smell in software systems [1]. This means that they do not influence the behavior of the code directly, but make it harder to understand and therefore harder to maintain [11].

A common way to treat long methods is to apply extract method refactorings, where parts of the long method are extracted and put into a new method. In practice, this is one of the most often applied refactorings [14].

The refactoring process using a modern IDE like ECLIPSE, NETBEANS or INTELLIJ IDEA [3] consists of the following steps. First, developers need to identify a sequence of statements that should be extracted. Second, they need to select the statements. Third, they call a tool that will, if possible, execute

This work was partially funded by the German Federal Ministry of Education and Research (BMBF), grant "Q-Effekt, 01IS15003A". The responsibility for this article lies with the authors.

© Springer International Publishing Switzerland 2016
D. Winkler et al. (Eds.): SWQD 2016, LNBIP 238, pp. 144–155, 2016.
DOI: 10.1007/978-3-319-27033-3_10

the refactoring. Fourth, before the refactoring can be applied by the tool, the developer needs to specify a name for the new method. Finally, the refactoring is executed.

Tool support makes refactorings much easier, but a developer still needs to select some source code within the method that they would like to extract. This can be complicated, time-intensive, tedious, and error-prone [8].

Problem Statement. Developers need to invest a considerable amount of time in finding the sequence of statements best suited for an extract method refactoring.

The majority of development tools only provide support to execute refactorings that are specified by the developer. In the context of long methods this means that the most time consuming step in shortening a method still needs to be done by developers themselves, which is a reason refactoring tools are not used as much as they could be [6].

Sometimes, even experienced developers select invalid refactoring candidates because they have overlooked a violation of preconditions that must hold for the extract method. In such cases, current tools give poor information on why no refactoring is possible [7].

Extract method refactoring suggestions are helpful for developers because they save time and make fewer mistakes during the candidate selection.

Contribution. We present an approach to automatically finding extract method refactoring suggestions for long methods in Java projects. The approach generates a list of possible refactorings and ranks those using a scoring function. The ranking focuses on readability improvement and reduction of code complexity. The scoring function uses structural information given by the developer to reward bonus points. Additionally, it takes into account the number of parameters needed by the new method. We evaluate our approach on three open source systems using a user study with ten experienced developers.

2   Related Work

There are several ways to suggest extract method refactorings which can be divided into four categories. Some use program slicing techniques to find recommendations for extract method, while others try to find suitable suggestions from graph representations of the code. Some rely on scoring functions to find the most appropriate refactoring candidate. Refactoring prioritization tries to identify methods that are actually worth for refactoring.

Program Slicing Based Approaches. Maruyama [5] presents a semi-automated mechanism for refactoring suggestions. It decomposes the control flow graph using block-based program slicing. The approach is adapted and implemented by the tool JDEODORANT by Tsantalis and Chatzigeorgiou [13] that improves behavior preservation. According to Sharma [9], approaches that use program slicing techniques cannot be fully automated as the user has to select a slicing criterion for every method that should be refactored. In addition, the suggestions depend heavily on the user's input. As we wanted to have an approach that is able to find extract method refactorings automatically, we did not rely on a program slicer.

Graph Based Approaches. Sharma [9] provides a mechanism to propose extract method candidates based on a data and structure dependency graph. Their suggestions are obtained by deleting the longest dependency edge in the graph. The resulting two disconnected subgraphs represent the statements that stay within the original method or which will be extracted to a new method, respectively. They are able to suggest non-continuous statements for extract method. We use a control and data flow graph to represent methods. We do not obtain suggestions from operations on the graph but determine valid candidates that are ranked using a scoring function.

Kanemitsu et al. [2] use a program dependency graph and recommend that users extract all nodes that are connected via edges not longer than a user-defined maximal length. Their approach was led by the design principle that one method should process only one thing. We consider the same design principle by rewarding bonus points to candidates that have comments or blank lines at the beginning or the end because they are often indicators that something new has been processed by the preceding or following lines. Our scoring function also considers code complexity reduction and the number of needed parameters.

Score Based Approaches. Silva et al. [10] suggest an approach to automatically generate candidates for method extraction. Their scoring function ranks candidates with respect to static dependencies between variables, types, and packages. Our approach was inspired by Silva et al. as the general procedure of candidate generation is similar and we were also not able to suggest candidates with non-continuous statements. The scoring function of our approach does not consider dependencies but mainly the reduction of length and nesting with the aim of reducing code complexity and increasing maintainability.

Yang et al. [15] consider long methods and suggest an approach to recommending refactorings that lead to as small a coupling as possible, automatically. Their scoring function is the benefit-cost ratio of the length of the extracted method and the numbers of needed input and output parameters. In contrast to Yang et al. we do not move variable declarations as far back as possible. Our scoring function also considers the number of parameters needed and we reward bonus points for comments or blank lines (which are a splitting criterion for Yang et al. to obtain their candidates). Additionally, reduction of code complexity has a high impact on the ranking.

Prioritization. Steidl and Eder [11] focus on the question of which findings should actually be resolved first. The question how to solve a given finding, i.e. a specific suggestion, is not addressed by their approach. They suggest a prioritization of quality defects that were found during a software quality analysis to maximize the developer's expected return of invest.

Steidl and Eder's approach is not appropriate for automated refactorings as it only gives a hint of where a developer should start refactoring.

3   Approach

We present an approach to finding extract method refactorings for long methods automatically. There are two fundamental steps: first, the generation of all possible refactoring candidates (i.e. all sequences of statements that can be extracted). Second, ranking all of them by applying a scoring function that considers reduction of complexity and structural information of the candidates. The candidates with the highest ranking will be suggested for an extract method refactoring.

3.1   Candidate Generation

The procedure of generating all possible candidates is quite similar to the one that Silva et al. [10] presented. They introduced a minimal number of statements, K, that ensures suggestions do actually have some benefit. In their evaluation they found that $K = 3$ is optimal and therefore, our approach also sets a minimal number of statements $K = 3$, which must hold for the number of statements of a candidate and the corresponding remainder of the long method.

To obtain valid refactoring candidates we use the software quality analysis tool ConQAT[1] and Streitel's implementation of control and data flow graphs [12] to check that several preconditions hold. Most importantly, an extract method candidate may not need more than one return parameter (see [7] for details).

3.2   Scoring Function

All valid extract method refactoring candidates obtained in the first step are ranked using a scoring function that focuses on code complexity reduction. We rely on length and nesting metrics as complexity indicators. The scoring function also takes structural information, like blank lines or lines with comments, and the number of parameters into account. For each scoring element (see Fig. 1) a score value is determined and all score values summed up lead to the total score of a candidate. The candidate with the highest score will be our first suggestion.

Length. We aim at suggestions that reduce complexity and consider length as an complexity indicator. Therefore, the length of a refactoring candidate influences its ranking. To avoid the effect of recommending nearly the whole method, the length score S_{length} depends on the length of the candidate L_c and the remainder L_r. For each line a constant number of points c_l is awarded, up to the upper bound $MAX_{scoreLength}$. This upper bound ensures that very long candidates are not ranked higher just because they are extraordinarily long. We set

$$S_{length} = \min\left(c_l \cdot \min\left(L_c, L_r\right), MAX_{scoreLength}\right),$$

where in our prototype $c_l = 0.1$ and $MAX_{scoreLength}$ is set to 3, i.e. the maximal length score is achieved by a length reduction of 30 or more lines of code.

---

[1] www.conqat.org.

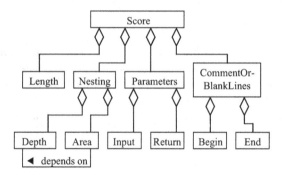

Fig. 1. Score elements

Nesting Depth. We use nesting depth as another indicator of code complexity. Let D_m be the nesting depth of the original method, D_r the nesting depth of the remainder, and D_c the nesting depth of the refactoring candidate. The score of a candidate obtained for reducing the nesting depth is set to

$$S_{nestDepth} = \min\left(D_m - D_r, D_m - D_c\right),$$

which means that (theoretically) there is no upper bound for $S_{nestDepth}$. But note that given a method with a nesting depth D_m the maximal reduction of nesting depth is $\lfloor \frac{D_m}{2} \rfloor$ and so, $S_{nestDepth} \leq \lfloor \frac{D_m}{2} \rfloor$ always holds.

Unfortunately, nesting depth often cannot be reduced by extract method if one considers both the remaining method and the candidate. It is often the case that there are several deeply nested statements that cannot be extracted at once without extracting the whole nesting structure: either one suggests a candidate that includes only some of these statements (which will not reduce nesting depth of the original method) or one chooses a candidate that extracts the whole deeply nested structure, leading to a new candidate which is as deeply nested as the original method was.

Nesting Area. To have a measure for nesting reduction that is more often applicable we consider the reduction of nesting area.

In formal terms, the nesting area of a sequence of statements S_1 to S_n, each having a nesting depth of d_{S_i}, is defined as $\sum_{i=1}^{n} d_{S_i}$. Intuitively spoken, it is the area under the single statements of pretty printed code.

As shown in the previous section, nesting depth is not always a suitable criterion to determine reduction of complexity as it might be complicated or even impossible to extract all deeply nested statements at once to reduce the maximal nesting depth of the remainder and the candidate. But even if nesting depth is not reduced, reduction of code complexity is possible by extracting nested statements. That is why we consider the reduction of nesting area. If nesting structure is simplified by extracting parts of it, we claim that complexity is reduced. The deeper the extracted statements are nested, the bigger the benefit is in terms of complexity reduction. We aim for maximizing nesting area reduction ($A_{reduction}$). That is the maximal nesting area of the remainder (A_r) and the candidate (A_c) is minimized: $A_{reduction} = \min(A_m - A_c, A_m - A_r)$, where A_m is the nesting area of the original method. For a given method with nesting area A_m an optimal candidate can achieve a reduction of at most $\lfloor \frac{A_m}{2} \rfloor$, similar to the maximal nesting depth reduction.

We assume that reducing the nesting area becomes more important as the nesting depth of the original method D_m becomes higher. Therefore, the upper bound of the score achievable for reducing the nesting area depends on D_m:

$$S_{nestArea} = 2 \cdot D_m \cdot \frac{A_{reduction}}{A_m}$$

The factor 2 is taken into account to obtain a score for the nesting area that is at most as high as D_m. As reduction of nesting area is nearly always possible, the achievable score for nesting area reduction is higher than the achievable score for reducing nesting depth. Remark that if nesting depth (i.e. complexity) is high, the other criteria have less relevance for the scoring of the candidates as nesting scores are not bounded while the other scoring criteria are bounded.

Parameters. To obtain the most independent candidates with respect to coupling, we consider the number of parameters that are needed for each candidate. The more parameters are needed to extract the candidate from the original method, the higher is the data dependency between the original and the extracted method. For the parameter score S_{param} there is an upper bound $MAX_{scoreParam}$. The number of needed parameters (n_{in} and n_{out}, where $n_{out} \leq 1$) will reduce the score, and each parameter decreases the score by one:

$$S_{param} = MAX_{scoreParam} - n_{in} - n_{out}$$

Fowler [1] claims that having a long parameter list is a bad smell. He proposes to not have more than three input parameters. As we have in Java at most one return parameter, we set $MAX_{scoreParam} = 4$.

Comments and Blank Lines. To capture additional developer's knowledge, we award bonus points for comments and blank lines. Developers often have comments that give information about the next source code line(s), especially if these perform something different than the previous ones. In other cases, blank lines separate such different tasks. But this is a violation of the design principle that one method should process only one thing (see [4]) and therefore, the following lines might be a good candidate for an extract method refactoring. The bonus we award for candidates that have such lines with comments or blank lines at the beginning or the end is as follows: for each such line (and the fact that these lines exist) c_p many points are obtained. In our experiments we saw that blank lines and comments at the beginning of a candidate are more relevant to identify the most suitable extract method refactoring candidate than the ones at the end because they give more information about itself. In the score formula the higher relevance is represented by the factor $f_b > 1$. In addition, several lines of comments before a sequence of statements indicate a more complex explanation which is more likely to describe a new functionality and therefore, more lines with comments or blank lines get more points.

The score depends on four variables: the existence of blank lines or comments (1) at the beginning (e_b) and (2) at the end (e_e) of a refactoring candidate. (3) the number of blank lines or comments at the beginning (n_b) and (4) at the end of a candidate (n_e), where $e_x \in \{0,1\}, n_x \in \{0,1,2,3\}$ and $x \in \{b,e\}$. If there are more than three blank lines or comments the same amount of points is awarded as if there were only three blank lines or comments. We set

$$S_{commentsBlankLines} = f_b \cdot c_p \cdot (e_b + n_b) + c_p \cdot (e_e + n_e)$$

For our prototype $f_b = 2$ holds, i.e. preceding comments result in twice as many points as comments at the end. c_p was set to 0.25 such that a candidate may get up to 2 points for having at least three comment or blank lines at the beginning, and up to 1 point for having at least three of such lines at the end.

Scoring Elements Intervals. The previous subsections gave detailed information about the single criteria for the score of a refactoring candidate. Table 1 shows the intervals of the single scoring elements. D_m stands for the nesting depth of the original method.

Table 1. Scoring elements and their intervals

Score element	Max score
S_{length}	3
$S_{nestDepth}$	$\lfloor \frac{D_m}{2} \rfloor$
$S_{nestArea}$	D_m
S_{param}	4
$S_{commentsBlankLines}$	3

Total Score. The candidates will be compared using the total score S. For each candidate the total score is the sum of all single scoring elements:

$$S = S_{length} + S_{nestDepth} + S_{nestArea} + S_{param} + S_{commentsBlankLines}.$$

3.3   Pruning

At the end of our suggestion algorithm, the list of candidates is optimized. As all possible candidates are generated, there are several ones that differ only in one or two statements at the beginning or the end. Those often have similar scores because they refer to nearly the same piece of code and the differing statements do not change the score that much. To obtain a wide range of suggestions, candidates are removed from the list if there is another candidate containing all of their statements, having the same input and return parameters, and having a better score.

4   Evaluation

This section evaluates our approach using a prototype that is implemented as a ConQAT analysis for Java projects. We constructed an online survey that presented ten long methods from open source Java projects with extract method refactoring suggestions.

RQ1: Are Suggestions Better than a Random (valid) Refactoring Candidate? This question considers a first criterion to have a useful scoring function. If random candidates are not significantly less preferred by developers than the suggestions of this approach, the approach with its scoring function would be useless.

RQ2: Do Developers Follow the Suggestions of this Approach? This question considers a much stronger criterion of usefulness than RQ1. The evaluation of this paper tries to find out, whether (and how often) this approach is able to suggest candidates that are taken as refactoring candidate from developers. The more often developers follow the suggestions of the prototype, the closer is the scoring function on their intuition.

RQ3: Should Several Suggestions be Made? This question addresses a result of Silva et al. [10]. They claimed that an implementation of their approach should preferably suggest only the best candidate. As the approach of this paper is structurally similar to their approach, we try to find out whether their result also holds for our prototype.

4.1   Design

For the survey, all participants received an HTML file that contained ten methods (survey object) that were considered during the survey. All these methods had between 48 and 73 lines. For each survey object there were three highlighted candidates. One of the candidates was always the first suggestion of the prototype, called *TOP1*. Another one was the second or third suggestion of the prototype (which one was determined randomly during the analysis but then was the same for each participant), called *TOP2/3*. The third candidate was a randomly selected valid candidate that was not one of the TOP3 candidates determined by the scoring function, called *Random*. All suggested candidates were highlighted in the same way such that the participants could not differentiate them.

Table 2 shows the study objects from which ten long methods were presented in the survey. We consider a method as long if it counts more than 40 lines. All study objects are Java open source projects. They all have long methods but

Table 2. Study objects

Name	Domain	Size (LoC)	# Methods	# Long methods	LoC of longest method
Agilefant	Backlog tool	36,116	2,841	31 (1.09 %)	143
JabRef	Reference manager	128,145	5,665	428 (7.56 %)	1,305
JChart2D	Charting library	50,728	1,849	72 (3.89 %)	641

some have – in relative terms – more long methods than others. All projects were selected for the evaluation because they are well-known Java open source systems and have a five star ranking (based on voluntary feedback from the users) on the open source distribution platform sourceforge[2].

Our online survey asked for each survey object the following questions:

1. Which candidate would you use more likely for an extract method refactoring? The participants could select exactly one suggestion.
2. Would you use the selected candidate for an extract method refactoring? In addition to "Yes" and "No", the participants could select "Yes, with slight modification (of 1–2 lines)".
3. Would you have applied an extract method refactoring on this method? Answering options were "Yes" and "No".

4.2   Results

Ten experienced developers participated in the survey that is used to answer RQ1–RQ3. All of them have between 6 and 24 (on average 12) years of development experience.

Are Suggestions Better than a Random (valid) Refactoring Candidate? (RQ1).
74 % of the selected candidates in the first survey question were the one that was ranked top most by the scoring function. The other 26 % were the TOP2/3 candidate. The random candidate was never selected by any of the participants and therefore one can assume that for the ten survey objects the suggestions generated by the prototype are much better than the selection of a valid random candidate.

Do Developers Follow the Suggestions of this Approach? (RQ2). 74 % of the selected candidates would have been applied without modifications (according to the answers to the second survey question). For other 12 % a quite similar refactoring would be applied (by only shifting the selected candidate about one or two lines). For the remaining 14 % the developers claimed that they would not have applied the selected refactoring. For 93 % of the survey objects developers would apply an extract method refactoring on the presented method. Five of the

---

[2] http://sourceforge.net/.

seven "No" answers concerned the last survey object, which was a method that contained a test case.

Should Several Suggestions be Made? (RQ3). 74 % of the selected candidates were the best one with respect to the order determined by the scoring function of this approach. The other 26 % were the TOP2/3 candidate. These values of course do only represent the average distribution. For none of the survey objects a similar distribution appeared: for half of them nearly all participants (nine out of ten) selected the TOP1 candidate and for the other half of survey objects the distribution was quite mixed, i.e. five participants selected TOP1 and the other five selected TOP2/3 or six selected TOP1 and four TOP2/3 (or vice versa).

4.3   Discussion

This section discusses the results of the analysis of the survey objects and the survey itself. Many participants gave additional and individual feedback and reasons for their answers which will also be included in the discussions.

Do Developers Follow the Suggestions of this Approach? (RQ2). For the survey objects, 86 % of the selected candidates (maybe slightly shifted) would have been chosen for an extract method refactoring. All of them were suggestions of the prototype. Nevertheless, several participants claimed (in their individual feedback) that for some survey objects there were redundancies in the code such that they would first try to eliminate those and then refactor the resulting method. But as they would not start with an extract method refactoring, they answered in such cases the third survey question with "No". As already mentioned, half of participants would not have refactored the last survey object because that method covered a test case. Thus, the participants claimed that it was better to keep the whole test case in the same method to have a better overview about the functionality that is tested by the given test case.

This means that not all methods that are considered lengthy by our prototype are candidates for developers for extract method refactorings. In general, the suggestions are helpful: if developers want to refactor a given method using an extract method refactoring, they often follow the suggestions of the prototype.

Should Several Suggestions be Made? (RQ3). Many participants mentioned in their feedback that there were some methods where they were quite sure which of the suggested candidates is the best one and that they would apply only this one extract method refactoring on the given method. For other survey objects, they would have applied both suggestions, the TOP1 and the TOP2/3 candidate for extract method refactorings. So, to answer the question in the survey, where they could select only one option, they had to select their answer more or less randomly between those two candidates. That might be an explanation for the mixed answers.

In practice, of course, several refactorings can be applied and often it is the best solution to refactor a long method by extracting several pieces of code into new methods. Hence, in some cases it really makes sense to suggest several candidates, at least the TOP3 candidates with respect to the ordering of the scoring function.

4.4   Threats to Validity

There are some threats to validity of the evaluation, which are summarized in the following.

Resolution of long methods is subjective (see [15]). First, there is no consensus in science when a method is actually long. This means that some may treat a given method as long where others do not. Second, there is no commonly accepted algorithm that splits a long method into suitable smaller ones. That actually is a threat to validity of this evaluation as several participants were asked which candidate according to their opinion is best for an extract method refactoring. Other participants might have selected other candidates. To handle this risk, ten experienced developers took part in the survey.

A threat of external validity is, as usual in software engineering topics, that the results of the evaluation need not necessarily hold for other software systems.

Ten survey objects do not represent the whole spectrum of methods that should be refactored using an extract method refactoring. They all covered (for long methods) only a few lines of code and did not represent all possible ways of designing a method. To have a fair overview the survey objects were selected from several open source systems and there from different packages. They have quite different code structures such that a wide range of ways how methods can be structured are covered by the evaluation.

5   Conclusion and Future Work

We proposed an approach to derive extract method refactoring suggestions for long methods in Java to improve maintainability and reduce code complexity. The approach determines extractable candidates from the control and data flow graph of a method. A refactoring candidate needs to fulfill syntactical preconditions, have an equivalent data flow and a minimal length. Each candidate is ranked using a scoring function that considers the following criteria: length, nesting depth and area reduction, and the number of input and return parameters. Bonus points are awarded for candidates having comments or blank lines at their beginning or end.

We used a prototype to evaluate our work in a survey. It showed that the suggestions of the approach for the survey objects are always better than a random candidate (RQ1). For 86 % of the suggestions for the study objects, the developers follow the suggestions made by the prototype (RQ2). This means that, at least for the study objects, the suggestions of the prototype are usually useful. We also addressed the question whether several candidates should be recommended (RQ3). For one half of the survey objects, nearly all participants selected the same candidate and claimed that they would use it for an extract method refactoring – in these cases one suggestion might be sufficient. But for the other half of survey objects, the participants would apply several extract method refactorings that were suggested by the prototype. So, for 50 % of the survey objects, at least the three best candidates should be suggested.

We think that our approach also works for methods with a high nesting depth (which is another code smell). In the future, we want to conduct another case study to test the validity of this hypothesis. We plan to do further research on the choice and weights of our scoring parameter.

Instead of suggesting several candidates from which developers can choose at least one, one could suggest a set of disjoint extract method refactorings. The scoring function then could consider the benefit of applying all these refactorings instead of ranking single suggestions.

References

1. Fowler, M.: Refactoring: Improving the Design of Existing Code. Addison-Wesley, Reading (1999)
2. Kanemitsu, T., Higo, Y., Kusumoto, S.: A visualization method of program dependency graph for identifying extract method opportunity. In: Proceedings of the 4th Workshop on Refactoring Tools, pp. 8–14. ACM (2011)
3. Marticorena, R., Lpez, C., Crespo, Y., Prez, F.J.: Refactoring generics in JAVA: a case study on extract method. In: 14th European Conference on Software Maintenance and Reengineering (CSMR), pp. 212–221. IEEE (2010)
4. Martin, R.C.: Clean Code: A Handbook of Agile Software Craftsmanship. Prentice Hall, Upper Saddle River (2009)
5. Maruyama, K.: Automated method-extraction refactoring by using block-based slicing. In: ACM SIGSOFT Software Engineering Notes, vol. 26, pp. 31–40. ACM (2001)
6. Murphy-Hill, E., Black, A.P.: Why don't people use refactoring tools?. In: Proceedings of the 1st Workshop on Refactoring Tools, pp. 60–61 (2007)
7. Murphy-Hill, E., Black, A.P.: Breaking the barriers to successful refactoring: observations and tools for extract method. In: Proceedings of the 30th International Conference on Software Engineering, pp. 421–430. IEEE (2008)
8. Opdyke, W.F.: Refactoring object-oriented frameworks. Ph.D. thesis. University of Illinois at Urbana-Champaign (1992)
9. Sharma, T.: Identifying extract-method refactoring candidates automatically. In: Proceedings of the 5th Workshop on Refactoring Tools, pp. 50–53. ACM (2012)
10. Silva, D., Terra, R., Valente, M.T.: Recommending automated extract method refactorings. In: Proceedings of the 22nd International Conference on Program Comprehension, pp. 146–156. ACM (2014)
11. Steidl, D., Eder, S.: Prioritizing maintainability defects based on refactoring recommendations. In: Proceedings of the 22nd International Conference on Program Comprehension, pp. 168–176. ACM (2014)
12. Streitel, F.: Incremental language independent static data flow analysis. Master's thesis, Technical University of Munich (2014)
13. Tsantalis, N. Chatzigeorgiou, A.: Identification of extract method refactoring opportunities. In: 13th European Conference on Software Maintenance and Reengineering, pp. 119–128. IEEE (2009)
14. Wilking, D., Kahn, U.F., Kowalewski, S.: An empirical evaluation of refactoring. e-Informatica 1(1), 27–42 (2007)
15. Yang, L., Liu, H., Niu, Z.: Identifying fragments to be extracted from long methods. In: Asia-Pacific Software Engineering Conference, pp. 43–49. IEEE (2009)

The Use of Precision of Software Development Effort Estimates to Communicate Uncertainty

Magne Jørgensen[(⊠)]

Simula Research Laboratory, Fornebu, Norway
magnej@simula.no

Abstract. The precision of estimates may be applied to communicate the uncertainty of required software development effort. The effort estimates 1000 and 975 work-hours, for example, communicate different levels of expected estimation accuracy. Through observational and experimental studies we found that software professionals (i) sometimes, but not in the majority of the examined projects, used estimate precision to convey effort uncertainty, (ii) tended to interpret overly precise, inaccurate effort estimates as indicating low developer competence and low trustworthiness of the estimates, while too narrow effort prediction intervals had the opposite effect. This difference remained even when the actual effort was known to be outside the narrow effort prediction interval. We identified several challenges related to the use of the precision of single value estimates to communicate effort uncertainty and recommend that software professionals use effort prediction intervals, and not the preciseness of single value estimates, to communicate effort uncertainty.

Keywords: Software cost estimation · Estimation uncertainty · Estimate precision · Human judgment

1 Introduction

There is a substantial uncertainty in required effort of software development projects, which is reflected in a high average estimation error. A review of seven surveys on software projects gave that the median effort overrun was 21 % [1]. Not only is the average error high, the proportion of projects with very high estimation error is substantial. A study of 3.650 software projects found that 12.8 % of the projects had a effort overrun of more than 105.9 % [2].

The sometimes very high effort uncertainty makes it essential to realistically assess and properly communicate the level of uncertainty of the produced effort estimates. The level of uncertainty may, amongst others, affect the pricing, cost-benefit analyses, prioritization, budgeting and planning of software projects [3–6], i.e., most of the different types of usages of effort estimates involves judgment of the uncertainty of the estimate. A client may, as an illustration, find a project worthwhile to invest in only if the effort uncertainty, and consequently the risk of high cost overrun, is low. Similarly, a software development company may choose not to bid for a project or to add high cost contingency when the effort uncertainty is high.

© Springer International Publishing Switzerland 2016
D. Winkler et al. (Eds.): SWQD 2016, LNBIP 238, pp. 156–168, 2016.
DOI: 10.1007/978-3-319-27033-3_11

More recently introduced software development approaches, such as incremental or continuous delivery or other elements of agile development, may give the perception that there is no more need for effort estimates, which would invalidate the need for communicating the uncertainty of estimates as well. The "no estimates"-movement (*zuill.us/WoodyZuill/beyond-estimates/*) seems to argue in this direction. This movement provides good arguments in favour of that there are several situations where we do not need effort estimates and where effort estimates can be harmful (see our own study on negative effect of too low effort estimates on software quality in [7]). Few, if any, of those within the movement do, however, claim that we *never* need to or should estimate, see for example *ronjeffries.com/xprog/articles/the-noestimates-movement/*. The "no estimates"-movement may also be accused of not being clear about of what is meant by an estimate. It seems, for example, that estimates of production capacity, e.g. answers to questions like "How much can be delivered in the next increment?" and "Is it likely that we will be able to deliver a certain amount of features within the client's budget?" are frequently not counted as estimates. Clearly, answers on these questions are based on estimates of effort and would benefit from assessing and communicating the estimation uncertainty. Even when applying a continuous delivery model there will frequently be a need for the client and/or provider to know the approximate need for effort before starting the development of new features. Also of interest is that the most successful agile projects, but not the less successful agile projects, seem to carry out as much up-front estimation and planning as the non-agile projects [8]. Finally, hardly any client, given that they have the choice not to build the software, is likely to start a software project without any knowledge about how much it will cost to meet their business needs. The value of such cost (and benefit) estimates would be limited if there was no communication of the uncertainty of them.

One possible means of communicating the estimation uncertainty in software projects is through the precision of the estimate, e.g., through the number of significant digits or trailing zeros of an effort estimate. For example, an estimate with low precision, such as 1000 work-hours (three trailing zeros), is likely to indicate a much higher effort uncertainty than an estimate with higher precision, such as 1075 work-hours (no trailing zeros). This paper examines the following topics: (i) To what degree the estimation precision is actually used to communicate estimation uncertainty, (ii) Challenges by using the estimation precision to communicate uncertainty, and (iii) How the estimation precision affects the assessments of the competence of the estimator, the trustworthiness of the estimate and, after the actual effort is known, the perceived accuracy of the estimate. If the actual effort is 1200 work-hours we may, for example, assess an estimate of 1000 work-hours to be more accurate, given the low precision which implied a large estimation interval, than the much more precise and clearly incorrect estimate of 1075 work-hours.

Research from many contexts [9–12], including software engineering contexts [13–15], reports a strong tendency towards over-confidence in the accuracy of one's estimates. As an illustration, in [16] the authors found that most software developers assessed it to be likely (at least 60 % likely) that the actual effort would be within +/− 10 % of the estimated effort. In reality, however, only 15 % of the project efforts fell within this narrow effort interval.

Research on answers given to so-called "almanac questions", such as the question *"How long is the Nile?"* suggests that more precise answers, e.g., that the Nile is 6180 km compared to that the less precise answer that it is about 7000 km, are interpreted as indicating increased confidence in the answer and more competence in the topic. The research also finds that more precise answers have larger influence on other people's decisions [17].

The only study on the use and effect of single value precision in a software development estimation context is, as far as we know, the study reported in [18]. That study failed to replicate previous result that more precise suggestions (estimation anchors) were more influential for subsequent predictions. An effort suggestion (estimation anchor) of 998 work-hours did not have more impact on the subsequent effort estimate than an effort suggestion of 1000 work-hours. A potential explanation for this difference in results is that an overly precise suggestion, such as 998 work-hours for a complex project, may be seen as indicating incompetence, rather than higher competence in a software development context. There may consequently be domain and context differences in the interpretation and judgmental effect of more precise predictions.

This paper aims at extending previous research by:

- Examining the use of the estimation precision to indicate software development effort estimation uncertainty (Sects. 2 and 3).
- Examining how the estimation precision is interpreted as indicator of estimator competence and estimate trustworthiness, and how estimation accuracy of overly precise effort estimates is evaluated (Sect. 4).

We discuss the findings and conclude in Sect. 5.

2   Measuring Single Value Effort Precision

The measurement of the precision of a single value effort estimate, in connection with the potential use of it to communicate estimate uncertainty, is not straightforward. It may be easy to agree on that precision and estimate uncertainty is, or at least should be, connected. An estimate of 1000 work-hours is for example expected to be less accurate, i.e., more uncertain, than an estimate of 830 work-hours. It is however not easy to formalize this connection in an effort estimation context. What is, for example, a reasonable interpretation of the uncertainty of an estimate of 830 work-hours? Should it be interpreted to communicate that the expected actual effort is in the interval [825, 835], in the interval [820, 840], or some other interval? How should a belief in that the actual effort is likely to be in the interval [810, 850] be communicated? An estimate of 800 work-hours indicates less precision than intended and an estimate of 830 work-hours may indicate too high precision. Also, the implied effort intervals have no obvious connected confidence level. We may argue that the estimator believes that it is likely that the actual effort will be inside the interval, but it is not clear whether that corresponds to, for example, 70 %, 80 % or 90 % confidence. In addition, the number of significant digits does not say anything about trailing value of 5, which may also be used to indicate uncertainty.

The use of the Fibonacci numbers in agile estimation of software development effort, see for example [19], may be argued to assume that the intended precision of user story-based estimates, typically in story points, is about +/-30 %, assuming non-overlapping uncertainty intervals. This is so, because the ratio of two succeeding Fibonacci numbers is always approximately 1.6. The estimated numbers themselves, however, do not necessarily communicate that level of uncertainty.

There may also be precision measurement challenges connected with the choice of units. Estimating values connected with work effort or calendar time means that the value 10 is not always the natural unit. Indicating that a task takes about one day of work may, for example, result in the seemingly very precise estimate of 8 work-hours.

From the above discussion, see also [20] for elaboration on several of the above challenges, we see that the precision of a single point estimate may not be an optimal method of communicating clearly about effort estimation uncertainty.

For the purpose of our studies, trying to address some of the above measurement challenges, we apply the following measures:

- *NumbTrailZero*: Number of trailing zeros. If there is at least one trailing zero, this indicates (but do not guarantee, since a trailing zero may be a significant digit) that some rounding has been taken place, or that the estimate has a high granularity.
- *RelPrec*: The relative precision (uncertainty) of an estimate measured as a function of trailing zeros and the estimate. We include the factor w to enable different precision interpretation and assume that all estimates are integer number. The need for the w-factor is motivated by the lack of commonly accepted precision interpretation in effort estimation. The interpretation of the meaning of, for example, 8000 work-hours could be 8000 +/- 500, 8000 +/- 1000 or something else.

$$RelPrec(w) = w \cdot 10^{NumbTrailZero} / Estimate \qquad (1)$$

Example: Assume that we observe the estimates 3000 work-hours and 3020 work-hours, where the first estimate has three and the second has one trailing zero. We then have that the relative precision, for the interpretation $w = 1.0$, is $10^3/3000 = 33$ % (corresponding to the interval 3000 +/- 1000 work-hours, assuming symmetric intervals) for the first estimate and 0.3 % (3020 +/-10 work-hours) for the second. Changing the w-value to be 2.0 gives a relative precision of 67 % (3000 +/- 2000 work-hours) and 0.7 % (3020 +/-20 work-hours). If the actual effort, for example, turns out to be 3655 work-hours we have that the implied effort interval, by assuming $w = 1$, of the estimate 3000 +/-1000 work-hours includes the actual effort (estimation error of 22 % and *RelPrec* of 33 %), while the assumed implied interval estimate 3020 +/-10 work-hours does not (estimation error of 21 % and *RelPrec* of 0.7 %). Notice that the number precision interpretation commonly applied in physics would be the one with $w = 0.5$ and is related to the reliability of measurement rather then expected accuracy of estimates. We are unaware of other studies applying the *RelPrec* measure for studies on numerical precision. This does not mean that the proposed measure in any way is innovative. If there had been a normative interpretation of how trailing zeros in software development effort estimates should be connected with effort estimation uncertainty, we would not need the w-factor and the measure would be trivial.

If the trailing zeros of estimates are successfully applied to indicate estimation uncertainty, with the interpretation indicated by the *w*-factor, we would expect that the average *RelPrec* is similar to the average absolute value of the relative error. In particular, if the average error tends to be much higher than *RelPrec*, then the effort estimate is likely to have been too precise to reflect the effort uncertainty. The lack of standardized precision interpretations in software effort estimates means, however, that we will examine different *w*-factors and also analyse which precision interpretation (which *w*-factor) that would give a good correspondence between precision and accuracy.

3   Effort Uncertainty Indicated by Estimate Precision

Table 1 summarizes our examination of the effort estimates of three different software project datasets. The datasets were selected based on availability and we do not make any claim that they will be representative for the software development industry as a whole. The purpose is mainly to indicate the existence and degree of systematic of use of precision of cost or effort estimates to indicate estimation uncertainty in software projects.

An important reason for high precision in software professionals' effort estimates is, based on our experience from several organizations, that the estimate of the total project effort is based on adding the effort of many activities, i.e., based on bottom-up based estimation processes. Consequently, adding one activity of about 2 work-hours with one with about 100 gives the sum of 102 work-hours, which is not likely reflect the total uncertainty given the presumably high uncertainty of the activity estimated to take 100 work-hours.

Trailing zeros may not always be a result of estimate rounding based on uncertainty considerations. They may also be a result of request for early, rough, perhaps analogy-based, estimates. We can, however, exclude this reason for trailing zeros in the examined data sets, since all estimates were based on bottom-up estimation processes where effort of many activities were added to find the total effort. Trailing zeros can, of course, also be significant digits.

Our analysis of the three data sets may be summarized to say that some software projects used estimate precision to communicate the effort uncertainty, but that most software projects communicated estimates with a precision much higher than warranted by the actual effort usage uncertainty. The variance in the *w*-factors that would lead to good correspondence between precision and uncertainty suggest that, even when trailing zeros are used, that there are various interpretations of what they mean in terms of estimate precision.

4   Competence, Trustworthiness and Accuracy

The precision of an effort estimate may not only be read as an indication of the estimation uncertainty. It may also be read as indication of competence of the source (the estimator) and/or the trustworthiness of the estimate. Our hypothesis was that

Table 1. Use of estimate precision in three data sets

Data set description	Precision indicated by trailing zeros
Data set 1: Seven very large (larger than 440 mill NOK, corresponding to larger than about 50 mill Euro) Norwegian software development projects with governmental client. Data set found at www.nrk.no/ fordypning/tvilsomt-om-kvalitetssikring-virker-1.11936733. Median estimation error of 21 %.	Only one project estimate (which were in mill. NOK) had trailing zeros. The other estimates were presented to the nearest million NOK. The only project estimate using trailing zeros to indicate relative precision (two trailing zeros, *RelPrec* = 29 %) had corresponding relative accuracy (31 %) for $w = 2$, but were seemingly over-precise, i.e., not reflecting the cost estimation inaccuracy of the software projects, for precision interpretations based on lower w-factors. For all other projects the estimates were too precise to reflect the observed estimation uncertainty.
Data set 2: Fifty-two medium large and small software development projects (average estimated effort of 850 work-hours) carried out by a Norwegian software provider for various clients. Median estimation error of 14 % (sixteen of the projects were not completed at the time of data collection). We asked the project leaders, at time of estimation, to assess the expected accuracy of the estimates, with the alternatives +/-10 %, +/-25 %, +/-50 % and more than +/-50 % error of estimates. Data set is available upon request to the author.	Twenty-one (40 %) of the project estimates had trailing zeros. The project estimates that used trailing zeros to indicate relative precision (median *RelPrec* of 18 % for $w = 1$) had corresponding relative median estimation accuracy (20 %). Seventeen of the twenty-one projects with trailing zeros of the estimates provided informed about the expected precision of the estimates. The relative precision of these estimates, with $w = 1$, corresponded well with the projects' expected precision. The +/-10 % estimation error category (n = 11) had a median relative precision of 6 %, the +/-25 % category (n = 5) had a median relative precision of 17 %, and the +/-50 % category (n = 1) had a relative precision of 50 %. This suggests that the project managers in these projects actually used the precision of the estimate to communicate the expected accuracy of the estimates.
Data set 3: Thirty Medium large projects (average estimated effort of 2300 work-hours) carried out in-house in a large Norwegian company. Median estimation error of 11 %. Data set is available upon request to the author.	Twelve (40 %) of the project estimates had trailing zeros. The project estimates using trailing zeros to indicate relative precision (median precision of 3 %, for $w = 1$) had not corresponding relative median estimation accuracy (9 %). Only two of the project estimates used two trailing zeros or more. These two projects were the only ones with correspondence between estimate precision and accuracy.

estimate precision, both in terms of less trailing zeros and narrower intervals, would be interpreted as increased competence of the source and increased trustworthiness of the estimate.

To test this we invited 236 project managers and software developers from six different software providers located in Poland, Romania and Ukraine. The mean length of experience was 6 years, varying from 0.5 to 35 years of experience. Twenty-four per cent were project managers. Eight per cent were female. The participants were asked to describe how they would interpret varying degrees and types of precision of effort estimates.

First, we gave the participants the following scenario and questions:

Four different developers (Developer A, B, C and D) are estimating the same project and spend about the same time to read and understand the requirement specification.

Developer A says: *"I think I will need 1020 work-hours to complete the project"*
Developer B says: *"I think I will need 1000 work-hours to complete the project"*
Developer C says: *"I think I will need between 900 and 1100 work-hours to complete the project"*
Developer D says: *"I think I will need between 500 and 1500 work-hours to complete the project"*

Assume that this is the only information you have about the four developers.

Question 1: Which of the developers would you think is the most and the least competent?
Question 2: Which of the estimate would you trust the most and the least?

The rationale behind the chosen estimates and estimation intervals were as follows:

- The precision of 1000 and 500–1500 work-hour estimates may be said to be similar in precision, assuming the precision interpretation corresponding to $w = 0.5$. Both represent a situation where the estimation uncertainty is high.
- The estimate of 1020 work-hours represents a situation with very precise estimate. Given that the other developers, especially B and D, communicate high estimation uncertainty, the participants have to choose between believing that the high precision is a consequence of high competence, i.e., low estimation uncertainty, or over-precision. If they believe that the estimate is likely to be over-precise, i.e., that the estimate precision does not reflect the actual effort usage uncertainty, they have to assess to what degree this is likely to be an indicator of low competence.
- The interval 900-1100 work-hours is a situation with very precise (narrow interval) estimate. Similarly to the situation with the 1020 work-hours estimate, the participants have to decide to what extent this indicates high competence and, if not, whether an overly narrow effort interval indicates low competence or not.

We suspected that the software professionals' responses on Question 1 and 2 would be strongly correlated, in spite of Question 1 requesting judgment of the developer and Question 2 requesting judgment of the estimate. If you, for example, do not think a developer is competent, you will hardly trust his/her estimate. The inclusion of both questions was mainly to see if they respondents tended to think that a developer with precise estimates would be the most competent, and at the same time not trusting his/her estimates. This may happen if, for example, the respondents thought that over-confident software developers are the most competent, but their estimates are usually less trustworthy.

There are several threats to the *external validity* of the results of this experiment. The above situation with four estimates on the same projects is not a typical situation for software professionals. Similarly, software professionals are not typically asked to evaluate competence and trustworthiness of the estimates based on characteristics of the estimates alone. Usually, they will know more about the context and the software professionals providing the estimates. These threats means that we should be careful about using the results to make claims about of what will happen in more realistic situations, e.g., situations where only one estimate is received and where the receiver knows much more about the context and the estimator. It is however our belief that we, in spite of these limitations, may get a first indication of how the precision of the estimate affects how software professionals think about those who provide the estimates and the estimate itself in situations with little context information. To what extent more context information in more realistic situations will over-ride the observed effects we will not be able to make claims about.

There are also threats to the *internal validity* of the results of this experiment. The software professionals were only allowed to select one developer as the most/least competent or having the most/least trustworthy estimate. This means that if, for example, one developer were judgment to be just slightly better by most respondents, this developer will turn up as the significantly most competent in our study. This is a limitation of just asking for the ranking and not allowing selecting more than one alternative. The direction of the results (the ranking) should, however, not be affected by this design choice.

When the participants had completed the first two questions, they were randomly divided into two groups and given a scenario where they were informed about the actual effort. For one group the actual effort was described to be 800 work-hours and for the other 1200 work-hours. We wanted to know how the estimate precision affected the participants' assessment of the accuracy of the estimate. For this purpose we asked them the following question:

Question 3: Assume that all four developers completed this project and that all of them used close to 800 (Group 1)/1200 (Group 2) work-hours to complete the project. Which of the developers do you think had the most and the least accurate estimate?

We had no prior expectation about which of the four estimates the participants would chose as the most and the least accurate. The actual effort values of 800 and 1200 work-hours are both outside the narrow interval of 900–1100 work-hours, i.e., Developer C may be said to be wrong about his/her estimate. The precise estimate of 1020 work-hours may also be said to be wrong, since it deviates quite much from both

800 and 1200 work-hours. The estimate of 1000 work-hours may be interpreted as less wrong if, for example, it is interpreted ($w = 2$) as 1000 +/- 200. The interval 500–1500 work-hours is clearly correct, but may be viewed as not informative enough to qualify for an accurate estimate.

The responses from the two first questions are displayed in Table 2 and for the last question in Table 3.

Table 2. Competence and trustworthiness

Estimate	Most competent	Least competent	Most trustworthy	Least trustworthy
Developer A (1020)	6 %	31 %	7 %	49 %
Developer B (1000)	11 %	13 %	7 %	14 %
Developer C (900–1100)	74 %	1 %	70 %	1 %
Developer D (500–1500)	9 %	55 %	16 %	36 %

Table 2 shows that the narrow interval of Developer C was assessed to indicate the highest competence of the source and the highest trustworthiness of the estimate by most participants. The least competent and trustworthy were assessed to be the wide interval by Developer D and, interestingly, the very precise estimate of Developer A. The results, consequently, suggest that precision in the format of narrow effort intervals makes an estimator look more competent and the estimate more trustworthy, while high precision of single value estimates has the opposite effect. We discuss limitations and possible explanations of this observation in Sect. 5.

We found no large differences in responses dependent on role (project manager or developer), gender, length of experience, or company.

Table 3. Accuracy (answers of the project managers in brackets)

Estimate	Most accurate when Act = 800	Least accurate when Act = 800	Most accurate when Act = 1200	Least accurate when Act = 1200
Developer A (1020)	1 % (0 %)	41 % (45 %)	9 % (12 %)	24 % (32 %)
Developer B (1000)	13 % (13 %)	7 % (10 %)	21 % (16 %)	18 % (16 %)
Developer C (900–1100)	69 % (68 %)	0 % (0 %)	55 % (60 %)	6 % (8 %)
Developer D (500–1500)	17 % (19 %)	52 % (45 %)	15 % (12 %)	52 % (44 %)

Table 3 reports the same tendency found in Table 2. There is again a positive evaluation of the narrow interval of 900–1100 work-hours. This was the case in spite of that the narrower effort interval did not include the actual effort, while the wider effort interval of 500–1500 work-hours did. The result corresponds with earlier research that reports that people tend to emphasize and reward informativeness rather than correctness [13, 21, 22]. While 500–1500 work-hours is a "correct" interval, it may be felt to give less useful information than the "incorrect" interval of 900–1100 work-hours.

The situation for the precise (1020 work-hours) and the less precise (1000 work-hours) single value estimate was, similar to the situation in Table 2, the opposite. Here the more precise estimate was considered by more participants to be the least accurate. This was the case even for the group with actual effort of 1200 work-hours, i.e., even in the situation when the precise estimate was closer to the actual effort than the less precise.

A limitation of the single value estimate comparison is that an estimate 1020 work-hours may be said to be clearly over-precise. The interval 900–1100 work-hours may also be said to be over-precise, but less over-precise than 1020 work-hours.

Another limitation is that our results may have been different if we had a pairwise comparison of estimates. The difference in responses for the 1020 and the 1000 work-hour estimate may, for example, be different if not the two other, effort interval alternatives were present.

In spite of the described limitations and threats, we believe that the observation that over-precise intervals but not over-precise single estimate are rewarded in terms of competence and trustworthiness points at challenges when it comes to communicating estimation uncertainty through estimate precision.

5 Discussion and Conclusion

Previous research, such as the study reported in [23] and the studies referred to in the introduction of this paper, tend to find that people with more precise estimates are, on average, more confident and more accurate. Previous research also suggests that people in many situations tend to convey the expected accuracy of their estimates by use of trailing zeros, i.e., by estimate precision. It is therefore not unreasonable to expect that less trailing zeros of an effort estimate and more narrow effort prediction intervals are interpreted as coming from a more competent and accurate source.

Our results only partly correspond with those of the previous research. We did, in accordance with previous research, find that more precise (more narrow) prediction intervals were interpreted as coming from a more competent source and to be more trustworthy. We did, however, not find the same effects for more precise single value effort estimates. Neither did we find that most software projects, but instead only a minority, tried to convey the expected uncertainty through the precision of single valued effort estimates.

The difference between our and the previous results may have been caused by differences in context, e.g., that software professionals know based on previous experience that people with overly precise single value effort estimates tend to be less competent than those with estimates with more trailing zeros or effort intervals. Then, however, we should perhaps expect to find the same effect for the more narrow effort prediction interval. In an earlier study, see [16], we found that software professionals with the high confidence and narrow effort prediction intervals did *not* give the most accurate effort estimates.

The differences between our and previous results may also be a result of the particular numbers and effort intervals selected for the scenario used in our study. A more precise effort interval than 900–1100 work-hours, e.g., the interval 950–1050, or a less precise single value estimate than 1050 work-hours, e.g., the value 1100, may have led to different results. More research is needed to get more insight into how different contexts affect the precision-related interpretations. (We conducted a follow-up study on with 83 software developers where we observed that very narrow intervals, such as 1100–1020 work-hours were considered to come from low confidence source. This study confirmed the finding that intervals are perceived to come from more confidence sources than single estimates with similar precision. The interval 1000–1200 work-hours was for example considered to come from a much more confidence source than the estimate 1100 work-hours).

Finally, the difference in results may also be a result of that the participants assumed different underlying estimation processes in the interval and the single value estimation context. The estimate 1050 work-hours may be interpreted as coming from a process with addition of most likely effort values without any uncertainty analysis. The effort interval 900–1100 work-hours may, on the other hand, be interpreted as coming from a more thorough, and consequently more competent and trustworthy, process where both minimum, most likely and maximum efforts have been considered.

The perhaps most surprising result is that the participants, including the project managers, even after knowing that the effort interval of 900–1100 work-hours was overly narrow, i.e., did not include the actual effort of 800 or 1200 work-hours, still thought that this was the most accurate interval. This suggests that effort prediction intervals are not interpreted as wrong or inaccurate when the actual effort is close, although not inside the interval. One possible reason for this result is that trailing zeros of the minimum and maximum values communicate that that these boundary values also have uncertainty. Our effort interval, where the boundary values have two trailing zeros, may consequently have been interpreted, for example, as the interval from 800 +/-100 to 1100 +/-100 or as "between around 900 to around 1100 work-hours". Another potential reason is that, in spite of not being able to include the actual effort, they expected that the prediction interval 900–1100 work-hours to be the most useful, i.e., a result in correspondence with the informativeness findings reported earlier. Estimation accuracy measurement by software professionals is then not a mechanical calculation of deviations, but also affected by the usefulness of the estimate.

The findings of our study and their *practical implications* (recommendations) include the following:

- The observed challenges related to the measurement and interpretation of different levels of precision of single value effort estimates suggest that uncertainty communication by use of estimate precision is, at best, unclear. Which level of effort usage uncertainty does, for example, an estimate of 1100 work-hours intend to communicate? Is it 1050–1150 work-hours ($w = 0.5$), is it 1000–1200 ($w = 1$) work-hours, or is it something else? In addition, how do an estimator convey that he/she expects the effort to be between 1300 and 1700 work-hours by the use of the precision of a single estimate? How should a group of software professionals proceed to agree on a proper w-value (interpretation of trailing zeros) and communicate this interpretation to other parties? While we, for the above reasons, would not recommend single value estimate precision to communicate effort uncertainty, we believe that the common practice of high precision (none or few trailing zeros) of highly uncertain effort estimates should be avoided to avoid communicating a higher certainty that is warranted. This is in particular the case when no other means, such as effort prediction intervals, are used to communicate the uncertainty.

- **Recommendation 1**: Do not use or rely on the precision of single effort estimates to communicate estimation uncertainty.
- **Recommendation 2**: Avoid high precision estimates in situations where the estimation accuracy is low. This also applies for the values used as minimum and maximum effort values in prediction intervals.

- The uncertainty communicated by use of effort prediction intervals also seems to have interpretation challenges, but perhaps less than the challenges connected with single value estimates. To enable reasonable clear communication of expected uncertainty of effort estimates, we therefore believe that effort prediction intervals, preferably including confidence levels, is to be recommended.

- **Recommendation 3**: Use prediction intervals to derive and communicate estimation uncertainty, i.e., use minimum-maximum effort intervals with connected confidence levels. Examples of how to do this can be found in [24, 25].

- Our results on the assessment of competence and trustworthiness suggest that software professionals, when providing effort estimates, will be more positively evaluated by those receiving the estimates when communicating narrow effort intervals rather than highly precise single value estimates.

- **Recommendation 4**: Be aware your tendency to interpret narrow effort intervals (but not highly precise numbers) as indicating high competence and trustworthiness, even when it is demonstrated to be over-confident. Use other means that the effort prediction interval itself, such as the estimation process and the relevant experience of the developer [16], to evaluate estimator competence and estimate trustworthiness.

References

1. Halkjelsvik, T., Jørgensen, M.: From origami to software development: a review of studies on judgment-based predictions of performance time. Psychol. Bull. **138**(2), 238–271 (2012)
2. Budzier, A., Flyvbjerg, B.: Making-sense of the impact and importance of outliers in project management through the use of power laws. In: Proceedings of IRNOP (International Research Network on Organizing by Projects), At Oslo, **11** (2013)
3. Little, T.: Schedule estimation and uncertainty surrounding the cone of uncertainty. Softw. IEEE **23**(3), 48–54 (2006)
4. Jørgensen, M.: Evidence-based guidelines for assessment of software development cost uncertainty. Softw. Eng., IEEE Trans. **31**(11), 942–954 (2005)
5. Moses, J.: Measuring effort estimation uncertainty to improve client confidence. Softw. Qual. J. **10**, 135–148 (2002)
6. Kitchenham, B., Linkman, S.: Estimates, uncertainty, and risk. IEEE Softw. **14**(3), 69–74 (1997)
7. Jørgensen, M., Sjøberg, D.I.K.: Impact of effort estimates on software project work. Inf. Softw. Technol. **43**(15), 939–948 (2001)

8. Serrador, P., Pinto, J.K.: Does agile work?—a quantitative analysis of agile project success. Int. J. Project Manag. **33**(5), 1040–1051 (2015)

9. McKenzie, C.R.M., Liersch, M., Yaniv, I.: Overconfidence in interval estimates: what does expertise buy you? Organ. Behav. Hum. Decis. Process. **107**, 179–191 (2008)

10. Cesarini, D., Sandewall, Ö., Johannsesson, M.: Confidence interval estimation tasks and the economics of overconfidence. J. Ecnomic Behav. Organ. **61**, 453–470 (2006)

11. Winman, A., Hanson, P., Jusling, P.: Subjective probability intervals: how to reduce overconfidence by interval evaluation. J. Exp. Psychol. Learn. Mem. Cogn. **30**(6), 1167–1175 (2004)

12. Klayman, J., et al.: Overconfidence: it depends on how, what and whom you ask. Organ. Behav. Hum. Decis. Process. **79**(3), 216–247 (1999)

13. Jørgensen, M., Teigen, K.H., Moløkken, K.: Better sure than safe? Over-confidence in judgement based software development effort prediction intervals. J. Syst. Softw. **70**(1–2), 79–93 (2004)

14. Jørgensen, M., Teigen, K.H.: Uncertainty intervals versus interval uncertainty: an alternative method for eliciting effort prediction intervals in software development projects. In: International Conference on Project Management (ProMAC), Singapore (2002)

15. Teigen, K.H., Jørgensen, M.: When 90 % confidence intervals are 50 % certain: on the credibility of credible intervals. Appl. Cogn. Psychol. **19**(4), 455–475 (2005)

16. Jørgensen, M., Faugli, B., Gruschke, T.: Characteristics of software engineers with optimistic predictions. J. Syst. Softw. **80**(9), 1472–1482 (2007)

17. Jerez-Fernandez, A., Angulo, A.N., Oppenheimer, D.M.: Show me the numbers precision as a cue to others confidence. Psychol. Sci. **25**(2), 633–635 (2014)

18. Løhre, E., Jørgensen, M.: Numerical anchors and their strong effects on software development effort estimates. submitted for publication (2014)

19. Cohn, M.: Agile estimation. Prentice Hall, Upper Saddle River (2006)

20. Ferson, S., et al.: Natural language of uncertainty: numeric hedge words. Int. J. Approximate Reasoning **57**, 19–39 (2014)

21. Yaniv, I., Foster, D.P.: Graininess of judgment under uncertainty: an accuracy-informativeness trade-off. J. Exp. Psychol. Gen. **124**(4), 424 (1995)

22. Yaniv, I., Foster, D.P.: Precision and accuracy of judgmental estimation. J. Behav. Decis. Making **10**(1), 21–32 (1997)

23. Welsh, M.B., Navarro,D.J., Begg, S.H.: Number preference, precision and implicity confidence. In: 33rd Annual Meeting of the Cognitive Science Society (CogSci 2011), Boston, USA (2011)

24. Briand, L.C., El Emam, K. Bomarius, F.: COBRA: a hybrid method for software cost estimation, benchmarking, and risk assessment. In: International Conference on Software Engineering, Kyoto, Japan. IEEE Computer Society, Los Alamitos (1998)

25. Jørgensen, M.: Realism in assessment of effort estimation uncertainty: it matters how you ask. IEEE Trans. Softw. Eng. **30**(4), 209–217 (2004)

Software Testing

Web Service Test Evolution

Harry M. Sneed[1,2,3(✉)]

[1] SoRing Kft., Budapest, Hungary
Harry.Sneed@T-Online.de
[2] Fachhochschule Technikum, Vienna, Austria
[3] Fachhochschule Hagenberg, Hagenberg, Upper Austria, Austria

Abstract. In order to remain useful test scripts must evolve parallel to the test objects they are intended to test. In the approach described here the test objects are web services whose test script is derived from the web service interface definition. The test script structure is automatically generated from the WSDL structure with tags and attributes, however, the content, i.e. the test data has to be inserted by hand. From this script service requests are automatically generated and service responses automatically validated. As with other generated software artifacts, once the structure of the interface or the logic of the targeted service is changed, the content of the test script is no longer valid. It has to be altered and/ or enhanced to fit the new interface structure and/or the altered service logic. In this paper the author proposes a semi-automated approach to solving this test maintenance problem and explains how it has been implemented in a web service testing tool by employing data reverse engineering techniques. The author also report on his experience with the approach when maintaining a test in the field.

Keywords: Web services · Automated web service testing · Test-driven development · Requirement-based testing · Test automation · Regression testing · Test maintenance · Test script evolution · Data reverse engineering

1 Background of this Work

Testing has become an essential part of the software development and maintenance process. Testers produce test models, test cases, test procedures, test scripts and test documents to supplement the models, documents and code produced by the developers [1]. These artifacts, referred to as testware, are part of the overall software product. When the software evolves, the testware has to be evolved along with it. When the requirement document is changed, the test cases based on that document have to be changed too. The same applies to the design model. In system testing, test cases and the scripts which implement them refer to functions and data contained in the system interfaces or data-bases. If these are altered, the test cases used to test them have to be changed in parallel to keep the system test synchronized with the system under test. This is an essential part of the maintenance process.

If the testware is developed manually it will also be maintained manually. It is only a question of cost and quality. Manual processes are known to be expensive and error

© Springer International Publishing Switzerland 2016
D. Winkler et al. (Eds.): SWQD 2016, LNBIP 238, pp. 171–185, 2016.
DOI: 10.1007/978-3-319-27033-3_12

prone. That is why in today's world more and more of the testware is generated automatically from the other software artifacts. In particular, test cases are often generated either from the design model, the interface descriptions, the GUIs, the database schemas or from the original requirements document [2].

The goal of the research presented here is to implement requirement-based testing in the testing of web services. However, as with code generated from a higher level design model, generated tests are not complete. Unless the data domains are specifically specified in the requirement document, the tester will have to assign test data values manually. A simple automat will not know what names are representative of a particular group of customers. Those names have to be assigned by the tester based on his knowledge of the application. Thus, automated test cases are really the result of an automated generation process combined with a manual enhancement process. When the automated process is repeated in regression testing, the manual enhancement process has to be repeated as well. The problem is that in regenerating the test cases, the manual enhancements made before are lost. If there are several thousand test cases involved, the costs of updating them become prohibitive. This is the main reason for not using test automation as pointed out in the literature on that subject [3].

2   Perennial Maintenance Problem

The maintenance problem is not new. It came up before in connection with code generation. Time and time again we have been promised that both code and test will be generated and that maintenance will take place only at the model level. This was the goal of the automatic programming project at M.I.T. in the 1970's, the goal of the CASE tools in the 1980's and the goal of UML modeling in the 1990's [4]. When the M.I.T. automatic programming project was finally terminated in 1980, Rich and Waters sadly conceded that any specification language from which complete code can be automatically generated, must be at the same semantic level as the code itself, i.e. it must contain all of the details down to the if condition level. This way, it inevitably becomes yet another programming language, only in a different syntax [5]. As noted by Swartout and Balzer back in the early 1980s specification and implementation are highly intertwined [6].

This fact also sealed the fate of the highly promised CASE tools of the 1980's. They were expected to revolutionize software development. The user need only to create a model of his application and that model would be transformed into executable code. The maintenance personnel would no longer deal with the code but only with the model expressed in terms of diagrams and decision trees. However there existed a tremendous gap between the abstract, logical model of an application and the physical environment in which the application should run. To bridge this gap, manual adjustment had to be made to the code. It was an illusion to believe that a complete and correct application could be automatically generated from a CASE model [7].

The author remembers well his attempt to automate software development at several large German users in the second half of the 1980's. The result was always the same. Up to 95 % or more of the code could be generated out of the model, depending on how diligent the users were in filling out the model, but no matter how complete this model was, there still remained the last 5 % which had to be hand coded. When the model was altered, as it always was, the code had to be regenerated. In regenerating the code the manual adjustments were lost. Of course, those could be saved and reinserted but this was an error prone process which often caused delay. So in the end the model was discarded and only the code remained. The elaborate CASE tools became useless and disappeared from the market. Obviously, it was easier to maintain the code manually than to start over each time from the model [8].

One would have thought that the IT community would have learned from this experience, but they did not. In the 1990's, object technology and UML were the big hope. Ivar Jacobson promised "UML all the way down" from the use cases to the executable code [9]. Tools were constructed to transform UML models into executable C++ and Java code. UML has no means of expressing decision logic, so the OCL language was added to the diagrams. By including OCL and ready-made patterns certain types of code can be generated, but here too, manual optimizations are required. And, when the model is altered, the code has to be regenerated, which means that the optimizations are lost. In the end the developers wind up maintaining the code directly and the model is left aside. For this reason there are hardly any maintenance shops with an up-to-date UML model. If they want to know, what is going on in the code they have to read the code or to reverse engineer a new model from the code. That is the solution most frequently used. This author knows of no single case where a system is actually maintained at the model level.

Now the exact same problem comes up with testware. Tests which are generated from requirement documents or from design models are only valid if they remain consistent with those sources. If those sources evolve, the test has to evolve along with them [10].

3   The Dilemma of Test Automation

Just as with generated code, generated tests are never 100 % automated. The test tool used here can extract the logical test cases from the requirements, from the system model, or from the data input structure, but it cannot assign specific test values to the data [11]. The information for doing this is missing unless the user has assigned predefined domains for all data used. As a rule only data relationships can be generated without any specific values. The test case generator can generate the assertion that variable CurrentDate must be greater than variable LastDate, but it cannot generate the assertion CurrentDate = "01.01.2010" since to do that it must know the significance of that date. Such values have to be added by the tester based on what the test case should achieve. For instance, if the credit rating of a customer is to be checked, then it should be tested with

- a good credit rating
- a bad credit raging and
- an undecidable credit rating.

In other words, the human tester has to finish off what the test case generator has started. Based on the requirement "check customer rating, reject customer if the credit rating is insufficient"– the test analysis tool will generate two test cases.

"Test when customer rating is sufficient" and
"Test when customer rating is not sufficient".

Unless the analyst has defined what sufficient is somewhere in the requirement documentation, the tool will not know what values to generate. It will only assign the symbolic values "sufficient", "not sufficient" and "undecidable".

assert input.CreditRating = "sufficient", "not sufficient", "undecidable";

It is left to the user to assign the actual representative values like

assert input.CreditRating = "2", "1", "0";

When the requirements are changed to add another rating class, for instance "excellent", the test case generator will generate the assertion:

assert input.CreditRating = "excellent", "sufficient", "not sufficient", "undecidable";

In so doing, it overwrites the previous values assigned by the tester. The tester will have to insert the new value along with the other old values.

assert input.CreditRating = "3", "2", "1", "0";

Not only that but all the other assertions he has assigned real values to will be overwritten by the newly generated symbolic values. He would have to go back and redo all of his assertions.

3.1 Changes to a Web Service Test

In the work described here, the test tool involved is a tool for testing web services. Test cases are generated from the requirement text by parsing the sentences to recognize actions, states and conditions. A test case is generated for each action such as "Add a customer to the customer file.", for each state such as "The customer credit rating is sufficient." and for each condition such as "Delete the customer if his credit rating is insufficient". The technique for extracting test cases from natural language text has been described in previous papers [12]. Once the test case table has been created, the tester has the possibility of editing and enhancing the test data contained therein. This is necessary because the test cases generated from the requirements are incomplete. They contain the operations and their parameter names, but not the test data values and the expected results. These have to be assigned by the tester [13]. Once that is done, the test scripts are generated from the edited test case table. Here again, the tester has the possibility of editing the test scripts.

Thus, there are three levels at which the tester can edit the test cases:

- At the level of the excel table produced from the requirement document.
- At the level of the test case database loaded from the excel table.
- At the level of the test scripts generated from the test case database.

If the requirement or business rule text is changed, such shown above, the test cases have to be regenerated (Fig. 1).

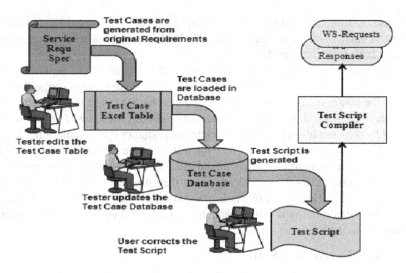

Fig. 1. Generating test cases top-down

There are two ways in which a web service test can change

- the service interface definition can change
- the requirements on the use of the service change.

In the first case the structure of the WSDL definition changes. Most often additional parameters are added or existing ones deleted. In the sample given above it could be that a new input parameter "CustAge" is added to the customer data input.

```
<complexType name="Customer">
  <sequence>
   <element name="CustNo" type="xs:int"/>
   <element name="CustName" type="xs:string"/>
   <element name="CustCreditRating" type="xs:int"/>
   <element name="CustAge" type="xs:int"/>
   <element name="PaymentMode" type="xs:string"/>
   <element name="Orders" type="ns1:ArrayofItems"/>
  </sequence>
</complexType>
```

Less often, but also possible is that the data types change. The preconditions of the unchanged data remain valid but there are no preconditions for the new data. The preconditions of the deleted parameters are no longer needed and the values of data whose type is changed may no longer be valid. The test script is based on the structure of the WSDL. Therefore it has to be restructured. In the sample given above, the new WSDL with the parameter has to be copied into the requirement document so that the data "CustAge" will be added to the test case table.

In the second case, the use case using the web service is changed. Additional steps may be added or existing ones deleted. The text describing the steps can also be altered.

In this case, additional test data values are required. This is achieved by mutating the existing test data. Data values are copied and altered by the tool using progression or regression analysis techniques [14].

The requirements fulfilled by a use case may also change. New requirements are added and existing ones deleted. The wording of the requirements can change. The same applies to the business rules which are implemented by use cases. If a business rule or a requirement changes, this may have an impact on several use cases. The business rule addressed by the sample is changed to "Delete the customer if his credit rating is insufficient and he is over 60 years old". Since the test cases are derived from the use cases and the use cases refer to the requirements and rules, the test cases have to be regenerated based on the revised use case specification, but then the previous test data definitions are no longer valid. Here we will get a new text case with the purpose "Delete the customer if his credit rating is insufficient and he is over 60 years old." This requires a new assertion using boundary analysis [15]:

    assert input.CustAge = {18:60};

3.2 Adapting Service Test Cases

If the structure of the interface changes, the pre-and post-conditions of the unchanged parameters remain valid but do not fit to the new interface structure [16]. A new test case table has to be generated based on the new interface structure but the old pre- and post-conditions can be reused. When a revised WSDL definition is taken over by the test tool user, the tool will generate a new test data table, but in doing so, it will check if a previous test data table exists. If so it will compare the names of the parameters. If a parameter existed before, it's pre- and post-conditions will be copied over into the new test data table. In this way all of the previous test data assignments are preserved within the new interface structure. For the new parameters the user will have to insert new pre- and post-conditions. This is the same as is done with the capture/replay tools for testing user interfaces.

    assert input.CustNo = "100000" + 10;
    assert input.CustName = "Jones", "Smith" "Wally";
    assert input.CustCreditRating = "2", "1", "0";
    assert input.CustAge = {18:60};

assert CustAge is added, all other assertions remain as they are.

    <element name = "Orders" type = "ns1:ArrayofOrderItem"/>

A change to the requirement text is more difficult to handle and the solution is the actual essence of this paper. The automated generation of test cases is based on the requirement text [17]. If that text changes the test cases must change with it. The easiest solution is to generate a whole new set of test cases based on the altered requirement text, but in so doing the test data added or overwritten by the tester to the previous test cases, is lost. The pre- and post-condition columns will be empty again.

This is a common problem to all automated testing solutions which are less than 100 % complete. The human tester must fill in the missing details. The same applies to generated code which is not 100 %. The developer must complete the job. If the specification changes, which it will evitable do, the details supplied by the human tester are lost when the test cases are regenerated. With test cases it is the definition of the test case pre- and post-states which can only be defined in terms of real data values supplied by the user. The assignment of the pre-condition states and the corresponding post-condition states is dependent on the goal of the test. If, for instance, the goal is to test the withdrawal of money from an account the pre-condition is a valid account number, a valid pin number and an account balance greater or equal to the amount desired. This information should be in the account data base somewhere, but it is not automatically recognizable from the requirement text.

The names used in the requirement text do not match to the names in the database schema. Human interpolation is required to select the proper account with the fitting pin number and the desired amount. If their requirement specification were to be written using the correct database names and the same names as in the code, the problem would be partially solved but there still remains the problem of interpreting the natural language description of what is done with the data.

The semantics of the natural language text must be understood in order to assign proper values to the action defined and to assign the correct output values. For instance, if the state of an account balance is 1000 before the withdrawal action and the amount withdrawn is 400, then the account balance after the withdrawal should be 600. This could be expressed as a formal rule from which test data can be generated.

@pre accountBalance > 0;
If (action = "withdrawal" & withdrawAmount > 0)
    @post accountBalance = @pre accountBalance − withdrawAmount;

However, if written in natural language such as:

"Deduct the withdrawal amount from the account balance if the action is withdrawal and the withdrawal amount is greater than zero",

it becomes a challenge to convert that text into a rule from which test data can be derived [18].

Natural language processing is becoming increasingly sophisticated but it is still not able to bridge the gap between an informally defined requirement and a formally defined test case. The human tester is needed to act as an interpreter.

This being the case, it is necessary for the human actor to complete the partially generated test cases as depicted in Fig. 2. The test case generator recognizes that the withdrawal is an action with three conditions and will generate four test cases to test it, but it will not know exactly what data is used and what the state of that data should be. Therefore it can only generate random test data values based on the data type. The tester must replace those values with the values required for each particular test case. If the test cases are regenerated then the values assigned by the tester are lost.

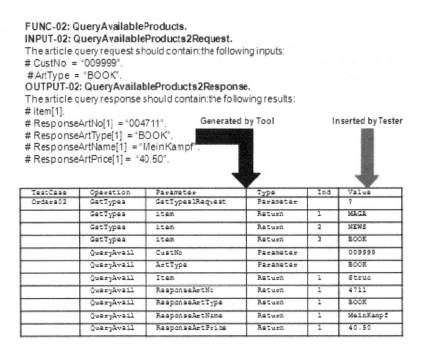

FUNC-02: QueryAvailableProducts.
INPUT-02: QueryAvailableProducts2Request.
The article query request should contain:the following inputs:
CustNo = "009999".
#ArtType = "BOOK".
OUTPUT-02: QueryAvailableProducts2Response.
The article query response should contain:the following results:
item[1].
ResponseArtNo[1] = "004711".
ResponseArtType[1] = "BOOK".
ResponseArtName[1] = "MeinKampf".
ResponseArtPrice[1] = "40.50".

Generated by Tool   Inserted by Tester

TestCase	Operation	Parameter	Type	Ind	Value
Orders02	GetTypes	GetTypes1Request	Parameter		?
	GetTypes	item	Return	1	MAGA
	GetTypes	item	Return	2	NEWS
	GetTypes	item	Return	3	BOOK
	QueryAvail	CustNo	Parameter		009999
	QueryAvail	ArtType	Parameter		BOOK
	QueryAvail	Item	Return	1	Struc
	QueryAvail	ResponseArtNo	Return	1	4711
	QueryAvail	ResponseArtType	Return	1	BOOK
	QueryAvail	ResponseArtName	Return	1	MeinKampf
	QueryAvail	ResponseArtPrice	Return	1	40.50

Fig. 2. Generating the test case table

Every time the requirement document changes the test cases have to be regenerated. That means, the tester will have to reassign all of the pre- and post-conditions. If the requirements change frequently, the tester will become frustrated and go back to making his test manually. This is the main reason for not using test automation.

The solution to the second problem is to save the test cases and to compare the new test case descriptions with the old ones. The test case description is a natural language sentence cut out of the requirement text. This sentence is assigned to a unique test case-ID. The nouns used in that sentence are extracted and placed in a separate column. The type of the test case is also added to the test case description as well as the requirement, the rule or the use case step targeted by this test case. A use case uses one or more operations of a web service. This is included in the use case specification. Thus a use case

- fulfills one or more requirements
- implements one or more rules
- uses one or more data objects
- invokes one or more service operations.

Besides a use case has, itself, several steps, each of which is described by the user.

A test case is generated for each and every requirement fulfilled, for each rule implemented and for each step of the use case. The text of that requirement – rule or step – is inserted in the test case description. Together with the Use Case-ID it makes the test case unique. The names of the input and output data are taken from the operations invoked by the use case. The result of the automated test case generation is a table with the

- use case id
- test case id
- test case type
- test data objects
- operations invoked
- input parameters of those operations
- predecessor test case
- data generation.

Missing are the input and output parameter values which must be filled in by the tester. Once that is done, the test case table is complete and is used together with the WSDL interface definition to generate the service test script.

3.3   Updating the Test Case Table

The solution presented here is a two level reverse engineering process. At the top level the newly generated test case table is updated from the previous test case database. At the bottom level the test case database is updated from the previous test script. Thus the user can alter both the test script and the test case database and still keep his test cases consistent. He can also regenerate new test cases and still preserve his old test data (Fig. 3).

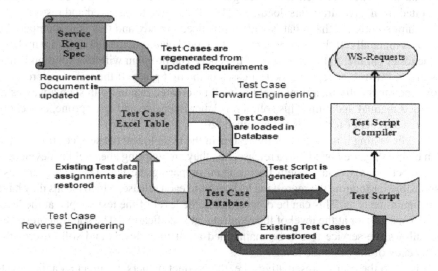

Fig. 3.   Updating the test cases bottom-up

When generating a new test case table from an altered requirement text, the test tool looks to see if there already exists a test case table for that service. If so, it compares each test case it creates new against the existing table. If the use case-id, the operation, the input/output parameters and the test case description match to an existing test case, it takes over the existing test case with its pre- and post-conditions. If not, it marks the test case as being new. Then it is up to the tester to fill in the pre- and post-conditions of the new test cases. This requires much less effort than having to resubmit all of pre-post-conditions again. Besides, the new test cases are marked and only those have to be retested.

This solution also works for changes to the structure of the service interface definition. If the interface definition changes, new parameters are introduced and older ones deleted. The tool will add test cases for the new parameters and delete those which address the deleted parameters. In this way the test case table will always be consistent with the actual service interface definition.

4   Alternate Solutions to Service Test Maintenance

Other possible solution would be to use the design model as a basis of the test and discard the requirement document. In that case the change requests would have to be targeted at the entities in the UML model, e.g. the different design diagrams. Changes are made first to the UML diagrams and then carried over into the code. The model-based test cases which were generated from the different model types have to be regenerated from the altered model types. If these test cases have been enhanced by the testers, e.g. data values have been added, then that information will be lost, unless the case have been saved. Then it can be reinserted back into the new test cases. In this respect, there is no essential difference between test cases generated from a UML model and test cases generated from a requirements document [19]. Both have to be saved and restored.

A third solution is that what is widely practiced already and that is to maintain the test cases manually. If the requirements or the model changes, the test cases are updated by the tester parallel to the changing of the code. The problem with this solution is that it is then not worth generating the test cases in the first place. If the test cases are to be maintained manually then they might as well be created manually in such a way as to ease their manual updating. This solution is labor intensive and error prone, especially if a large number of test cases are involved [20].

In agile testing it is the task of the testers in the team to test the services used by the team before they are bound into a release, i.e., they are working ahead of the developers as members of a special system testing team preparing the way [21]. They are also responsible for running the regression tests prior to each release, which means they have to maintain the tests. This can be done either at the level of the test scripts, at the level of the test cases, or at the level of the requirement specification. The solution presented here allows the service test to be maintained at all three levels and still ensures the consistency of the semantic levels.

It is up to the user representatives, i.e. the product owners, to direct an agile development by means of stories. The stories are the basis not only for the development, but also for the test. Therefore they have to be carefully reviewed and converted into a testable form. The review of the stories is concerned with discussing and analyzing the stories with the view of enhancing and improving them. They should also be checked for testability. The user representative might overlook something or fail to cover all the functions adequately. It is up to the testers in the team to point this out and to clear the missing and unclear issues with him. Special attention should be paid by the testers to the non-functional aspects of the stories like security and usability. In any case the stories need to be purified before the developers start to implement them. Testers need stories they can interpret and test.

In order to establish a testing baseline, the testers should convert the informally defined user stories into an, at least semi-formal, requirement specification. A significant portion of what is referred to as technical debt is caused by missing functions, but who is to know that they are missing when they are not specified anywhere. All of the exception conditions, security checks and other quality assuring functions of a system should be noted down as non-functional requirements or as business rules. They should be specified in such a way as to be recognizable, for instance with key words and to be convertible into test cases. For every business rule and non-functional requirement at least one test case should be generated to ensure that the possible exceptions and security threats are tested. In this way the requirements can be used as an oracle for measuring test coverage. The key feature of the test approach presented here is that the service test is based on the service requirements document as suggested by Canfora and DiPenta.

5   Experience with Web Service Testing

The WebsTest test tool has been in use for more than two years now to test web services, based on their requirement specifications [23]. Experience with the first testing projects has shown that the service interfaces change only slightly but that requirement changes are more frequent. In the one project for the order entry web service there were six requirement changes within an 8 month period. All six requirement changes resulted in new test cases, altogether some 19 additional test cases. Each time the requirement document was changed, the test cases were regenerated. At the beginning there were 215 test cases, after the six changes there were 234. Each time the test case table was recreated, the previous table was secured and the existing data value assignments copied over into the new table. If this had not been done, the tester would have had to edit the test data for all 234 test cases. That would have cost at least 8 person hours for each of the six changes at 30 test cases per hour. By having the tool restore the pervious test data, the tester only had to assign data to the new test cases. For the 19 additional test cases only 1,5 person hours were needed, resulting in a net savings of 6,5 person hours per change, or 39 person hours in all. Instead of 48 h for updating the test cases, only 12 were needed. This underlines how important it is for a testing tool to be able to preserve existing test cases [24].

It is difficult to pass judgement on the usability of the web service test tool. As it stands now the tool is not easy to use, but that has more to do with the complexity of the process than with the way the tool is implemented in Delphi using a Paradox database. It may be that the goal of the tool is too ambitious, going from a free text service requirement document to a validated service test. There are currently too many steps in the process. For the future the process has to first be simplified and then the tool re-implemented.

6 Related Work

There are many other tools for testing web services, both in academia and in industry. Already in 2007 Bokzurt, Harman and Hassoun from Kings College of London published a survey on testing web services, in which they listed out more than 150 tools [25]. SOAP-UI is one of the tools that have been around the longest. It is an open source tool and can be easily used [26]. Like most of the other web service testing tools, it generates a GUI interface from the WSDL schema – the form editor and allows the user to edit the requests. Storm is another open source tool for testing web services. It allows testers to test web services written using the dynamic invocation of web service operations, even those with complex data types. The GUI is simple and easy to use [27]. JMeter from Apache, although developed for testing web applications, can also be used for testing web services. Like WebsTest it facilitates the creation of test scripts with assertions [28]. Another tool which deals with the test of evolving web services is QuickCheck presented by Li, Thompson, Lamela Seijas and Francisco at the last ACM SIGPLAN Workshop on Partial Evaluation and Program Manipulation. The key components include the automatic generation of initial test code, the inference of web service interface changes between versions, the provision of a number of domain specific refactorings and the automatic generation of refactoring scripts for evolving the test code. The main motivation of that tool is very much in line with that of WebsTest, but it is not based on a natural language requirement specification [29].

Unlike these tools that are all running in dialog mode with the user via a GUI interface, WebsTest runs in the background. The user only generates the service requests and starts the test. The rest is fully automated. The requests are dispatched to the server and the responses are automatically collected and validated. The degree of automation is in the case of WebsTest much higher since there in no user interaction during the test.

7 Conclusion

WebsTest is a tool for automatically generating test cases from a service requirement specification. There is no exact empirical data on the effect of automated testing on test productivity when testing services in industry, at least as far as WebsTest is concerned. To get that data it would be necessary to test the same services both manually and automatically. However, there is some comparative data on the service testing exercises made at the Vienna-Fachhochschule. Students there were able to finish the same test exercises with a tool within an hour, which when done manually required more than three hours to do. That is a test cost savings of 67 %. This is good as long as the test specification does not change. If it changes, the test cases have to be regenerated, thus losing information added to the test cases after their generation. The paper has proposed a solution for solving that problem by saving the manual enhancements and reinserting them back into the test case table. This solution has been demonstrated on an existing web service to order articles from an online store. The solution is acceptable, but still not optimal. The optimal solution is to generate the test cases 100 % from the beginning so that manual enhancement is no longer necessary. To attain that goal the service interface definitions have to first be extended to include sample data values with assertions as to their possible use. This should become a goal for the web service provider community.

The perennial problem of test automation is that of keeping the test synchronized with changing data structures and evolving requirements. This problem came up with the first capture/replay tools. Adapting existing test cases to changing data structures has become simplified by generating and validating data at the level of elementary data types. It doesn't matter in what superstructure the data is embedded, it can be identified by name and type.

Adapting existing test cases to evolving requirements is not so simple. When the requirement document is altered it is best to regenerate new test cases from it and then to compare those with the test cases from the previous version. For those use cases, types and target condition are still the same, the asserted pre- and post-conditions are taken over from the previous test cases. For those that do not match, i.e. the new cases, the tester has to write new assertions. These are highlighted in the requirement text. That means that the newly generated test case table has to be recycled back into the requirement text so that the enhancements can be made there. The intention here is to maintain only one document as a basis for the test. It should be possible to create a new test at any time from that one document. It may be that the code is handwritten or generated from some model, but the test is always generated from the requirement specification. For this reason, the requirement document must always reflect the current state of what the software should be. It is the test oracle.

As a consequence of this approach all change requests must point to the requirement document. The users who fill out the change request forms must identify which section, requirement, rule, object or use-case is targeted by the change. If a new requirement, rule or use-case is introduced then the responsible analyst must decide where to insert it in the document. Since the requirement document is the basis of the test, it must always be up to date.

8 Further Work

The current solution of the test case update problem is to compare the old and new test cases when the test case table is generated and to copy over the manual enhancements to the old test cases into the new ones. This way, the tester only has to enhance those test cases which have been added to the test case table as a result of changes to the service requirement specification. To improve this solution it would be necessary to extend the service interface schemas to include value domains within the data type definitions. The providers of web services should at least prescribe sample values – metrics or strings – for each input type. This would give a starting point for the generation of additional data. As far as the outputs are concerned, boundary values should be given to limit the scope of what the outputs could be. This too would give the tester a starting point as to what results are valid.

The Schematron convention for extending WSDL interface definitions by XML notations provides syntax for adding such additional semantic information. It should be exploited to define test cases build into the service interface [30]. That would make the testing of the service much easier.

References

1. Everett, G., McLeod, R.: Software Testing – Testing Across the Entire Software Development Life Cycle, p. 29. IEEE Press, Wiley, Hoboken (2007)
2. Polo, M., Reales, P., Piattini, M., Ebert, C.: Test automation. IEEE Soft. **30**(1), 84 (2013)
3. Sneed, H.: Bridging the concept to implementation gap in software testing. In: 8th International Conference on Software Quality (QSIC 2008), Oxford (2008)
4. Eriksson, H.-E., Penker, M.: Business Modelling with UML. Wiley, New York (2000)
5. Rich, C., Waters, R.: The programmer's apprentice. IEEE Comput. **21**(11), 10–25 (1988)
6. Swartout, V., Balzer, R.: On the inevitable intertwining of specification and implementation. Commun. ACM **25**(7), 112 (1982)
7. Fetzer, J.: Program verification – the very idea. Commun. ACM **31**(9), 479 (1988)
8. Sneed, H.: The myth of top-down software development. In: Proceedings of ICSM-1989, Miami, p. 22, October 1989
9. Jacobson, I.: UML – all the way down. In: Keynote Speech, ICSM-2001, Florence, November 2001
10. Reiss, S.: Incremental maintenance of software artifacts. IEEE Trans. SE **32**(9), 682 (2006)
11. Sneed, H.: Testing against natural language requirements. In: 7th IEEE International Conference on Software Quality (QSIC2007), Portland, p. 380, October 2007
12. Sneed, H.M.: Testing web services in the cloud. In: Winkler, D., Biffl, S., Bergsmann, J. (eds.) SWQD 2013. LNBIP, vol. 133, pp. 70–88. Springer, Heidelberg (2013)
13. Sneed, H., Verhoef, C.: Natural language requirement specification for web service testing. In: IEEE Proceedings of MESOCA-2013, Eindhoven, p. 19, September 2013
14. Jia, Y., Harman, M.: An analysis and survey of the development of mutation testing. IEEE Trans. SE **37**(2), 649 (2011)
15. DeMillo, R., Offutt, J.: Constraint-based automatic test data generation. IEEE Trans. SE **17**(9), 900 (1991)
16. Andrikopoulos, V., Benbernou, S., Papazoglou, M.: On the evolution of services. IEEE Trans. SE **38**(3), 609 (2012)
17. Martin, R., Melnik, G.: Tests and requirements, and tests – a mobius strip. IEEE Softw. **25**, 54 (2008)
18. Meservy, T., Zhang, C., Lee, E.T.: The business rules approach and its effect on software testing. IEEE Softw. Mag. **29**(4), 60 (2012)
19. Mesbah, A., Deursen, A., Roest, D.: Invariant-based automatic testing of modern web applications. IEEE Trans. SE **38**(1), 35 (2012)
20. Mens, T.: State of the art survey on software merging. Trans. SE **28**(5), 449 (2002)
21. Linz, T.: Testing in Scrum Projects, p. 11. dpunkt, Heidelberg (2013)
22. Canfora, G., DiPenta, M.: Testing services and service-centric systems – challenges and opportunities. IT Prof. **8**, 10 (2006)
23. Sneed, H., Huang, S.: The design and use of WSDLTest – a tool for testing web services. J. Softw. Maintenance Evol. **19**(5), 297 (2007)
24. Sneed, H., Verhoef, C.: Cloud service testing. Prof. Tester Mag. **5**, 36 (2014)
25. Bozkurt, M., Harman, M., Hassoun, Y.: Testing Web Services – A Survey, Software Test Verification and Reliability, vol. 18, no. 2. Wiley Interscience (2007). doi: 10.1002/000
26. Soap-UI – the home of functional testing. http://www.soapui.org
27. Storm. http://storm.codeplex.com
28. Apache apache JMeter. http://jmeter.apache.org/

29. Li, H., Thompson, S., Lamela Seijas, P., Francisco, M.A.: Automating property-based testing of evolving web services. In: Proceedings of the ACM SIGPLAN 2014 Workshop on Partial Evaluation and Program Manipulation, pp. 169–180, January 2014
30. International standard organization (2006). ISO/IEC-19757-3 Document Schema Definition Languages (DSDL) - Rule-based validation — Schematron, Geneve (2006)

Integrating a Lightweight Risk Assessment Approach into an Industrial Development Process

Viktor Pekar[1], Michael Felderer[1]([✉]), Ruth Breu[1], Friederike Nickl[2], Christian Roßik[2], and Franz Schwarcz[2]

[1] Institute of Computer Science, University of Innsbruck, Innsbruck, Austria
{viktor.pekar,michael.felderer,ruth.breu}@uibk.ac.at
[2] Swiss Life Group, Munich, Germany
{friederike.nickl,christian.rossik,franz.schwarcz}@swisslife.de

Abstract. Risk assessment is dependent on its application domain. Risk values consist of probability and impact factors, but there is no fixed, unique guideline for the determination of these two factors. For a precise risk-value calculation, an adequate collection of factors is crucial. In this paper, we show the evolution from the first phase until the application of a risk assessment approach in the area of an international insurance company. In such a risk-aware field we have to systematically determine relevant factors and their severity. The final results are melted into a calculation tool that is embedded in the companies development process and used for decision support system. This paper shows the results and observations for the whole implementation process achieved via action research.

Keywords: Risk assessment · Risk-based testing · Risk management · Test process improvement · Software process improvement · Software process · Action research

1 Introduction

Risk assessment helps to support decisions during development and testing. For instance, risk assessment is a key activity in every risk-based testing (RBT) process because it determines the significance of the risk values assigned to tests and therefore the quality of the overall process [1,2]. Also for development activities, risk assessment helps to decide which activities to prioritize and where to invest effort. In this paper, we present a risk assessment approach that has the goal to support stakeholder decisions on whether projects are worth the effort and in which sequence tasks should be performed. According to Boehm [3], risk assessment comprises the activities of risk identification, analysis and prioritization.

The contribution of this paper is twofold. On the one hand we present an initial case study in form of action research and on the other hand we provide guideline proposals for researchers and practitioners to perform similar lightweight risk

D. Winkler et al. (Eds.): SWQD 2016, LNBIP 238, pp. 186–198, 2016.
DOI: 10.1007/978-3-319-27033-3_13

assessment implementations in different contexts. We follow the action research concept because of our active involvement while implementing the risk assessment approach. Moreover, the project goals changed over time, which requires a dynamic research method that can be adapted throughout the process. The action research takes place at the insurance company Swiss Life Germany.

Our risk assessment is connected to artifacts, called use case specifications. These specifications are the sub-parts for a system specification and their implementation order is flexible. Until now, the ordering decision is based on expert opinions and this process needs to be supported by risk assessments based on use case specifications. Furthermore, we provided tool support, which we will discuss in detail.

Such a tool needs to be based on a properly chosen set of criteria to determine impact and probability. It is crucial that such factors are chosen according to the current environment, otherwise the risk assessment will fail. We show how to perform such a selection process and explain its threats.

In the following Sect. 2 we present related action research. Section 3 describes the industrial context at Swiss Life Germany. The applied research method and research questions are stated in Sect. 4. In Sect. 5 we explain the steps for the implementation of the risk assessment approach, which might be used as guidelines for alternative domains. Our results are presented in Sect. 6 and threats to validity are discussed in Sect. 7. Finally, in Sect. 8 we conclude our work.

2 Related Work

Although several studies on risk assessment are available [4–6], only a few of these perform action research.

Iversen et al. [7] perform action research on software process improvement. One goal of the paper is to contribute knowledge on risk management to software engineering activities. Differing from our work, requirements engineering (RE) is not specifically addressed in the paper. The improvement takes place in form of advices and a framework, which can be used by practitioners as well as researchers. Furthermore, the author pursue the alternative collaborative action research, which also differs from our approach.

Lindholm et al. [8] conduct action research in the domain of medical device development. The authors present their experiences from performing risk management with an organization. The paper focuses on risk identification, whereas we focus on the actual risk assessment. Another difference is the domain of the study.

Felderer and Ramler perform a case study [9,10] as well as a multiple case study [11] on risk-based testing, especially also taking risk assessment aspects into account. The authors investigate risk assessment and risk-based testing in one and three industrial cases, respectively, but do not consider action or change, which distinguishes action research from case studies [12].

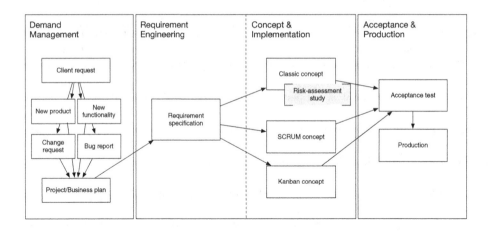

Fig. 1. Development process

3 Context

In this section, we provide the context of our study. It takes place at the international insurance company Swiss Life Germany. Approximately fifty employees are directly involved with the risk assessment approach as authors of artifacts. Furthermore, about a hundred persons are affected by the risk assessment within project management or quality assurance.

Figure 1 shows an overview of the applied development process. It consists of the following three stages: (1) demand management, (2) requirements engineering as well as concept and implementation, and finally (3) acceptance and production. After successful completion of one stage, the next stage is entered. Demand management describes the process of receiving an order by a client. The procedures can be activities like a client request for a new product or changes in functionality. Furthermore, collection of information (like cost-profit probabilities) and business plans conceptualization is performed in this stage. Then, the process enters the critical stage of requirements engineering (RE), concept and implementation. Even though this is basically one stage, we distinguish the RE part from the concept and implementation part. The reason is a variety of different software development procedures, which can be classic, SCRUM or Kanban-based. The RE process may slightly differ according to the chosen concept, but always is a inherent part of this stage. When we talk about concept, we simply mean one of the three mentioned software development methods. The decision about what concept is applied depends on several criteria, which are for example human resources, state of requirements specifications or project type.

The last stage is independent of its predecessor stages. It consists of the necessary steps for the product acceptance and final production. In this paper, these steps are not relevant and therefore not considered further.

Our risk assessment approach is part of the concept and implementation stage for classic software development projects. The classic concept is in use for a longer period of time than the two agile alternatives and therefore more suitable for experimental approaches. The classic concept basically follows the V-Model XT [13] starting with the product requirements specification (see Fig. 2). Based on that, the IT specification consists of the specifications for single or multiple systems. The implementation is performed due to technical specifications. The first testing stage comprises system tests that take place on the layer of the system specification. In the next test stage, system integration tests are performed according to the IT specification. The last test stage comprises the user acceptance test.

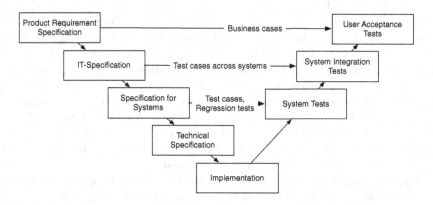

Fig. 2. Optimization method classification

Approximately, there are 25 new system specifications per year. Each system specification comprises several use case specifications, which is the artifact type we use as basis for risk assessment. Use case specifications describe functionality with considerably varying effort. The project manager decides which use cases' have the highest priority and in which order they are implemented. It is possible that the implementation of use cases is canceled due to limited resources or business policy reasons. The risk assessment shall support this decision.

4   Research Method

We make use of the canonical action research (CAR) method proposed by Easterbrook et al. [14]. Easterbrook et al. state that "most empirical research methods attempt to observe the world as it currently exists, action researchers aim to intervene in the studied situations for the explicit purpose of improving the situation". Action research is the right research method in our context since the authors from the University of Innsbruck were directly involved in the improvement process. Direct involvement includes the introduction and explanation of approaches, organizing and moderating workshops and finally providing the tool support. The actual action research approach is defined by Davison et al. [15] and states five principles: (1) The principle of the researcher-client agreement (RCA); (2) the principle of the cyclical process model (CPM); (3) the principle of theory; (4) the principle of change through action; and finally (5) the principle of learning through reflection. We do not discuss details about the first principle since it contains confidential information about our industry partner. The CPM consists of the steps *diagnosis, action planning, intervention, evaluation* and *reflection*. The third principle of theory is slightly based on the risk-based testing procedure proposed by Black et al. [16] meaning that we do not follow all guidelines of risk-based testing, since our risk assessments shall not influence the test management in the first place. Besides Black's guidelines, we refer to the risk management standard ISO 31000 [17], which defines a vocabulary and factor set for the risk management domain. Even Davison et al. state that the *Principle of Theory* is considered problematic in AR, as Cunningham et al. [18] states that it is highly improbable that theory can be exactly known before a project takes place. The fourth principle *Change through Action* is essential for our research, since the final goal becomes visible during the process. The research and client side was motivated to improve the situation right from the beginning, but proposals were denied, which lead to direction changes, which are described in Sect. 6. Related to the fifth principle of *learning through reflection* we only reflect on one cycle. The establishment of our approach is nothing that is possible to be reviewed in a cyclic way. We plan to review the usage of the new approach for multiple cycles in further research.

Davison shows 31 criteria according to the five CAR principles but additionally states that it is unlikely to follow these steps in a statical way. We do not refer specifically to the criteria but use them as non-committal guideline. This paper addresses the following research questions: (1) How to determine important factors for risk probability and impact?, (2) How to integrate risk assessment into an existing industrial product development procedure?, and (3) What tooling is necessary for a risk assessment implementation?

The ultimate research goal is to show the process of establishing a risk assessment procedure into an existing software development environment. For that, the first and most important requirement is a specific collection of factors related to risk impact and probability. This issue is addressed with the first research question discussed in Sect. 6.1. The actual integration procedure is in focus of the second research question. The third question addresses the tool support for the previously mentioned goals and is a key element for the overall success. In Sect. 6.2 we cover the second and third research question. As a basis for discussing the research questions, Sect. 5 provides background on guidelines for lightweight risk assessment.

5   Guidelines for Lightweight Risk Assessment

In this section, we describe the generic implementation procedure of the lightweight risk assessment approach for no specific environment. The steps might be used by practitioners for other domains than the insurance area. We use this sequence of events for our action research and present our results in Sect. 6. We consider the approach as lightweight, since the assessment is performed manually and based on expert opinions. It can flexibly be integrated into an existing requirements engineering process and does not have notable impact on existing infrastructure. An alternative lightweight approach for risk assessment is presented by Rapp et al. [19].

5.1 Factor Determination

The first phase in establishing the new risk assessment procedure is to determine the relevant factors for the respective organization and domain, i.e., Swiss Life Germany and insurance, respectively. As factor basis for impact and probability we suggest the proposal of Black et al. in [16] for assessments that take place on higher levels, like product specifications. Alternatively, the ISO 31000 [17] standard provides factor proposals, which are more adequate for artifacts closer to the software level, like software requirements specifications. Basically, the standard defines a vocabulary and factor set for risk management. This original set needs to be adapted, which is done in several iterations and consists of two phases shown in Fig. 3. In the first phase, decisions are discussed with one expert (for instance, an IT analyst) and re-factored according to his feedback. There is no fixed limit for the iteration-repetitions and it is up to the experts to decide whether the modified set is appropriate or not. The second phase is a council consisting of all experts. The session can be moderated by a person with no related business expertise. The previously adapted set of factors needs to be discussed factor-by-factor. A transcriber needs to note the decisions, which are the basis for the re-factoring that takes place after the council. It is crucial that every factor is discussed so that every attendee has the same understanding of the factor meaning. Since factors are written in natural language there is the risk of ambiguity and misinterpretation. Examples and clearly defined explanations reduce the risk of misunderstanding during the council. If controversies appear, it might become necessary to return to the first phase and prepare a new council-meeting. The final step is an approval by all experts after the final re-factoring.

Fig. 3. Factor determination phases

5.2 Risk Assessment Procedure

The risk assessment procedure is dependent on the following factors: (a) tooling, (b) frequency of risk assessment, (c) related artifacts and (d) expert know-how. The goal of risk assessment is to find representative values for a given artifact in a specified time range. The decision about what tool is used for collecting risk assessment data is mostly restricted to organization policies. Basically, any system, i.e., from a manual approach to an automated survey tool, can be used. Depending on the frequency, the assessment procedure should be adjusted according to effort. An assessment that takes place every six months can require more effort than a monthly-triggered procedure. Related artifacts can be static or dynamic. Quickly changing artifacts need to be assessed more often than more stable specifications. The experts who assess the risk may differ with regard to their know-how which becomes a problem if somebody cannot assess certain factors accordingly. Therefore, it is important to have the adequate set of factors for the right experts. This aspect has to be considered in the factor determination phase.

6   Results

In this section, we present the results of factor determination and risk assessment.

6.1 Factor Determination

We describe the procedure for determining factors for impact and probability in Sect. 5.1. In the following, we present our experience and results from implementing the procedure at Swiss Life Germany. For the first phase and iteration we needed to decide what factor types to choose. We considered ISO 31000 [17] and the factor proposal of Black et al. [16] as two possible starting points. The standard is based on the software quality criteria aligned with the ISO/IEC 25010:2011 standard on software product quality [20]: functional suitability, performance efficiency, compatibility, usability, reliability, security, maintainability and portability. Since this factor selection is partially close to code-aspects, for instance, portability is taken into account, it is not suitable in our case. It is necessary to use factors that assess the risk for a whole product development process instead of just the software development part. Black et al. proposes these risk factors for likelihood: complexity of technology and teams, personnel training, team conflicts, contractual problems, geographical distribution, legacy, quality of used technology, bad management, time and resource pressure, lack of earlier quality assurance, high rates of artifacts, high defect rates and complex interfaces. Furthermore, he proposes the following factors for risk impact: feature usage-frequency, potential image, financial or social damage, loss of customers, legal sanctions, license loss and lack of reasonable workarounds. We used this set as starting point. During several iterations in the first phase the set of factors changed to the following probability factors: complexity of technology, new functionality, poor maintainability, system size, complexity of interfaces, insecure code, deadline pressure, pressure due to limited resources, poor quality of previous test management; and impact factors: usage frequency, risk for corporation image-damage, risk for financial loss, risk for efficiency deficit, legal issues, performance, security, data privacy, compliance violation. The decisions for changes are purely based on expert opinions, which are highly dependent on the environment. We consider this fact as threat to the research validity, because the applicability to other scenarios is decreased. We discuss this issue in more detail in Sect. 7.

The last phase includes the council of experts and the goal to finalize the previous factor set. The sequence of events in the meeting is a moderated discussion that iterates through all factors. First, every factor is explained until all attendees agree to have the same understanding. The researchers from University of Innsbruck took the role of moderators and explained each factor, which was then discussed by all attendees of the discussion. Afterwards, the attending experts, consisting of project managers, process owners, enterprise architects as well as business and IT analysts, discussed for each factor whether it is important in the context of Swiss Life Germany and how it should actually be defined. The finally selected set of factors is presented in Table 1.

Table 1. Final factor collection

Probability factors
Business complexity
Technical complexity
New functionality
Maintainability
Pressure due to deadlines
Limited resources
Existing test infrastructure
Level of requirement-detail
Impact factors
Usage frequency
Potential damage for image of organization
Potential financial loss
Potential efficiency loss
Performance
Compliance

6.2   Risk Assessment Procedure

After a final agreement on the set of factors was achieved, a tool for risk assessment was implemented (see Fig. 4 for a screenshot) that enabled a user to estimate the risk. It is essential that such tool support is accepted by the users who will have to deal with it besides their everyday work. Approximately fifty employees are directly involved with the risk assessment tool as authors from IT- and business-domains. Additionally, another hundred employees, for instance from project management or quality assurance, are affected as readers. We assume 25 new system specifications per year; each of them with several use case specifications. A single risk assessment should require an effort of 5 to 10 min.

The factor assessment is based on several Likert scales. It means that factors can have different Likert scales depending on their meaning. In the end a calculation that aggregates all assessments is required. This is why the intuitive Likert scales are the upper layer visible to assessing experts. The used numerical scale ranges from one to hundred. After an expert chooses a value from the Likert scale it is transformed into a numerical value that is consistent across all factors. For instance, the factor *existing test infrastructure* needs a scale like *extensive, regular, poor*. On the other hand, the factor *usage frequency* has to be assessed with *very rare, rare, normal, frequent* and *very frequent*. The two scale examples show that the quantity of rating levels may vary. The decision for different quantities is based on expert opinions.

The calculation procedure is purely based on numerical values that are mapped from the Likert scale. The mapping is performed according to a quadratic function, i.e., x^2, depending on the risk criticality. In our case, very low is mapped to 1^2 ($= 1$), low to 2.75^2 ($= 7.5625$), normal to 5.5^2 ($= 30.25$), high to 7.25^2 ($= 52.5625$), and very high to 10^2 ($=$ 100). The reason for this decision is

Risk Assessment		
Artifact ID:		
Author ID:		
Date of assessment:		
Comment:		
Probability		
Business complexity	Intermediate	▼
Technical complexity	Low	▼
New functionality	Very poor	▼
Maintainability	Intermediate	▼
Pressure due deadlines	Intermediate	▼
Pressure due resources	Very low	▼
Existing test infrastructure	Bad	▼
Probability: 21.8		
Impact		
Usage frequency for features	Very low	▼
Possible damage for organization	Intermediate	▼
Possible financial loss	Poor	▼
Performance	Very unimportant	▼
Security	Rather important	▼
Compliance	Important	▼
Impact: 23.3		
Risk Value:	**5.1**	

Fig. 4. Risk assessment tool

simply to assign more critical weights to factors with higher risk. Prototype tests with experts showed that x^2 weighting has a intuitively correct effect on the risk assessment compared to higher exponent values. The reason for this effect is the severity of high risk ratings. For instance, an artifact that has only one very high risk while the rest is very low, should have a higher overall risk value than an artifact with some intermediate risk rating and no high risk. It requires more research to test different settings and adaptations for alternative environments.

The overall risk value consists of the two parts probability and impact factors. The median over the factor values is calculated for both categories each. Finally, the probability and impact values are aggregated to the final risk value.

Figure 4 shows the tool that we used for the actual risk assessment procedure, which is based on an Excel spreadsheet. It consists of meta data fields where information about the related artifact and the expert has to be entered. Furthermore, the factor fields are built as drop-down menus and offer different Likert scales depending on the actual factor. The factors are analog to the presented final set, shown in Table 1. We decided to use the following constraints for the assessment: (1) The user is not allowed to skip a factor. This means that only after all factors are estimated, an overall risk value is calculated. Until then, a message is shown that informs the user about missing informations. (2) There is no option to select a neutral value. The reason for both constraints is to achieve comparability between all assessed artifacts.

The calculated risk values are entered and linked to the assessed use case specification. In Sect. 3, we explained the workflow process and we assume that all use case specifications have risk assessments. It enables to make and justify decisions based on the comparable risk values. At this point, we do not consider the priority of use case specifications, so this information needs to be combined with the risk values by the decision maker. In future, the risk assessments should be used to compare the criticality across several projects.

In the following, we present the results from the first risk assessment iteration. On the one hand, we (1) consider the usability of the tool and (2) the precision of the assessed risk values. For the usability aspect, we performed tests with experts and surveyed them for their experience. The precision aspect is hard to evaluate, as no regular assessment results were available to us at the time the paper was written. A sample set of six use case specifications was assessed by several experts. The previously mentioned expert council had the task to judge these estimations according to the intuitive perception of risk related to the use case specification. The overall feedback was positive, which is why we can say that the tool provides useful risk calculations. Nevertheless, to provide certainty, more and long-term evaluation is required as future work.

We define the tool usability according to the following criteria: (1) easy to use, time-effort for (2) initial and (3) regular usage, (4) functionality, (5) usefulness of risk values. We collected the data with a survey, measured time and noted observations. Overall, we performed tests with six experts, of which three took place remotely and three on site. The time effort range was between 5 to 10 min, except in one case, which took slightly more time than 10 min. The reason were misunderstandings related to the meaning of factors. The understandability was also a problem for the other attendees, because of ambiguous or unclear meaning of the factors. The even greater threat than not-understanding the meaning of a factor are wrong assumptions. We therefore included a list with explanations and examples to avoid this threat. The usage itself did not bring any problems and was considered as easy and not error-prone. The tester did not miss any functionality or factors to perform the risk assessment. Two of six testers did not see any purpose in the risk assessment; one attendee even described it as "waste of time". The rest of testers understood the meaning and value of the process. The fact that risk assessment does not need to be self-explanatory led us to adding an explanation about the purpose. The description is now shown to the expert in the workflow before one can fill in the spreadsheet.

7   Threats to Validity

A major threat is the tight dependency on the industrial case. Even though we consider our results as valuable beyond the insurance domain, the procedure needs to be adjusted when used in different environments.

We describe the factor determination process in Sect. 5.1. The decisions for the factor modification and selection are purely based on expert decisions. Obviously, the changes are specific for the Swiss Life Germany environment and project context. The authors, from the University of Innsbruck, hold the observers position and analyzed the decisions from a research point of view. We believe that those changes are applicable in other environments as well, but the lack of proof is a major threat to validity.

In Sect. 6, we showed the results for the first prototype tests considering six persons. Even though it is a valuable input for the evaluation of the risk assessment tool, the small number of test persons can be considered as threat.

Baskerville states in [21] that "action research processes and typical organizational consulting processes contain substantial similarities". Even though our motivation is to help our client, the main focus remains on scientific prospects.

8   Conclusion

In this paper, we explained how a new risk assessment approach was embedded into the existing product development process of the insurance company Swiss Life Germany. The evaluation showed that the method is usable and easy to integrate beside other workflows. Yet, it is necessary to observe the application for a longer period of time and to evaluate the benefit in a long-term. During the process we learned that the factor determination is the most fundamental step, which requires experts who have a good overview about the product. It is likely that developers and tester choose different factors than project managers and quality assurance employees. The right choice of experts depends on the level where the risk assessment takes place. In our case, the risk of the product or sub-parts of the product are in scope, therefore the experts have their expertise mainly on business level. The provision of tool support for assessing the risk for artifacts was important in terms of user acceptance. Disapproval would be fatal for the risk assessment approach, even with the most perfect set of factors. Therefore, we performed user tests during the prototype development and afterwards to assure a good usability. Our first results show promising assessment results for product risk that match with the intuitive estimation of business experts. In future, the effect and usage quality of the introduced risk assessment needs to be evaluated further, especially in a long term context, where the precision and quality of risk assessments becomes measurable. Additionally, we plan to elaborate a fully developed risk-based testing method [22] at Swiss Life Germany based on a refined version of the actual risk assessment approach.

Acknowledgements. This research was partially funded by the research projects MOBSTECO (FWF P 26194-N15) and QE LaB - Living Models for Open Systems (FFG 822740).

References

1. Felderer, M., Haisjackl, C., Breu, R., Motz, J.: Integrating manual and automatic risk assessment for risk-based testing. In: Biffl, S., Winkler, D., Bergsmann, J. (eds.) SWQD 2012. LNBIP, vol. 94, pp. 159–180. Springer, Heidelberg (2012)
2. Felderer, M., Haisjackl, C., Pekar, V., Breu, R.: A risk assessment framework for software testing. In: Margaria, T., Steffen, B. (eds.) ISoLA 2014, Part II. LNCS, vol. 8803, pp. 292–308. Springer, Heidelberg (2014)
3. Boehm, B.W.: Software risk management: principles and practices. Softw. IEEE **8**(1), 32–41 (1991)
4. Sulaman, S.M., Weyns, K., Höst, M.: A review of research on risk analysis methods for it systems. In: Proceedings of the 17th International Conference on Evaluation and Assessment in Software Engineering, EASE 2013, pp. 86–96. ACM, New York (2013)
5. Erdogan, G., Li, Y., Runde, R.K., Seehusen, F., Stølen, K.: Approaches for the combined use of risk analysis and testing: a systematic literature review. Int. J. Softw. Tools Technol. Transf. **16**(5), 627–642 (2014)
6. Felderer, M., Haisjackl, C., Pekar, V., Breu, R.: An exploratory study on risk estimation in risk-based testing approaches. In: Winkler, D., Biffl, S., Bergsmann, J. (eds.) SWQD 2015. LNBIP, vol. 200, pp. 32–43. Springer, Heidelberg (2015)
7. Iversen, J.H., Mathiassen, L., Nielsen, P.A.: Managing risk in software process improvement: an action research approach. Mis Quart. **28**(3), 395–433 (2004)
8. Lindholm, C., Notander, J.P., Höst, M.: A case study on software risk analysis in medical device development. In: Biffl, S., Winkler, D., Bergsmann, J. (eds.) SWQD 2012. LNBIP, vol. 94, pp. 143–158. Springer, Heidelberg (2012)
9. Felderer, M., Ramler, R.: Experiences and challenges of introducing risk-based testing in an industrial project. In: Winkler, D., Biffl, S., Bergsmann, J. (eds.) SWQD 2013. LNBIP, vol. 133, pp. 10–29. Springer, Heidelberg (2013)
10. Felderer, M., Ramler, R.: Integrating risk-based testing in industrial test processes. Softw. Qual. J. **22**(3), 543–575 (2014)
11. Felderer, M., Ramler, R.: A multiple case study on risk-based testing in industry. Int. J. Softw. Tools Technol. Transf. **16**(5), 609–625 (2014)

12. Runeson, P., Host, M., Rainer, A., Regnell, B.: Case Study Research in Software Engineering: Guidelines and Examples. Wiley, Hoboken (2012)
13. Rausch, A., Bartelt, C., Ternité, T., Kuhrmann, M.: The v-modell xt applied-model-driven and document-centric development. In: 3rd World Congress for Software Quality, vol. 3, pp. 131–138. Citeseer (2005)
14. Easterbrook, S., Singer, J., Storey, M.A., Damian, D.: Selecting empirical methods for software engineering research. Guide to Advanced Empirical Software Engineering, pp. 285–311. Springer, London (2008)
15. Davison, R., Martinsons, M.G., Kock, N.: Principles of canonical action research. Inf. Syst. J. **14**(1), 65–86 (2004)
16. Black, R., Mitchell, J.L.: Advanced Software Testing-vol. 3: Guide to the ISTQB Advanced Certification as an Advanced Technical Test Analyst. Rocky Nook, Santa Barbara (2011)
17. ISO: ISO 31000 - risk management
18. Cunningham, J.B.: Action Research and Organizational Development. Praeger, Westport (1993)
19. Rapp, D., Hess, A., Seyff, N., Peter Spoerri, E.F., Glinz, M.: Lightweight requirements engineering assessments in software projects. In: RE 2014. IEEE (2014)
20. ISO/IEC: ISO/IEC 25010:2011 systems and software engineering-systems and software quality requirements and evaluation (square)-system and software quality models (2011)
21. Baskerville, R.L.: Investigating information systems with action research. Commun. AIS, **2**(3es) (1999)
22. Felderer, M., Schieferdecker, I.: A taxonomy of risk-based testing. Int. J. Softw. Tools Technol. Transf. **16**(5), 559–568 (2014)

Fast Feedback from Automated Tests Executed with the Product Build

Martin Eyl[1(✉)], Clements Reichmann[1], and Klaus Müller-Glaser[2]

[1] Vector Informatik GmbH, Ingersheimer Straße 24, 70499 Stuttgart, Germany
martin.eyl@vector.com
[2] Institute for Information Processing Technology, KIT, Karlsruhe, Germany

Abstract. Nowadays Continuous Integration (CI) is a very common practice with many advantages and it is used in many software projects. For large software projects checking out the source code, building the product and testing the product build via automated tests during CI can take a long time (e.g. many hours). So the software developers do not get fast feedback about their changes. Often the test report contains the results of many changes from several software developers or the feedback is not accurate enough according to the developer's source code changes. This paper describes a novel approach to reduce the feedback time and to provide test results for only these changes the developer has committed.

Keywords: Continuous integration · Automated testing · Test case prioritization

1 Introduction

One software development practice of Extreme Programming is to provide small releases of the software product in short, regular intervals during the development of a new product release [1]. The demand on the quality for these releases is high. Also the overall quality of the software shall stay high from the start of the development until the final release. One reason for this practice is that the customer or product manager should always be able to validate the new developed features of the software. If a false implemented requirement is detected by a customer during the validation on the verge of a final release, the rework of the software can cause the release to be postponed for weeks or even be cancelled by the customer because the customer lost his confidence in the skills of the supplier [2].

Another reason for this practice is that the later a defect or failure is detected, the higher the effort to fix it [3]. All defects found during the development by the developer who caused the defect can be fixed with a little effort. At this very moment the developer knows the source code very well. There is no documentation for the bug necessary and no involvement of other people. If other people especially product manager and tester are confronted with the defect, the effort to solve the defect will increase significantly: A ticket has to be created in a bug tracking system. The defect has to be described in detail so that it can be reproduced. A product manager has to review the ticket and decide when to fix the bug. A project manager has to plan the ticket and assign it to a developer.

D. Winkler et al. (Eds.): SWQD 2016, LNBIP 238, pp. 199–210, 2016.
DOI: 10.1007/978-3-319-27033-3_14

The developer has to reproduce the bug, learn the source code and then resolve the problem in the source code. The solution has to be verified by a tester and if necessary it has to be reworked.

If the defect becomes relevant for the customer, there are even more problems. A service pack might be necessary and often this also entails a considerable damage to the supplier's image.

To avoid all these problems, defects should be detected and solved as early as possible during development. The developers should receive hints about new created defects shortly after making their changed or new source code available to all project members.

Contributions. The contribution of this paper is a novel approach based on continuous integration to provide the developers with valuable and fast feedback (in minutes or hours) on their changed source code.

Fast and accurate feedback for the software developer is essential for identifying the source of the problem and fixing the defect immediately before the developer is distracted with other work and before other people get involved with the bug.

2 Continuous Integration

Continuous Integration (CI) [4–6] is one step towards solving the problems described above. Depending on the size of the software product and the number of configured tests, a complete CI run can take a long time. Without any optimization and for large software products a complete check out and build of all source code can take hours [7] and the execution of all tests several days or even weeks [8]. To get fast feedback and to have a reasonable number of CI servers optimizations are necessary. The build time and test execution time has to be minimized.

There are several possibilities to reduce the build time: Incremental build, build parallelization, distributing builds [9]. Maven [10] is one possibility to implement an incremental build with dependency management. Maven allows you to define a project object model with the dependencies between the projects. By changing the source code of one project only the project itself and all direct and indirect dependent projects have to be rebuilt. In the worst case scenario all projects have to be rebuilt because of changes in projects with many dependent projects. Therefor the build time can still be substantially large for the CI run and possibly only a few binaries have been changed with the build.

The following modifications regarding the test execution are useful to have a reasonable number of CI servers and to get fast feedback:

1. All tests are executed overnight using several servers instead of triggering the test execution with every commit of source code. The disadvantage is that it is not clear which code changes caused which failed tests because all changes of the complete day are input for the tests. Another disadvantage is that the developer has to wait for the feedback a whole day.

2. A build pipeline is used [4]. The commit build is executed when someone commits source code. During this build only a few tests are executed and only tests are used with short execution time. The secondary build is not triggered with every commit of source code but from time to time and more and longer running tests are executed. The drawback of the commit build is that only some general tests can be executed which might not test the changed source code at all. The secondary build is very similar to the overnight build and has the same disadvantages.

The following goals shall be achieved by the solution described in this paper:

1. Reduce the feedback time for the developer
   a. Minimize the build time
   b. Lower the test execution time
2. Improve the quality of the feedback with the test results
   a. Execute tests with the product build in an environment which is similar to the production environment
   b. Provide only test results for the changed code of the developer
   c. Provide information whether a test has failed because of the last change of the developer or because of a previous change

3   Overview

The solution described in this paper is based on Continuous Integration with automated test execution whereby each commit of source code triggers its own continuous integration run. This ensures that the test results belong only to changes of one developer. Also the automated tests are executed with the product build in an environment which is similar to the production environment. The execution of automated tests on the developer's computer in the Integrated Development Environment (IDE) is not good enough for a reliable statement about the quality.

A fast product build is achieved by storing binary files in the Source Code Configuration Management (SCM) repository and automated test execution time is reduced by an elaborated selection of automated tests which are relevant for the changed source code. After the continuous integration run the developer gets per email feedback about the test results and can then fix the defects before the defects cause more problems.

The solution was developed and implemented for Java and the Eclipse IDE [11] and is called Morpheus. Morpheus is currently used in a team of about 30 developers for the development of a 3-tier application on base of Eclipse with more than 1000 plugins and about 4 million source lines of code.

4   Fast Build

Eclipse provides the feature "Continuous Build", which means that every save of a source file triggers a build[1]. During the build a Java compiler translates the Java source

---

[1] When the option "Build Automatically" is activated in the Eclipse IDE.

file to a class file (the binary file). So, the developed application can be started at any time (e.g. for debugging purpose). When the developers update their source code from the Source Code Configuration Management (SCM) repository to retrieve changes of other developers, all updated source code files are immediately built.

After the developer has committed the changed source file into the SCM repository, the source file is again translated during the Continuous Integration (CI) build and again on every computer of all developers when the source code is updated. There is actually no reason to compile the same file again and again. Instead the class file could be committed along with its Java source file in the SCM repository. Then the class file from the repository can be used to update the product build before the execution of the automated tests. All other developers can also take over the class files during updating their source code to avoid a local build. The commit and update of class files does not cause additional effort for the developer.

The following modifications and extensions are necessary to benefit from storing the class files in the SCM repository for a fast product build and no local build in the Integrated Development Environment (IDE).

4.1   Eclipse IDE Integration

There are several SCM integrations for the Eclipse IDE available for different SCM repositories. SCM integration allows committing and updating of source code inside the IDE very comfortable. The developer can select which changed files shall be committed and which plugins shall be updated. For our development Subversion [12] with the Eclipse IDE integration Subclipse [13] have been used. The following features have been developed in a Subclipse/Eclipse extension which is part of Morpheus.

Force Commit of Class Files and Depended Class Files: Binary Files are usually ignored by Subclipse. But it is of course essential for our feature that for each Java source file the corresponding class file will be committed. The developer should not be responsible for selecting the correct class files during commit. So, Morpheus ensures that for each committed source file also the class file will be committed.

In some situations the compiler creates a changed class file although the corresponding source file has not been changed. For example in the source file "Const.java" the following constant value has been defined:
```
public static final int LOCKED = 428;
```

The constant value is used in a second source file "Class.java".
```
int errorCode = Const.LOCKED;
```

Let's assume that the constant value has been changed from 428 to 429, then the compiler creates two new class files "Const.class" and "Class.class" although only one source file ("Const.java") has been changed. The reason is that the value 429 is directly included in the class file "Class.class". A second example is the change of the data type of a method parameter. If the method parameter changes from "int" to "double", the source file where this method is called does not need to be updated but the corresponding class file will change.

The Eclipse IDE knows the dependencies between the source code plugins. If the user selects a source file which shall be committed, Morpheus search for all depended and changed class files and adds those files to the commit set automatically.

If the source file of the depended and changed class file has also been changed and the developer has not selected the source file for commitment, there is a conflict situation which has to be made aware to the developer. Sometimes the developer works in parallel on two different bugs and the developer wants to commit only the changed source code for one bug. In these situations this conflict can occur and the developer will be requested to commit a larger set of files to keep the source files and class files consistent. The dependencies analysis is not that detailed and fine granular enough so that conflicts are signaled which really should not prevent the separate commitment of different source and class files. Here is potential for improvement for Morpheus.

The conflict errors can help the developer to detect a false selected set of files to be committed. If the developer selects not all depended changes for a bug fix and commits this incomplete set into the SCM repository, possibly the SCM repository contains source code which has syntax errors and the CI build will fail. For example the developer has added a new parameter to a method but not all source code files with the corrected method call with the additional parameter have been selected for the commit. All these not committed source files will have a syntax error in the SCM repository because the method signature is not correct. So the conflict detection can help to prevent these kinds of errors.

Prevent a Build After Update: Source files and class files are updated from SCM repository and so for each source file the translated class file is instantly available. There is no reason for a build and so Morpheus suppresses the build in Eclipse but with two exceptions:

1. With every update, merge conflicts are possible. If the incoming changes from the SCM repository affect the source files which have also been changed locally, those conflicted source files have to be merged. Of course the class files will have merge conflicts, too. But a merge of a class file would be very difficult. Therefore Morpheus resolves the merge conflict for the class file by taking over the class file from SCM repository and marking the plugin where the file belongs to. The build of these marked plugins will not be suppressed and the compiler creates a new class file from the merged source file.
2. Eclipse shows all currently present syntax errors in a separate view. The list of syntax errors will be updated during the build. If there is no build, the list will not be updated and so possibly solved syntax errors are still displayed to the developer. Therefore Morpheus will rebuild all plugins with syntax errors after the update to update the error list. This problem is only relevant for syntax errors which existed in the source code loaded from the SCM repository and this should be an exception.

If the developer wants to update source code, all plugins have to be updated because the above explained potential dependencies between the files. So it is ensured that all source and class files are consistent. This is not really a drawback because updating only parts of the source code can always lead to syntax errors because not all dependent changes could have been updated.

Prevent a Commit or Update During a Build: The execution of a build indicates that not all source files are yet compiled and some class files are not consistent with their source files. So, Morpheus prevents the commitment of source files during a build because possibly not compiled class files would be committed. Morpheus also ensures that the option "Build Automatically" (Continuous Build) is activated in the Eclipse IDE.

If the developer tries to update the source code during a build, the developer can decide whether to continue or to wait for the build to be finish. If the developer wants to continue with the update, the build after the update will not be suppressed and the class files will be updated via the build. If the developer decides to wait for the build to be finished, a new build after the update is not necessary. So, any conflicts between updating the class files and creating the class files via the build are prevented.

4.2   Creating the Product Build

For a fast feedback during CI we need a really fast product build which can be achieved by using the class files stored in the SCM repository. The class files can only be used to update an existing product build. So, at the very beginning a product build is created via a "normal" automated build.

When the developer commits some source and class files, Morpheus is triggered to provide a new product build. Therefore, Morpheus retrieves the change sets from Subversion which contains information about all committed files since the last product build update and analyses these change sets. It identifies the affected plugins and searches for the plugins in the product build. Then the class files are retrieved from Subversion and Morpheus replaces the class files in the plugins with the new class files from Subversion. If the plugin is a Java Archive (Jar), the plugin has to be unpacked before the replacement can be done. Then the updated product build can be used for the execution of automated tests.

In some cases Morpheus will find out that an update of the product build is not possible, for example when a new plugin has been created or an existing plugin has been deleted. Then a new product build has to be created from scratch and the execution of the automated tests is delayed. But very often change sets contain only changed source and class files and then the fast product build can be used.

We lose one big advantage of CI with this approach creating the product build: Potentially existing syntax errors in the source code in the SCM repository cannot be detected because a build is not really executed. So we need two kinds of CI runs: CI builds for detecting syntax errors and CI runs for automated test execution with the fast build. The later CI runs should be executed with every commit of source code so that the developers only get feedback for their changes.

If a CI build fails because of syntax errors, the execution of the automated tests with the fast build might also fail. So, what we really need is a mechanism which prevents any syntax error in the SCM repository in the first place. We are currently working on a solution for this problem.

4.3 Results

The above described approach has been validated in the development of an application based on Eclipse with 1000 plugins and 4 million source lines of code.

Without any optimization the update of source code in the Eclipse IDE varies very much depending on how many plugins and which plugins have been changed. If the update contains several changed plugins which have many dependent plugins, the local build can take up to ½ h[2] because Eclipse has to rebuild many depending plugins. The Eclipse IDE build is an incremental build with dependency management and so the build time is comparable with a product incremental build. With Morpheus no build at all is necessary. Of course the update time of the local workspace is higher than without the class files but usually the update time is within the range of few minutes.

The build time for a complete product build for continuous integration is about 1 ½ h without Morpheus and by using the fast product build provided by Morpheus within the range of few minutes of course depending on the number of changes.

5   Selection of Automated Test

After lowering the build time we have to bring down the automated test execution time. A significant improvement can be achieved by reducing the number of tests to be executed. Only tests which test the changed source code should be selected. Then the developer retrieves only test results which are directly connected to his or her changed source code. Four different strategies have been implemented to find and select the most appropriate tests.

Requirement Oriented Test Selection Strategy: There is always a specific reason why a source code has to be changed. For example a new requirement has to be implemented or a bug has to be fixed. To ensure that the implemented functionality for the requirement will still work in the next releases and the bug will not reappear, automated tests should be created to test the requirement or the solution of the bug.

All this information can be linked together: the changed source code can be linked with the reason for change (requirement or ticket) [14] which again can be linked with test cases [15] (e.g. requirement A is tested by test case X). The test cases can again be linked with the source code of the automated tests. This information is very valuable and should therefore be permanently stored for example in a data base. Among others we can use those linked artifacts to determine the right tests for source code changes.

We use an Application Lifecycle Management (ALM) tool (in our project we use PREEvision [16]) to store requirements, tickets and test data and the links between these artifacts in one data backbone. Besides these artifacts the links into the source code also have to be stored permanently. The link between changed source code and the reason for change is created by entering a unique id of the requirement or ticket into the change log during the commit of the source code. This unique id allows us to uniquely identify the artifact in the ALM repository. By viewing the history log of a source file the

---

[2] Depending on the hardware of the developer's computer.

developer can find all the ids of the requirements and tickets which are the reasons for the changes of the source code. The link between test case and the source code of the automated test is created by storing the full qualified name of the class plus the name of the method in a property of the test case.

How can this information be used to determine the automated test for a source code change? Before the developers commit their changes, they create a new test case with the method name of the automated test or they use an existing test case. They link the test case with the requirement or ticket. Then the developers commit the source code changes with the id of the requirement or ticket in the change log. Morpheus retrieves the change log of the change set and searches for the requirement or ticket in the ALM repository via the unique id. Then Morpheus only has to follow the links from the requirement or ticket via the test cases to the source code of the automated tests.

With the help of the history of the changed source file it is possible to ensure that already existing functionality is not broken by the last change. Therefore, Morpheus identifies all requirements and tickets of previous changes in the source file and selects the according tests for execution.

Software Architecture Oriented Test Selection Strategy: There is the common practice in Eclipse to separate the automated tests from the productive source code into their own test plugins. For each product plugin one test plugin should be created with automated tests verifying the code of the product plugin. By using a naming convention[3] Morpheus can find the test plugin for a product plugin. When the developer changes the source code of a plugin, Morpheus considers all tests of the according test plugin.

Side-Effect Test Selection Strategy: Sometimes code is executed for a certain functionality which is not obvious and surprising for the developers. For example a developer is changing a class for a certain requirement and suddenly a completely different functionality is broken. The measurement of the code coverage can be used to find tests for this kind of defects [17].

There are several tools available which analyze the code coverage during the execution of a test. For the Morpheus project JaCoCo [18] has been used to measure the code coverage. During the execution of a test JaCoCo stores all visited classes for a certain test class in an execution file. Morpheus uses these files to find for a changed class the test classes and adds those test classes to the list of tests to be executed.

Changed Test Code Selection Strategy: New automated test code is created or existing automated test code is changed during the product development. In the continuous integration run Morpheus selects all changed or new test code automatically for execution.

One could argue that the Side Effect Test Selection Strategy should be the only selection strategy. But the combination of all selection strategies is useful because of the following reasons. At the very beginning there is no information available about the executed code of a test class until the first run. Also the list of all visited classes is just

---

[3] For example the test plugin could be named as the product plugin plus the postfix ".test".

a snapshot and can change significantly with every code change. For very basic functionality (e.g. database access layer) the selection strategy will deliver a large number of tests but there might be only a few test classes which test the functionality very thoroughly in a short period of time.

The strategies can provide a large or only a small number of automated tests depending on how many tests are available. If the number is too large, the feedback for the developer takes too long. In this case the number of tests has to be reduced by prioritizing the tests so that test execution time does not exceed a defined maximum. This can be done for example by favoring one test selection strategy over the other. The number of executed tests is a compromise between extensive testing and detecting and fixing problems in the changed source code at a very early stage. Because not all tests might be executed the continuous integration run with the execution of all tests cannot be omitted and is still necessary (e.g. a continuous integration run overnight).

6   Feedback for the Developer

A continuous integration run is triggered by committing the changed source code and the according class files. The developer provides the reason for the change by entering the id of a requirement or ticket in the change log. Then in parallel in two threads Morpheus creates the product build and determines the automated tests to be executed by using the selection strategies. In our case (the development of a 3-tier application) the database is set up, the middleware and the client is created and started. The selected automated tests are executed and the results are summarized in a report. Then Morpheus sends this report back to the developer via email. The report contains following information:

- Information is provided about the change set of the commitment which triggered the test run (change log, time of commitment, committed files).
- The report contains an overview about all found and executed tests with the results (success or failure). Also in the case of a failure the information is provided how often the test has already failed. The test can fail because of other changes in the past or the test fails the first time because of the last change of the developer.
- The report contains URLs to web pages with detailed information about the failed tests (which exception has been thrown and the stack trace).
- A code coverage report of all executed tests is provided. This report allows the developer to verify whether the tests have really executed the changed source code and whether the code coverage of the written test is good enough.

7   Results

In our Eclipse based development project with 1000 plugins and 4 million source lines of code we started with the following procedure: The developer commits the source code and was supposed to check the results of the automated tests after the test executions had been finished during the course of the next day. The developer has to guess which test results are relevant and whether a test has failed because of his/her changes or the changes of someone else. After implementing Morpheus the developer gets automatic feedback via email about the committed source code within a period of 10 min up to 3 h depending on the number of executed tests. The test results are related directly to the developer's code changes.

One goal was to minimize the feedback time. The build time is now so short that the feedback time is substantially determined by the number of executed tests and the time needed to execute a test. For the system tests the test execution time has to be further optimized. The setup and tear down time of the tests are too long (e.g. starting the application, creating test data and deleting the test data after test execution).

We introduced Morpheus for the development of service packs of an already released version of our product and in the middle of the current trunk based development. For the service pack development the developers get very good feedback from Morpheus because almost all automated tests are green and newly created defects are becoming often visible by one or more failing tests. For the trunk based development there are currently several automated tests failing because of larger modifications in the source code. If an automated test has already failed before committing the source code, new created defects cannot be recognized. Therefore the number of failing tests should always be very low. Our expectation is that using Morpheus from the beginning of a new release the number of failing tests should remain low because failing tests and the cause for the failure can be early detected and solved.

Another problem is that Morpheus sometimes cannot find any automated tests to execute because of legacy source code without any automated tests. To improve this situation the developer can only close a bug found in legacy source code when automated tests have been created and connected to the bug in the Application Lifecycle Management repository or the developer gives a reason why an automated test is not possible.

8   Related Work

Continuous Testing (CT) [19] provides fast feedback about the quality of the code by automatically running regression tests in the background while the developer is changing the source code. There are a couple of commercial products available. One product is NCrunch [20] which provides several interesting features. NChrunch uses among others the code coverage for the selection of tests to be executed. The tests can be executed in the Integrated Development Environment (IDE) on the computer of the developer or on a server.

CT is very well suited for unit and component tests which test e.g. a method or a class. The developer can detect local problems, e.g. the method does not function as before and the method or the test has to be corrected. Although NCrunch also supports the execution of integration tests it seems not useful to execute integration or system tests during the development of source code because the probability that these tests will fail is quite high and not particularly bad because the developer has not yet finished. CT provides test results about the current change rather than test results about all done changes because already executed tests are not necessarily executed again. Source code of other developers which is developed at the same time is also not considered.

Van der Storm [9] introduced a concept for an incremental build for Continuous Integration. By considering the dependencies between the software components only the changed and the dependent components have to be rebuilt instead of building all components.

The application CompilerCache for C/C ++ compilers [21] caches the binaries to avoid rebuilds. The cache is used only locally and is not shared with other developers.

Test case prioritization (TCP) has received quite a lot attention from the research community [8, 15, 17, 22, 23] because it can help to reduce the costs for regression tests. Most of those suggested techniques are code coverage based. PORT [15] also considers the customer assigned priority of requirements, the implementation complexity, the requirements volatility and fault proneness of requirements.

9   Conclusion and Future Work

The subject of this paper is to provide valuable, precise and fast feedback about the quality of the source code, which has been committed into the Source Code Configuration Management (SCM) repository, so that defects can be found and fixed as early as possible. This can be achieved by testing the product build with automated tests which test only the changed source code. Four different selection strategies for the automated tests have been implemented. To reduce the build time we store the binaries along with the source code in the SCM repository and so, the compiling of source files over and over again is avoided.

We are currently working on the following improvements: Firstly, syntax errors in the source code of an SCM repository shall be prevented. So that, there is always a product build available. Secondly, the links from the artifacts in the Application Lifecycle Management repository into the source code has to be improved. The artifacts and the source code are very loosely coupled and the link can break by refactoring the source code (e.g. rename or move methods and classes). Thirdly, we plan to reduce or to avoid the effort for merging source code. When several developers change the same code, they have to merge their changes and this is costly and error-prone.

References

1. Lindstrom, L., Jeffries, R.: Extreme programming and agile software development methodologies. Inf. Syst. Manag. **21**(3), 41–52 (2004)
2. Mogyorodi, G.: Requirements-based testing: an overview. In: International Conference on Technology of Object-Oriented Languages. IEEE Computer Society (2001)
3. Building a better bug-trap. Economist Magazine, June 2003
4. Fowler, M., Foemmel, M.: Continuous integration. (Thought-Works) (2006). https://www.thoughtworks.com/continuous-integration
5. Duvall, P.M., Matyas, S., Glover, A.: Continuous Integration: Improving Software Quality and Reducing Risk. Pearson Education, United States (2007)
6. Beck, K.: Embracing change with extreme programming. Computer **32**(10), 70–77 (1999)

7. McConnell, S.: Daily build and smoke test. IEEE Softw. **13**(4), 144 (1996)
8. Elbaum, S., Malishevsky, A.G., Rothermel, G.: Prioritizing test cases for regression testing, vol. 25(5). ACM (2000)
9. van der Storm, T.: Backtracking incremental continuous integration. In: 12th European Conference on Software Maintenance and Reengineering, 2008, CSMR 2008. IEEE (2008)
10. Maven. https://maven.apache.org/index.html
11. Eclipse Foundation. http://eclipse.org
12. Collins-Sussman, B., Fitzpatrick, B., Pilato, M.: Version Control with Subversion. O'Reilly Media, Inc., Sebastopol (2004)
13. Subclipse. http://subclipse.tigris.org/
14. Asklund, U., Bendix, L., Ekman, T.: Software configuration management practices for eXtreme programming teams (2004)
15. Srikanth, H., Williams, L., Osborne, J.: System test case prioritization of new and regression test cases. In: 2005 International Symposium on Empirical Software Engineering. IEEE (2005)
16. PREEvision. https://vector.com/vi_preevision_en.html
17. Beena, R., Sarala, S.: Code Coverage Based Test Case Selection and Prioritization (2013). arXiv preprint arXiv:1312.2083
18. JaCoCo. http://www.eclemma.org/jacoco/
19. Saff, D., Ernst, M.D.: Continuous testing in Eclipse. In: Proceedings of the 27th International Conference on Software Engineering. ACM (2005)
20. NCrunch. http://www.ncrunch.net/
21. Thiele, E.: CompilerCache. http://www.erikyyy.de/compilercache/
22. Yoon, M., et al.: A test case prioritization through correlation of requirement and risk. J. Softw. Eng. Appl. **5**(10), 823–835 (2012)
23. Rothermel, G., et al.: Test case prioritization: an empirical study. In: Proceedings of the IEEE International Conference on Software Maintenance, 1999 (ICSM 1999). EEE (1999)

E-Government Applications

Approach of a Signature Based Single Sign on Proxy Solution

Klaus John[(✉)] and Stefan Taber

Research Group for Industrial Software (INSO),
Vienna University of Technology, Vienna, Austria
{Klaus.John,Stefan.Taber}@inso.tuwien.ac.at

Abstract. Many e-government applications need certificates, which are stored in the client's browser certificate store to gain access into a service. The problems of such an authentication methodology at first are, a client has to store all certificates on every device, with whom access will be gained into e-government services and secondly, if the client lost such a device (e.g. notebook etc.) than all involved certificates have to be exchanged, otherwise it exist the danger to be compromised. To phase such a problem and to provide a secure single sign on solution, we implemented a secure proxy solution with integrated encrypted certificate storage, where citizens can store all their certificates to use e-government services. Our solution – we call "proxy authenticator" – enabled us to omit any alteration of existing protocol structure or amending of software architecture for all Austrian e-government applications. This saved time, effort, and costs, by connecting the existing e-delivery services in Austria into the myHelp portal through the proxy authenticator.

Keywords: e-government · Quality management · Test · IT-strategy · Single sign on

1 Introduction

In recent years, the use of Information and Communication Technology (ICT) in administrative procedures (e-government) has gained much attention in efforts to modernise government. Within the framework of the STORK1 [1] EU project an electronic e-delivery service has been implemented for the Austrian government. At the beginning, citizens who wanted to access this service in Austria were required to install a certificate and private key into the client browser, through which citizens were enabled to authenticate themselves to an e-delivery service and been enabled to download delivered documents from this service. This solution has come under criticism because of the possibility of unauthorised occupance onto the client's browser and in particular onto the certificate and private key. If the certificate and private key is not protected by a password, which can only be set personally by the citizen, the citizen risks unauthorised access to an e-government application e.g. the client's e-delivery inbox.

© Springer International Publishing Switzerland 2016
D. Winkler et al. (Eds.): SWQD 2016, LNBIP 238, pp. 213–228, 2016.
DOI: 10.1007/978-3-319-27033-3_15

S. J. Leonetti has summarised the security issues as followed: "If the government is unable to protect information collected through electronic channels there will be a loss in public confidence towards government and worse yet, could contribute to crimes related to identity fraud. Privacy protection must explore a balance between privacy and service delivery" [10].

This paper describes the technical concept of a proxy based solution; we call it proxy authenticator, to move the storage of the certificate and private key from the client's browser into a trusted centralised authority service and for security purposes. The proxy authenticator is embedded in the myHelp[1] service and as a typical e-government application this e.g. enables citizens to download a document from various external e-delivery services via myHelp. This trusted centralised authority enables a single sign on (SSO) at e-government services, without requiring further login by employment of the citizen card. The SSO solution is in accordance with the Austrian law (Sect. 35 ZustG [2]) and has been implemented in myHelp or in the business service portal ("Unternehmens Service Portal (USP[2])").

The citizen logs into the web portal – myHelp.gv.at – which operates as a proxy service. After logging into the myHelp portal an additional automatic login into the e-delivery service will be passed on and executed. There is no legal relationship between them two – the myHelp portal functions as a proxy service, whereas the e-delivery service operates as an e-government service that transfers documents between citizens and government administration.

The remainder of this paper is structured as follows. A description of the technical background is given in Sect. 2. In Sect. 3 we descript the legal and technical background. Section 4 descripts the technical architecture of the proxy authenticator. Details about the implemented solution and its usage are given in Sect. 5. The paper finishes with a conclusion and ideas for further work in Sect. 6.

1.1   Methodology

This paper will commence by introducing the legal and technical aspects of the proxy authenticator. Furthermore, this paper intends to illustrate secure methodology in Austria with focus on legal requirements for document transmission from e-delivery services via the proxy authenticator. To emphasise the importance of security, the authors of this paper created a table of mayor security leaks, which have been collected in the IT security architecture list over the past years. A comparison of all security requirements with the ICT secure architecture list was then conducted by listing only those security patterns necessary for running the proxy authenticator. Furthermore, only best practices and industrial standards were used to meet security requirements. The proxy authenticator's use cases are described in detail, with focus on the communication sequences. Finally, the proxy authenticator is evaluated in relation to the list of possible security leaks.

---

[1] http://www.myhelp.gv.at/.

[2] https://www.usp.gv.at/.

We used for IT security the ISO/IEC 27001 standard, which is available for different domains in industry. In our case we concentrated on three domains in the ISO/EEC standard (a) to formulate requirements and objectives for IT security, (b) to consider cost efficiency management of security risks and (c) to secure conformity with laws and provisions. These base domains have been transferred as IT security requirements into the table, which enabled us to create a checklist through which we have been enabled to categorise our measurements against hacking attacks. This is a similar structure as D. P. Gilliam et al. developed. [11] We analysed the whole live cycle as D. P. Gilliam et al. states. We started with security risk analysis and requirements gathering, through design and development, testing and integration. This included operations and maintenance. Decommissioning was not in our focus yet but a modular structure in Java allows us an easy and smooth decommission of the proxy authenticator from the myHelp service when its running time is over.

We put huge efforts into security measures to protect the proxy authenticator in the myHelp service in the internet. H. Ki introduces a best practice approach of security violation processing. [12] It defines best practices, for prompt and accurate response to physical, logical and performance security violations. We also took into consideration in our architecture internet security violations, resulting from hacking and viruses [12].

2   Related Work

In Austria e-government applications are starting to employ Security Assertion Mark-up Language 2.0 (SAML V2.0) [6] in the Portal Group Protocol (PVP[3]). The SAML standard is used for exchanging authentication and authorisation data between security domains.

In Austrian e-government services the Portal Group Protocol (PVP) is used. Austria's government portals team up with each other to form a portal group and share the existing infrastructure. The advantage of the portal group concept is that many applications are available from a single entry point but this was not the case for the e-delivery services in Austria. The goal is that citizens as users only need to identify once when they first log on to the myHelp portal in order to access an e-delivery or other services.

Pashalidis and Mitchell [7] describe different methods to receive a SSO. They also exhibit pseudo architecture for SSO. The architecture is similar to the architecture illustrated in this paper. However, Pashalidis and Mitchell do not combine different techniques like SSO component, reverse proxy and certificate storage.

Participation of the portal group in Austria, who offers e-government services, is governed by a Portal Group Agreement, between the application providers and the base portal providers, who take care of user management. This agreement creates an environment of trust and allows communication within the portal group is managed, both technically and organisationally, by the portal group protocol (PVP) and the use of security classes. Application providers determine over which portals their applications will be available.

---

[3] https://www.digitales.oesterreich.gv.at/site/6568/default.aspx 28.08.2015.

SAML V2.0 is a protocol using XML. SAML V2.0 also uses security tokens containing assertions to pass information about a principal (in this case the citizen) between a SAML authority (the a-trust authority in Austria), which is an identity provider, and a SAML consumer (the myHelp-service), which is an e-government service provider. SAML V2.0 enables web-based authentication and authorisation scenarios including cross-domain single sign-on.

In this approach the possibility to use SAML V2.0 protocol [6] as a technical solution for SSO after Austrian law Sect. 35 Abs.3 ZustG was assessed. However, it turned out that the applications did not support SAML V2.0 and an adaption was impractical. That is why a solution had to be developed providing SSO functionality – just as SAML – though without any changes, neither in the architecture nor in the application layer.

Therefore, the certificate and the private key are stored encrypted in the proxy authenticator. If the citizen is authenticated and the certificate and the private key are necessary to perform the citizen request (e.g. collect the documents from the e-delivery service) only then the certificate and the private key will be decrypted during this request. To meet such high security requirements several security mechanisms were implemented (see Sect. 5.4).

A citizen card from a European member state using a qualified electronic signature, after Directive 1999/93/EC of the European Parliament [15] – in STORK it equals to QAA level 4 [16], can be used to ensure European citizen authentication in Austria for to gain access into an e-government portal. Both, citizen card and mobile signature are utilised by myHelp. The Austrian mobile signature works similar to the mobile TAN system in online banking and is a two-factor authentication [3].

3   Legal and Technical Background

Another solution is similar to the one of M. Dyrda et al. to set up a security layer were the credential from the user's wallet are used to authenticate and to create a delegated credential in a deployed service [9].

In Austrian law article Sect. 35 ZustG controls the document collection from existing e-delivery services (a) BRZ-Zustelldienst[4], (b) meinBrief and[5] (c) Postserver[6]. Authorised citizens who have registered to one or more of these e-delivery services have to verify their identity and authenticity by usage of their citizen card [8] or mobile signature (mobile signature card). Instead of using the citizen card, which requires a card reader, it is possible to use mobile signature, which only requires a mobile phone. In comparison to any other hardware platform, the mobile phone is the most frequently accessed technology in Austria with about 88 mobile phone contracts per 100 citizen in use in 2005 [13]. Since then the number of mobile contracts was rising in Austria. Verification of the identity is carried out by the citizen card or mobile signature.

---

[4] https://www.brz-zustelldienst.at/.

[5] https://www.meinbrief.at/.

[6] https://www.postserver.at/.

The verification of the authenticity will be achieved through adjustment with the central population register (ZMR) and generation of an area specific personal identifier in Austria ("bereichsspezifisches Personenkennzeichen (bPK)").

In accordance with the Austrian law ZustG, identification and authenticity can be executed through a special agreement by usage of a secure technology called "automated triggered signature". The article Sect. 35 Abs. 3 ZustG in Austria specifies that the verification of both elements, identification and authenticity, is necessary. The verification of only one element, e.g. bPK, is inappropriate after Austrian law.

To correlate with the Austrian law, the following conversion took place.

1. Implementation of a data base instance to enable encrypted storage of certificates and the appertaining keys.
2. Development of a key encryption process (e.g. PKCS12 key), [17] for key generation and storage in the data base as a replacement of a Hardware Security Model (HSM) [18] to maintain security, to assure trust into e-government services and assure trust in data protection in Austria.
3. Development of interfaces and a configuration of a generic encryption respectively decryption based on Java classes.
4. Development of an upload procedure via form, to upload the e-delivery certificate including hash value validity check, user interaction, error handling, and delete functionality.
5. Integration of a Single-Sign-On (SSO) [7] between myHelp portal and other e-government services e.g. e-delivery services, without repeatedly using of the citizen card for an additional login. This includes all calls to any e-government services from myHelp portal. All calls have to include now all necessary header information which includes the decrypted certificate and key to gain access e.g. to pieces of correspondence at an e-delivery service.
6. Development of proxy authenticator server, in which the previous enumerations 1 to 5 described methodologies are integrated as a secure private citizen certificate and key storage, which enables the citizens, when changing the hardware equipment e.g. notebook that all certificates and keys for e-government services do not have to be transferred into the new hardware.

4 Technical Architecture

Figure 1 shows the technical architecture of the proxy authenticator in the myHelp portal. The initial registration process (marked by ① in Fig. 1) is comprised of the establishment of secure connection to the e-delivery service and the download of a certificate and private key.

The citizen opens the browser and sets up a TLS encrypted connection to myHelp portal. The small doted grey lines mark communication with MOA-ID (this equals to MOA-ID STORK) and MOCCA server (online citizen card environment) for authentication and validation. [4, 5] To gain access to the myHelp portal, the citizen can use the citizen card or mobile signature. In the e-delivery service the citizen has to generate a certificate and private key, which enables the citizen to download documents

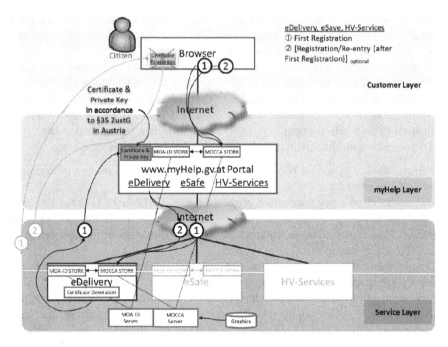

Fig. 1. Storage of a certificate and private key in myHelp portal including first registration and re-entry

from an e-delivery service in Austria. In order to enable citizens to download documents from the e-delivery service, the certificate and private key at first needs to be uploaded into myHelp portal. In the past the certificate and private key was uploaded into the citizen's browser (see grey arrows) - crossed of in the browser in customer layer.

The registration or re-entry process (marked by ② in Fig. 1) comprises the establishment of secure connection to pieces of correspondence at the e-delivery service.

5 Proxy Authenticator Solution

Basically the proxy authenticator solution can be divided into three domains: citizen (Private User Domain), provider (myHelp Domain) and administration (Administration Domain). These three domains are displayed in Figs. 2 and 3 represents a re-entry into myHelp and an e-delivery service in Austria. The Certificates and keys are created and downloaded into myHelp proxy authenticator.

The Administration Domain represents independent e-delivery services, where our described solution has no control. The e-delivery services are hosting all documents for the citizens. In order to collect these documents, the citizens have to use their certificates and his private keys. The myHelp Domain represents our solution and it includes the secure certificate storage. It includes also myHelp (the frontend), the proxy authenticator (the backend) and the key share holder.

Between all components and therefore between the domains, only TLS connections are implemented. The key shareholder is used to store parts of the shared key, which is used to encrypt and decrypt the uploaded certificate and private key, of the citizen. The private key will be stored encrypted. Each citizen has a unique constructed shared key.

To collect documents from any e-delivery service in Austria, the citizen uploads the certificate and private key into the trusted myHelp Domain. Afterwards the citizen can download the documents using the proxy authenticator. The proxy authenticator loads the certificate of the authenticated citizen and establishes a secure connection to the e-delivery service[7]. The citizen is always connected with the proxy authenticator and under no circumstances connected directly with the e-delivery service. Therefore, the proxy authenticator works like a reverse proxy to the e-delivery service.

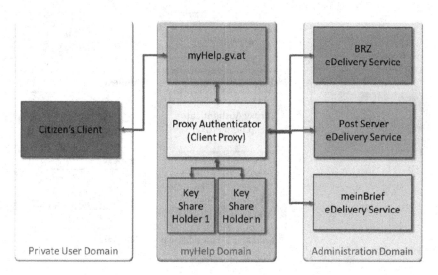

Fig. 2. e-Delivery service and its three Domains: Private User, MyHelp and Administration

As a project requirement, security was one of the highest priorities. Not only that the solution should be secured from outside attacks but also from inside intrusion. Further, the privacy of citizens is particularly worth protecting. Nobody except the citizens them self are allowed to get access to their own certificate or private key.

In the following selection the processes of the certificate and key upload (Sect. 5.1), the deletion/modification of certificates and keys (Sect. 5.2) and the retrieval of documents from e-Delivery services (Sect. 5.3) are described in detail. Further in Sect. 5.4 the used security mechanisms are listed.

---

[7] The proxy authenticator authenticates the on myHelp authenticated citizen to the e-delivery service.

5.1   Upload of the Certificate and Private Key

Upload of the certificate and private key is one of the main functionality of the proxy authenticator. As already mentioned the proxy authenticator acts as a single sign one component in the e-government system. In order to collect documents from existing e-delivery systems the citizen has to upload his certificate and private key to the proxy authenticator. The proxy authenticator stores the certificate and the private key encrypted in the internal storages of MyHelp domain. Figure 4 shows how citizens save their certificates and private keys.

Basically, the citizen sets-up a HTTPS secure connection between their client and the frontend of the proxy authenticator in myHelp domain. In the frontend the citizen will be authenticated using his citizen card or mobile signature and the request will be validated.

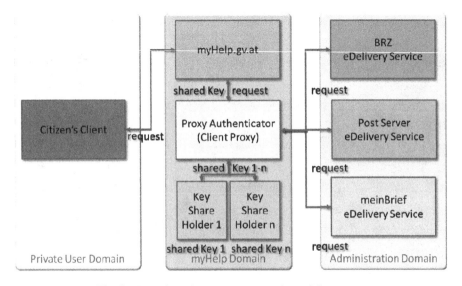

Fig. 3. Domain and component overview of the system

Validated certificate upload requests will be transferred to the backend (myHelp Domain) of the proxy authenticator. The shared key is reconstructed by combining several key shares retrieved from the key shareholders and used to encrypt symmetrically the uploaded certificate and private key. Finally the encrypted certificate and private key will be stored in the database.

5.2   Delete, Change of the Certificate and Private Key

In the section Delete, Change of the Certificate and Private Key, the limitations of certificates are pictured primarily as limited validity. For the Austrian e-delivery services it is a maximum of six months. Therefore a function has to be enabled that can automatically erase an active certificate after six month or change an expired certificate in the proxy authenticator. Also a message has to be sent out in such a way that there are two options of message retrieval is possible. Either an error message in a pop-up window in myHelp portal is displayed or an e-mail or SMS with information about the expiration date of the certificate is mailed.

To change the certificate and private key, a citizen goes to the proxy authenticator in myHelp domain and generates a new certificate including the private key. Afterwards the citizen deletes the current registered certificate and private key on the proxy authenticator. Finally the citizen uploads the new generated certificate and private key using the upload function, described in Sect. 5.

5.3 Retrieval of Documents from e-Delivery Services

To collect the citizen's documents from an e-Delivery service a secure (TLS) connection to myHelp will be established. Citizens authenticate themselves using the citizen card or mobile signature. This includes their area specific personal identifier ("bereichsspezifisches Personenkennzeichen (bPK)") as an identifier. Afterwards, they are allowed to collect their documents using the proxy authenticator. After authentication the proxy authenticator is able to reconstruct the shared key (the parts of the shared keys are located for security reason on independent shared key holder).

Then the certificate and private key (PKCS12 container) are loaded decrypted from the proxy authenticator database by using the area specific personal identifier from then citizen. There is no key installed at the client's browser. The decryption is necessary to prevent attackers from stealing private keys. All requests to the frontend are validated before they are transferred to the backend. Following decryption, the backend establish a connection to the e-delivery service to retrieve data (e.g. to collect the waiting documents). For the TLS connection the certificate and private key of the citizen is used for client authentication. All messages between citizen and e-delivery service are transferred through the proxy authenticator. A direct connection between citizen and e-delivery service is prohibited because it would result in an unauthenticated request due to the fact that the citizen does not have the private key installed in his browser. Therefore, the proxy authenticator has to modify all URLs in the e-delivery provider response before transmitting documents to the user to guarantee that the citizen does not leave the proxy domain.

5.4 Quality Management: Security Mechanism

Under the circumstances of quality management and security mechanisms, all citizen data needs to be protected by the data protection legislation in Austria (Sect. 12 Abs. 2 des Datenschutzgesetzes 2000). [14] This is the reason why the proxy authenticator solution includes various security solutions from the below-mentioned best practice table (see Table 1) to guarantee an adequate data protection. The measures are listed and explained in detail. The table includes different strategies and methodologies in protecting data in internet. It is a paradigm to reduce all risk to zero. To find an acceptable solution,

Table 1. Implemented security measures

Measures	Description	Advantage
Encrypted database	Database will be encrypted	This guarantees that a possible attacker, who gains access to the database, cannot read or interpret any data in the database. It will be set up as an extra hurdle for the attacker
Shared key concept to encrypt and decrypt the certificate and the private key of the citizen	To encrypt and decrypt the certificate and private key of a citizen, it is necessary to possess all parts of the shared key. The different parts of the key are stored on different machines. Further a secure share key is reconstructed which means that information about parts of the keys does not help to reconstruct the final key	Through the assembled key it is guaranteed that data can be read only if all parts of the shared key are available. This raises the security of the data protection and reduces any abuse through administration personal
Secure end-to-end connection	A connection between two components will be adjusted via HTTPS	This intends to prevent a Man-in-the-middle attack
System structure (1): Fragmentation of components	Proxy authenticator will be divided into two components. The frontend validates requests and filters all corrupt requests. The backend manages sessions and de- or encryption of the certificate and private key. Both the shared key and private key of the citizen never leave the backend. The backend builds ups a HTTPS connection with the e-delivery service, by using the certificate and the private key of the citizen	This architecture should prevent an attacker to retrieve confidential data of any citizen. For outsiders only the frontend is visible. If an attack was successful and an attacker reaches the backend, then the attacker would not have any possibility to sniff or recalculate the shared key. Furthermore, all certificate and private keys of all existing citizens are stored in the secure area DMZ of the backend

(Continued)

Table 1. (*Continued*)

Measures	Description	Advantage
System structure (2): Fragmentation of Modules	The Frontend and the backend are fragmented into modules	This fragmentation does not only create more flexibility of the system, it also contributes to higher security. Through the fragmentation of the modules it refines a more secure access right model. During data delivery the backend module only requires reading rights, whereas the module for key-upload requires access rights for writing in the database
Encryption certificate and private key	Certificate and private key is encrypted by the prior reconstructed shared key and is saved encrypted in the database	Protection is guaranteed through encryption of all certificate and private keys, which are securely stored in the database. In case an attacker gains access to the database account, the attacker needs the individual shared key for every saved certificate and private key
Secured configuration	Important configuration files are encrypted, as for example, database implementation	Due to the encryption, an attacker cannot read any database password and therefore cannot gain access to the database
Code Scramble	All Jar files are obfuscated	This prevents any binary analyses or reverse engineering of an attacker. Otherwise an attacker could gain access onto internal processes
Hash	To reconstruct the shared key, hashes are used. The hash algorithm is SHA-256 to fulfil actual security standards	SHA-96 for high security application is still usable but SHA-256 provides a higher security level

(*Continued*)

Table 1. (*Continued*)

Measures	Description	Advantage
Separate saving of private keys and certificates	The private keys and the certificates are saved separately, i.e. instead of a single container	There is not only a performance increase, but also enhanced security. If only the certificate is needed, the whole container does not need to be decrypted. This implies less decrypting and avoids that the private key is unprotected as visible text in the code readable

we concentrated at risk mitigation. This helped us to reduce risks by choosing certain security measures to a minimum. The Table 1 includes all relevant measure, which we used for our risk mitigation.

6 Conclusion

This paper assesses the issue of a secure certificate proxy authenticator, which requires a strong security solution. The necessity derives from the proxy, which is accessible via the myHelp portal. This paper has exhibited that the challenge of quality assurance, such as supported ICT secure architecture (see Sect. 5), lies not only in fulfilling various security standards or technical security aspects of software, but also in IT-security strategies within all IT-processes of the secure proxy authenticator, e.g. separating the system into frontend, backend and data base. In the frontend all request are validated against unauthorised requests and only the frontend communicates with e-government services, i.e. BRZ e-delivery service. All relevant access data to gain communication with an e-government service via certificate and private key, this secure information is stored encrypted in the data base and scrambled by different parts to join the relevant key. When using certificate and private key, they never leave the backend. Bearing this in mind, a new combined SSO solution for e-government portals in Austria has been established, using for identification citizen card technology or mobile signature, which is a strong alternative to SAML V2.X for secure login into any Austrian portal service. All workflow changes that needed to be considered required a detailed evaluation with strong focus on security and quality aspects as well as subsequent intensive testing. The IT strategy advocates in this paper a combination of security measures that allows for our predefined security requirements to be met. These predefined best practices of measure keep the quality high. As a result, a mechanism similar to SAML V2.0 was created. This allows citizens to download any document from any e-delivery service in Austria, e.g. meinBrief or BRZ-Zustelldienst etc. without saving a certificate and private key into the citizen's browser.

The previous solution saved the certificate and private key in the citizen's browser. This relied on the citizen's understanding of security to protect the data with a strong password. The architecture of the previous solution furthermore leads to a limitation when a certificate and private key is saved in the citizen's browser; only this browser is allowed to download documents from an e-delivery service in Austria.

The here presented solution does not compromise the citizen's online security when using an Austrian e-delivery service provided by myHelp. All citizens' certificate and private keys are saved within the myHelp portal. This is an extended private secure data store to gain access to e-government service for citizens. The new solution furthermore enables all citizens to download documents from any computer they wish, e.g. Internet café, computer at work etc., thereby significantly increasing accessibility. A citizen will gain access to myHelp by using a citizen card or mobile signature, using a mobile phone.

The developed technology is a smart technology and directs e-government towards a more citizen friendly usability. The future success of Austrian e-government 2.0 lies upon an increased comprehension of citizen requirements in order to raise user friendliness. Naturally, this is not limited to Austria, but the success of e-government globally.

Appendix

Appendix A: Sequence Diagram of Certificate Upload.

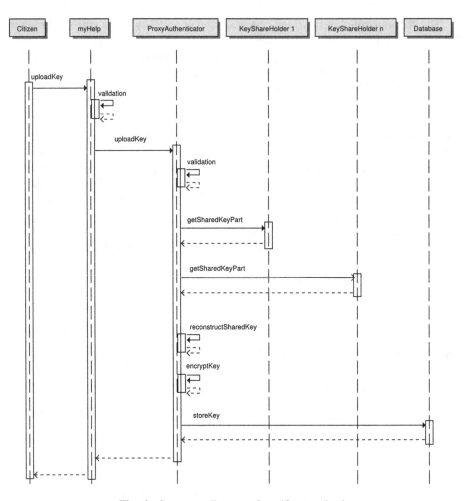

Fig. 4. Sequence diagram of certificate upload

Appendix B: Sequence Diagram of e-delivery Message Retrieval (Fig. 5).

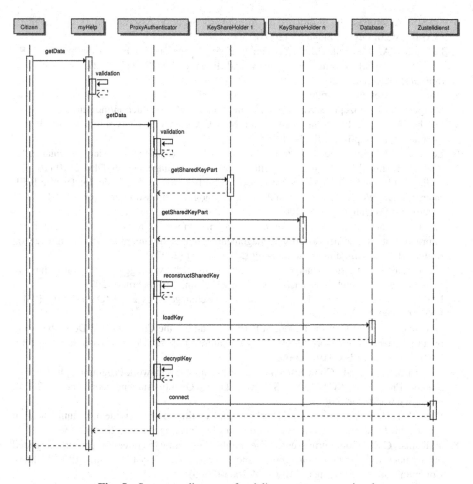

Fig. 5. Sequence diagram of e-delivery message retrieval

References

1. STORK: Secure electronic identity across Europe. https://www.eid-stork.eu/pilots/index.htm, 24 March 2013
2. Austrian Government (no Date): Bundesgesetz über die Zustellung behördlicher Dokumente (Zustellgesetz - ZustG) StF: BGBl. Nr. 200/1982 (NR: GP XV RV 162 AB 1050 S. 110. BR: S. 421.) Sect. 35 Ab. 1 bis Abs. 9
3. E-Government Innovationszentrum: Two Factor Authentication (2012). http://demo.egiz. gv.at/plain/projekte/signatur_im_e_government/webservice_schnittstelle_fuer_das_signatur pruefservice
4. E-Government Innovationszentrum: MOA-Modules for signature check-up (2013). http:// demo.egiz.gv.at/plain/projekte/signatur_im_e_government
5. E-Government Innovationszentrum: MOAModules, Pre-Screencast-Dokumentation (2013). http://screencasts.exthex.com/exthex-EGIZ-Screencast-Indroduction.pdf

6. OASIS: Assertions and Protocols for the OASIS Security Assertion Mark-up Language (SAML) V2.0, OASIS Standard (2005)
7. Pashalidis, A., Mitchell, C.J.: A taxonomy of single sign-on systems. In: Safavi-Naini, R., Seberry, J. (eds.) Information Security and Privacy. LNCS, vol. 2727, pp. 249–264. Springer, Heidelberg (2003)
8. Hollosi, A., et al.: Einführung in die österreichische Bürgerkarte (2004). http://www. buergerkarte.at/konzept/securitylayer/spezifikation/aktuell/introduction/introduction.html
9. Dyrda, M., et al.: Providing security for MOCCA component environment. In: IPDPS, International Symposium IEEE (2009)
10. Leonetti, S.J.: Government Electronic Service Delivery (ESD) and privacy in Ontario. In: Fifth International Conference on Digital Information Management, ICDIM 2010 (2010)
11. Gilliam, D.P., et al.: Software security checklist for the software life cycle. In: Twelfth IEEE International Workshops on Enabling Technologies: Infrastructure for Collaborative Enterprises (WETICE 2003) (2003)
12. Ki, H., et al.: Study on developing a security violation response checklist for the improvement of internet security management systems. In: International Conference on Multimedia and Ubiquitous Engineering (MUE 2007) (2007)
13. Die Presse: Die meisten Handyverträge gibt es mit 120 Verträgen je 100 Einwohner in Luxemburg. Österreich liegt leicht über dem EU-Schnitt, 07 February 2005
14. Datenschutzgesetzes: Sect. 12 Abs. 2 des Datenschutzgesetzes 2000 (DSG 2000), BGBl. I Nr. 165/1999
15. Directive 1999/93/EC of the European Parliament and of the Council of 13 December 1999 on a Community framework for electronic signatures. http://eur-lex.europa.eu/legal-content/DE/TXT/?uri=CELEX:31999L0093
16. Timmermans, J., et al.: Competitiveness and Innovation Framework Programme, ICT Policy Support Programme (ICT PSP) – STORK - D2.3 - Quality Authenticator Scheme (2009). https://www.eid-stork.eu/
17. Peng, Y.: The application of PKCS#12 digital certificate in user identity authentication system. In: IEEE World Congress on Software Engineering, WCSE 2009 (2009)
18. Williams, C.K.: Configuring enterprise public key infrastructures to permit integrated deployment of signature, encryption and access control systems. In: IEEE Military Communications Conference, MILCOM 2005 (2005)

Author Index

Printed in the United States
By Bookmasters